MAESTRO GLORIOSO

MAESTRO GLORIOSO

TEN ESSAYS IN CELEBRATION OF SIR JOHN BARBIROLLI

RAYMOND HOLDEN

The Barbirolli Society

First published by The Barbirolli Society, 2021

The Barbirolli Society
11 Cranbrook Drive, Kennington, Oxfordshire, OX1 5RR, UK

www.barbirollisociety.co.uk

ISBN: 978-0-9556710-4-3

Printed in the United Kingdom
by QuayDigital, Bristol

For Mary

and in memory of Sir John Pritchard CBE and Professor Cyril Ehrlich

CONTENTS

FOREWORD   ix

PREFACE   x

CHRONOLOGY   xii

ESSAY ONE: In Defence of the Realm: Barbirolli and British Music
(Part One) – Boy Cellist to Novice Music Director   17

ESSAY TWO: A Knight at the Opera: Barbirolli and the Lyric Theatre   29

ESSAY THREE: In Defence of the Realm: Barbirolli and British Music
(Part Two) – From New York to Manchester   45

ESSAY FOUR: A Life Recorded: Barbirolli and the Gramophone   57

ESSAY FIVE: A Cockney Down Under: Sir John Barbirolli in Australia   69

ESSAY SIX: From the Cradle to the Grave: Barbirolli, Elgar and
In the South (Alassio)   83

ESSAY SEVEN: Bruckner 8: Sir John Barbirolli's London Swansong   101

ESSAY EIGHT: What the Papers Say: Barbirolli, Sibelius and the Critics   117

ESSAY NINE: From Mystery to Monument: Barbirolli, Mahler and
the Second Symphony   129

ESSAY TEN: Barbirolli on the Art and Craft of Conducting   149

APPENDIX ONE: Bruckner's Eighth Symphony –
Tempo Chart and Score Examples   159

APPENDIX TWO: Mahler's Second Symphony –
Tempo Chart and Score Examples   166

NOTES   172

INDEX   196

FOREWORD

Some memories remain sharp. It's a Saturday morning in the spring of 1983 and I'm with my mother on the top floor of the HMV store in Northumberland Street, Newcastle. I'm here to buy my first LP. My eyes land on a black and white photo of an orchestra and conductor who are clearly very caught up in *English String Music*. 'Sir John Barbirolli', says my mother 'you'll like that'. And so began my life-long admiration for the conductor whose music-making has inspired me more than any other. As my record collection grew, new worlds opened up for me and I soon became familiar with the distinctive sounds of the great orchestras and conductors. But my devotion to 'J.B.' never wavered and, to this day, his Puccini, Mahler, Brahms, Elgar, Delius and Vaughan Williams remain the discs I cherish most.

When I first conducted the Hallé in 2000, there were still a handful of players in the orchestra from Barbirolli's day and I lost no time in collecting first-hand reminiscences from them. His reputation for thoroughness in rehearsal seems justified: 'he stopped 179 times in the first movement of the *Eroica* – I know because I counted them'. The word *atmosphere* kept cropping up, something I think is crucial in understanding the essence of Barbirolli's conducting – his innate ability to bring the sound-world of a work with him into the room and, almost miraculously, preserve it in the recording studio. In music with which Barbirolli had a particularly close affinity, such as that of Frederick Delius, this heightened atmosphere is tangible even in the silence before the pieces start.

His legendary capacity for sheer hard work was central to the transformation of the Hallé in the 1940s; rehearsals for woodwind, brass and percussion in the morning, strings in the afternoon, and then everyone in the evenings spawned lyrics to Hindemith's *Symphonic Metamorphosis*: 'Come and join us, come and join us; ten till one, two till five, six till nine'. I asked a long-standing Hallé subscriber if the audience noticed a change in the sound of the orchestra when Barbirolli took over – 'Immediately. From the first concert. It was like night and day. We felt that we were the luckiest people alive to have this great man with us here in Manchester'. And he stayed in Manchester and gave us one of the greatest partnerships between conductor and orchestra in history.

John Wilson
London, February 2021

PREFACE

Having had the chance to reflect fully on the remarkable life and career of Sir John Barbirolli during the preparation of this book, I am reminded of Arturo Toscanini's insightful remark: 'in life, democracy; in art, aristocracy'. A musician who believed passionately in the universal right of all human beings to access great music through sovereign performances, Barbirolli, or J.B. as he was affectionately known, was an artist who touched the hearts and souls of millions around the world. As a young musician growing up in far-off Australia during the 1960s, I was one of those millions and soon found myself enthralled by this diminutive man with the big sound. A guiding light whose recordings never failed to reveal the true content of the music he was interpreting, Barbirolli represented for me the pinnacle of musical achievement. Whether it was with the Hallé Orchestra or the Berlin Philharmonic, his discs for HMV and Pye were the very definition of great performances. The works of Elgar, Mahler, Brahms, Sibelius and others all spoke to me with great intensity thanks to the artistic insights of Barbirolli. That intensity has not diminished with time and it is no exaggeration to say that my life in music would have been far less rich had I not encountered the artistry of that remarkable Englishman with the Italian name all those years ago.

When I was asked by the Barbirolli Society to write a book to mark the fiftieth anniversary of J.B.'s death, I was adamant that it should not be a biography. Both Charles Reid and Michael Kennedy had written marvellous accounts of Barbirolli's life in the early 1970s and it seemed to me both pointless and impertinent to try and compete with these beautifully crafted and meticulously researched documents. I was keen, however, to explore key elements of J.B.'s performance style and felt that the best way of doing this was in essay form. Based on lectures, broadcasts and articles that I have given and published in Britain, Europe, North America, Asia, Africa and Australia over the last thirty years, the ten essays found in this collection examine his activities as a music director of orchestras in Britain and North America, his work as a recording artist, his years in the opera house, his impact as a touring musician and his approach when interpreting great masterworks. Each of the essays can be read independently with only the third being a continuation of the first. As this volume was always intended for a broad readership, I have tried to keep the more technical aspects of the art and craft of conducting to a minimum.

But it would be doing Barbirolli a complete disservice as a performing musician if his highly developed set of practices and principles were not considered in at least a few of the essays found in this book. With this fine balancing act in mind, I have restricted my more detailed analyses of Barbirolli's performance style to the concluding sections of the essays on Elgar, Bruckner and Mahler.

Throughout the preparation of this book, I have received enthusiastic support from the Barbirolli Society and would like to thank particularly the late Pauline Pickering and my friend, Paul Brooks, for all the advice, material and help that he has given me. I would also like to thank John Wilson, Professor Jonathan Freeman-Attwood, CBE, Philip White, Henry Kennedy, Alice Filon, Dr Stephen Mould, Dr Margaret Dziekonski, David Llewellyn Jones, Sir Mark Elder, CH, Professor Timothy Jones, Janet Snowman, Katherine Adamson, Dr Adrian Müller, Dame Gwyneth Jones, DBE, Dr David Patmore, the late Lady Barbirolli and Gabriele-Strauss-Hotter for their unstinting help and kindness. But my greatest debt of gratitude is to my wife, Mary, for her unfailing optimism and encouragement. She sustained me throughout this project and without her support, this book would not have been written.

Raymond Holden, AM
Emeritus Professor of Music
Royal Academy of Music
London, 2020

CHRONOLOGY

1899: Born Giovanni Battista Barbirolli on 2 December at Southampton Row, London

1910: Enters Trinity College of Music, London, as a cello student

1911: Makes first recordings as a cellist with his sister, Rosa, for Edison Bell

1912: Performs an unidentified cello concerto by Saint-Saëns at the Queen's Hall, London, before entering the Royal Academy of Music, London, as a cello student

1913: Gives first cello recital at the Aeolian Hall, London, and performs as a chamber musician at the Royal Academy of Music

1914: Plays Bruch's *Kol Nidrei* with the Royal Academy of Music Orchestra at the Queen's Hall

1915: Plays movements from Sir Alexander Mackenzie's Piano Quartet with fellow students at the Royal Academy of Music's Duke's Hall

1916: Leaves the Royal Academy of Music and joins the Queen's Hall Orchestra as a rank-and-file cellist

1917: Gives two recitals at the Aeolian Hall with the pianists, Ethel Bartlett and Harold Craxton, and plays at a charity concert at the Queen's Hall

1918: Joins the British Army and is stationed at the Isle of Grain where he conducts a concert for the first time

1919: Demobilised from the British Army

1920: Plays the cello for Pavlova's Russian Ballet Company and is the soloist for Tchaikovsky's *Variations on a Rococo Theme* with Dan Godfrey and the Bournemouth Municipal Orchestra

1921: Performs Elgar's Cello Concerto with Dan Godfrey and the Bournemouth Municipal Orchestra

1922: Conducts a performance for the London Violoncello School and gives a recital at St. Andrew's Hall, Norwich, with Ethel Bartlett

1923: Travels to Paris as a member of the Philharmonic String Quartet

1924: Establishes the Guild of Singers and Players Chamber Orchestra

1925: Forms the Chenil Chamber Orchestra

1926: Tours Spain with the Music Society String Quartet and engaged as a conductor with the British National Opera Company

CHRONOLOGY

1927: Makes first recording as a conductor for the National Gramophonic Society and conducts the London Symphony Orchestra at the Queen's Hall for an indisposed Sir Thomas Beecham

1928: Makes first recording as a conductor for HMV with the John Barbirolli Chamber Orchestra and conducts at the Royal Opera House, Covent Garden, for the first time

1929: Conducts the Orchestra of the Royal Philharmonic Society at the Queen's Hall

1930: Conducts the Scottish Orchestra for the first time

1931: Conducts the BBC Symphony Orchestra for the first time

1932: Marries the singer, Marjorie Parry

1933: Appointed Music Director of the Scottish Orchestra and conducts the Hallé Orchestra for the first time

1934: Conducts an all-Elgar programme with the Hallé Orchestra for an indisposed Sir Edward Elgar

1935: Conducts in Helsinki and Leningrad

1936: Performs with the New York Philharmonic-Symphony Orchestra as a guest conductor

1937: Appointed Music Director of the New York Philharmonic-Symphony Orchestra

1938: Conducts the Detroit Symphony Orchestra and records for Victor

1939: Divorced by Marjorie Barbirolli (*née* Parry) and marries the oboist, Evelyn Rothwell

1940: Records for Columbia and conducts the Vancouver Symphony Orchestra, the San Francisco Symphony Orchestra, the Philharmonic Orchestra of Los Angeles and the Chicago Symphony Orchestra

1941: Conducts the Philharmonic Orchestra of Los Angeles for three concerts at the Hollywood Bowl in August and returns for a series of thirteen concerts in November and December with the orchestra in Los Angeles, the Hollywood Bowl, the Los Angeles environs and San Diego

1942: Performs with the Seattle and Cincinnati Symphony Orchestras and returns to Britain during the summer for wartime concerts with the London Philharmonic, London Symphony and BBC Symphony Orchestras

1943: Appointed Permanent Conductor of the Hallé Orchestra and returns to HMV

1944: Conducts in recently liberated Italy and Belgium with the Orchestra del Teatro di San Carlo, the Friends of Music Symphony Orchestra, the Orchestra Sinfonica Roma della RAI and the Hallé Orchestra

1945: Performs at the Cheltenham Festival for the first time

1946: Conducts the Philharmonia Orchestra and joins the Turner String Quartet for a concert at St. Helens

1947: Performs with the Orchestra dell'Accademia Nazionale di Santa Cecilia in Rome, the Vienna Philharmonic and the Vienna Staatsoper

1948: Tours Austria with the Hallé Orchestra

1949: Knighted by King George VI and conducts three concerts with the Berlin Philharmonic at the Edinburgh Festival

1950: Awarded the Gold Medal of the Royal Philharmonic Society and makes first tour of Australia for the Australian Broadcasting Commission

1951: Returns to the Royal Opera House, Covent Garden, for performances of Puccini's *Turandot* and Verdi's *Aïda*

1952: Divides his time between the Hallé Orchestra and the Royal Opera House, Covent Garden

1953: Tours with the Hallé Orchestra to Africa for thirteen concerts in Bulawayo and conducts at the BBC Proms for the first time

1954: Conducts the Orchestra del Teatro La Fenice in Venice

1955: Makes second tour of Australia for the Australian Broadcasting Commission and launches commercial television in Britain by conducting Elgar's *Cockaigne (In London Town)* with the Hallé Orchestra from the Guildhall, London

1956: Leaves HMV and records for Pye

1957: Tours with the Hallé Orchestra to Italy for four concerts at Ravello

1958: Becomes an Honorary Freeman of Manchester, announces that he is stepping down as Permanent Conductor of the Hallé Orchestra to become its Conductor-in-Chief and begins a three-month tour of North America

1959: Conducts the New York Philharmonic for the first time since 1943 and performs in Denmark, Italy and Spain

1960: Returns to North America for a second major tour within twelve months and conducts concerts in Czechoslovakia, Hungary, Israel, Italy and Portugal

1961: Appointed Music Director of the Houston Symphony Orchestra, becomes a regular guest conductor of the Berlin Philharmonic, tours Scandinavia and travels with the Hallé Orchestra for concerts in Switzerland

1962: Returns to the Los Angeles Philharmonic for five concerts in Los Angeles and environs, conducts the Berlin Philharmonic at Coventry, performs ten concerts with the Israel Philharmonic Orchestra at Tel Aviv, Haifa and Jerusalem, gives eight concerts with the New York Philharmonic and returns to HMV

1963: Tours with the Philharmonia Orchestra to South America and conducts in Hungary

1964: Records Mahler's Ninth Symphony with the Berlin Philharmonic for HMV, the first British conductor to record with the orchestra since Sir Thomas Beecham in 1937 and 1938

1965: Tours with the New Philharmonia Orchestra to South America and the Caribbean

1966: Travels with the Hallé Orchestra to Germany for concerts in Essen, Leverkusen, Hanover, Hamburg, Kassel, Frankfurt am Main, Nürnberg, Düsseldorf and Viersen

1967: Relinquishes the music directorship of the Houston Symphony Orchestra and tours Eastern Europe with the BBC Symphony Orchestra

1968: Appointed Conductor Laureate of the Hallé Orchestra and tours with it to Central America, South America and the Caribbean

1969: Appointed Companion of Honour by Queen Elizabeth II, conducts five concerts with the Concertgebouw Orchestra of Amsterdam and returns to the Los Angeles Philharmonic Orchestra for nine concerts in Los Angeles and environs

1970: Suffers a coronary thrombosis on 29 July at Huntsworth Mews, London, and is taken to the Middlesex Hospital where he is pronounced dead on arrival

IN DEFENCE OF THE REALM: BARBIROLLI AND BRITISH MUSIC (PART ONE) – BOY CELLIST TO NOVICE MUSIC DIRECTOR

Described erroneously as '*Das Land ohne Musik*' by the Wilhelmine critic, Oscar Adolf Herman Schmitz, in 1904,[1] Edwardian Britain was, in fact, a vibrant artistic centre that was home to a string of highly professional composers and a plethora of remarkably gifted virtuosi. Like so many other catchy comments both before and since, Schmitz's disingenuous remark was not only deceptive musically but damaging historically. Carefully crafted to imply that Britain was better suited to importing musical masterworks than producing its own, the German's artistic poison dart was designed to help bring British cultural life to its knees at a time of rising tension between the two countries. Vying openly with London for economic, industrial and military supremacy in Europe, Berlin was also conscious of the propaganda value of cultural domination. While it is true that the German-speaking countries acted as a powerful artistic magnet for aspiring British musicians throughout much of the nineteenth century, Britons had begun to find their own compositional voices by the time Schmitz penned his aphorism. Even so, it was clear to local performers that the music of their compatriots had been severely impugned and that it was up to them to be indefatigable in the defence of their musical realm.

Born and educated in London during this period of heightened cultural rivalry, Sir John Barbirolli was a committed interpreter of British music from his earliest years. Something of an evangelist when it came to the compositions of his fellow countrymen, Barbirolli began his lifelong advocacy of them as a young cello student at the Royal Academy of Music. With fellow pupils, Josef Shadwick (violin), Wolfe Wolfinsohn (viola) and Leo Levins (piano), he flew the flag for British music for the first time when he performed the opening two movements of Sir Alexander Mackenzie's Piano Quartet, Op. 11, at the Academy's Duke's Hall on 18 February 1915. A Scotsman by birth, Mackenzie was a remarkably versatile artist and something of a musical polymath. A distinguished conductor who was also a gifted violinist and composer, Mackenzie had been appointed the Academy's Principal in 1888.[2] Throughout his still-unsurpassed thirty-six-year tenure, he impressed all who entered his educational orbit and acted as a lifelong cultural role model for his devoted pupils. A proud musical father figure who never failed to follow his students' progress even in retirement, Mackenzie had a particular professional soft spot for Barbirolli and continued to keep a watchful eye on his progress as he began to rise through the ranks of the music profession. The great man's affection for the younger musician never wavered and in 1927 he wrote touchingly to J.B.:

> I think it most kind of you to send me the invitation to see [you conduct Rossini's *Il barbiere di Siviglia* at the King's Theater, Hammersmith]; and I assure you that nothing would have given me greater pleasure [than] to hear and meet my dear friends again. I may tell you that I am very proud of you for having reached this position which you already occupy, and which is bound to increase in public estimation. This which appeals to me is, that you have done it <u>yourself</u>, and in a modest, quiet way: without – vulgarly speaking – gassing or swank. I liked you as a student, and still more now when I see you "arriving" quickly. Now, I am more than sorry that I am unable to come to your performance to-night. The fact being that I am tired out with an amount of work during this past months, and which is not to [be] attempted again. Further, I am leaving for a short holiday of four weeks to-morrow forenoon: and as I have no end of errands during the day, I am <u>advised</u> not to journey to Hammersmith this evening – not being quite so sprightly as I once was. I have passed on the tickets to a friend by this post.[3] Now, do me [a] favour to give my most cordial sincere wishes to [the singers and former Academy students] [Robert] Radford, [Percy] Heming (and the others) and tell them how much I would have enjoyed meeting my "boys", for such I ever regard them. I still look forward to an "ensemble" with you all but believe me, with every good wish – my dear <u>Barbirolli</u> – yours very faithfully A. C. Mackenzie[4]

No doubt disappointed that Mackenzie was unable to attend the performance, Barbirolli never lost his admiration for his former Principal and went on to give multiple performances of his music at Edinburgh, Dundee and London in the mid-1930s.[5]

Barbirolli's quick 'arrival' as a conductor was not as quick as Mackenzie's letter suggests. For nearly a decade after leaving the Academy, Barbirolli had worked primarily as an orchestral and chamber musician before taking up the baton professionally. As a member of the Philharmonic, Phillis Tate, Kutcher and Music Society String Quartets, he performed throughout much of the United Kingdom and Western Europe. Works by British composers were given regularly by these quartets and they were never afraid to challenge local audiences with their compatriots' music when performing abroad. At a concert at Bad Homburg in August 1925, for example, the Music Society String Quartet gave an all-English programme that included compositions by Purcell, Gibbons, Vaughan Williams, J. B. McEwen and Bridge.[6] Perched picturesquely on the southern slopes of Germany's Taunus Mountains, Bad Homburg was an upmarket health spa whose wellness-seeking clientele would have been more at home with the familiar strains of Strauss-family waltzes rather than the more demanding compositional styles of Ralph Vaughan Williams and Frank Bridge. Probably something of an artistic cold shower for the thermal-loving visitors to the spa, the programme would have done little to encourage the locals to explore British music further and, if anything, would have simply added to their sense of cultural chauvinism.

A composer whose music was also heard frequently at Barbirolli's chamber concerts was Eugene Goossens. Like Mackenzie, Goossens was a violinist, conductor and conservatory principal but, unlike Mackenzie, his sound-world as a composer no longer looked back longingly to the works of Mendelssohn and Brahms but forward to the music of Debussy, Ravel and Delius.[7] Within weeks of Goossens's 'Phantasy' Sextet being published in 1925, Barbirolli and the augmented Philharmonic String Quartet gave it at Brussels.[8] Three months later, Barbirolli, now a member of the Kutcher Quartet, recorded the composer's *By the Tarn* and *Jack O'Lantern* for Vocalion,[9] before setting down McEwen's *Peat Reek* and Vaughan Williams 'Phantasy' Quintet with an enlarged Music Society String Quartet for the National Gramophonic Society the same year. But it was at concerts with his duo partners, the pianists Harold Craxton, Hugo Anson and Ethel Bartlett, that Barbirolli returned time and time again to the music of his fellow countrymen. Their programmes at the Wigmore Hall, the Aeolian Hall, the Steinway Hall, St. Andrew's Hall (Norwich) and on the BBC were not only peppered with the works of Purcell, Goossens, Delius, Herbert Hughes and Ireland, but also those of Bartlett and Anson themselves.

Having turned eighteen in December 1917, Barbirolli enlisted in the British Army the following February. But any dreams of glory on the Western Front evaporated rapidly after he was posted to the Isle of Grain later that year.[10] Duties were light and boredom was omnipresent. Allowed to take his cello with him to pass the time,

Barbirolli quickly joined the garrison's Voluntary Orchestra and soon impressed his fellow islanders with his innate artistry and eagerness to learn. Having fantasised about a life on the podium since boyhood, he got his first chance to conduct when he deputised for the orchestra's regular conductor at a concert in May 1918. Amongst the works given in the garrison's mess that night were Coleridge-Taylor's *Petite Suite de Concert* and Fraser-Simson's Suite from *The Maid of the Mountains*. Described in old age by Barbirolli as 'charming', Coleridge-Taylor's work seems to have had a particular significance for him, as he nostalgically claimed it to be the first work that he conducted that evening and, by extension, the first of his career.[11] A surviving programme from that performance tells a different story, however, and it seems that it was with Suppé's popular Overture to *Dichter und Bauer* that Barbirolli began his career on the podium and not with Coleridge-Taylor's suite.[12]

Keen to become a professional conductor after being demobilised in 1919, Barbirolli faced the same dilemmas that confront all aspiring conductors: what is the most effective route to the podium and how soon can they get there? Some enter competitions, some join opera companies, while others form chamber orchestras at their own expense. As conducting competitions were virtually non-existent during the early decades of the twentieth century, and as Barbirolli's rudimentary keyboard skills precluded him from becoming a répétiteur at an opera house,[13] the third option offered the best, and perhaps only, chance of realising his professional dream at that time. From the 1930s onwards, artists such as Adolf Busch, Edwin Fischer, Karl Münchinger, Karl Richter, Nikolaus Harnoncourt, Sir Neville Marriner, Sir John Eliot Gardiner and Mark Wigglesworth have founded chamber orchestras and have used them to further their careers. But it was the young Barbirolli in the early 1920s who was one of the earliest to realise the potential that this type of ensemble offered and who was arguably the first to exploit it in both the concert hall and the recording studio.

Founded in 1921 by the bass, John Goss, the Marylebone-based Guild of Singers and Players was established 'to enable performers to cooperate in programmes of greater variety and artistic interest than those which they could give singly'.[14] Performing at a number of inner-London venues,[15] the Guild soon caught the public's imagination and had 434 members by 1925, rising to 525 the following year.[16] Already secure in its audience base by 1924, the Guild decided to allow the young Barbirolli the chance to conduct a series of concerts with a small string orchestra that he had formed at his own expense. Along with music by Mozart, Debussy, Vivaldi and Tartini, Barbirolli gave works by Hughes, Purcell, Warlock and Delius. Combining high technical standards with intimacy and novelty, these concerts attracted a large and devoted audience. While healthy box-office receipts were always welcome, some supporters were concerned that there was a danger that the concerts' defining qualities might be sacrificed on the pyre of commercial gain. *The Times* recognised this and was quick to caution that:

> It would be an odd fate for a series of concerts to be destroyed by its own success. Yet the Guild of Singers and Players will have to watch that their subscription concerts are not driven by increasing audiences from the intimacy of the room at the Court House, Marylebone, into the more frigid atmosphere of the ordinary concert hall. When these concerts were resumed on Friday there was a full house to hear a delightful programme … Mr. John Barbirolli got from the Guild Chamber Orchestra a tone both keen and clean and a kind of contrapuntal regard for the inner parts which made the whole thing pulse with life.[17]

On 5 June 1925, the New Chenil Galleries opened in the King's Road, Chelsea.[18] A stylish combination of exhibition spaces and performance areas, the Galleries was a multi-purpose venue that not only displayed the plastic and visual arts, but also promoted concerts. Overseen by a music committee that included Eugene Goossens, Peter Warlock,[19] John Ireland, E. J. Moeran, Ralph Vaughan Williams and John Goss,[20] the Galleries' distinctive concert series needed an equally distinctive performance vehicle to deliver its artistic message to the public. Impressed by Barbirolli's work with the Guild of Singers and Players, Goss knew that the young *maestro* was the right man for the job and so the Chenil Chamber Orchestra was formed.

With its vibrant art scene and its sophisticated and well-educated audiences, Chelsea provided Barbirolli and his players with a unique opportunity to explore their interests in all things new and unfamiliar. Surrounded by paintings, etchings, sculptures and drawings by some of Britain's most celebrated contemporary artists, J.B.'s dynamic ensemble soon became known for its interesting programmes and its exacting musicianship. The young musicians thrilled their audiences with works by Warlock, Elgar, Holst, Goossens, Bax, Delius, John Cooper, Gibbons and Purcell. Given with a flair and commitment that quickly captured the attention and admiration of the musical press, Barbirolli's performances at the Galleries were seen as an exciting alternative to the more traditional fare on offer at some of London's larger venues. But as remarkable as the performances surely were, tempting the capital's conservative audiences away from Portland Place and Kensington Gore was far from easy.[21] And even after two years of successful music-making in Chelsea, *The Musical Times* felt the need to write:

> Having heard, within five days, the Chenil Chamber Orchestra and another one four times its size, I pronounce for the Chenil. Perhaps this is mere anti-jumboism, a disease as mischievous as its opposite … Whatever the complaint that fostered it, there was utmost enjoyment for one listener at the Chenil Gallery. Everything was matched in scale and quality—the orchestra, the conductor (Mr. John Barbirolli), and the hall being small and excellent. So, too, was Arnold Bax's new work, called a 'Romantic Overture' … [There] was not a fault to find anywhere, either in the interpretation or in the playing of this select and musicianly [*sic*] little orchestra. It is said that these concerts are endangered by public neglect. Chelsea, no doubt, does its bit, but London is to blame. Let the *Musical Times* offer its advice to those about to go to a concert: Chenil Gallery, King's Road, is just as accessible as the Albert Hall, no more and no less.[22]

Aware that putting all his eggs in the one musical basket would undoubtedly prove professionally problematic in the long run, Barbirolli decided to test the artistic waters outside Chelsea by rebranding his players as the John Barbirolli Chamber Orchestra for a concert at the Wigmore Hall on 14 December 1924. Joined by the Kutcher String Quartet for a reading of Bernard van Dieren's Third String Quartet, J.B.'s band performed an extract from the Dutch-Born, British composer's unfinished opera, *The Tailor*, with John Goss as soloist.[23] A challenging and enigmatic composer who had the unnerving habit of writing some works without bar-lines, van Dieren had something of a cult following during the 1920s and the 1930s, and amongst his friends and champions were the sculptor, Jacob Epstein, the painter, Augustus John, and the musicians, Peter Warlock and Constant Lambert.[24]

Whether through curiosity or personal acquaintance, the administrator, singer, and composer, Frederic Austin, was also in the hall that night to hear van Dieren's works. A colourful character who had sung under Sir Edward Elgar, Sir Thomas Beecham, Sir Hamilton Harty and Sir Henry Wood, Austin was also the artistic director of the British National Opera Company (BNOC).[25] A musical polymath with a knack for spotting talent, Austin immediately recognised in Barbirolli the makings of a fine operatic conductor. *The Musical Times* also recognised Barbirolli's very obvious abilities and chirped that 'the *opéra bouffe* on a witty libretto by Robert Nichols … was excellently … conducted by Mr. John Barbirolli'.[26] Keen not to allow such a naturally gifted artist to slip through his fingers, Austin engaged Barbirolli as a staff conductor with the BNOC from the beginning of the 1926–7 season. While he performed no British operas with the company, J.B. cut his teeth as a jobbing conductor with it by performing works by Gounod, Wagner, Puccini, Rossini, Verdi and Humperdinck. In later years, Barbirolli never forgot the debt that he owed Austin and was able to repay him, at least in part, by performing his Sonata for Cello with the pianist, Rae Robinson, at the Marylebone Court House in 1928 and his orchestral works, *Paalsgard* and *Spring*, with the Scottish and Hallé Orchestras in 1935 and 1946 respectively.

But as Barbirolli was not scheduled to start work with the BNOC until the autumn of 1926, his professional life continued to revolve around the Chenil Chamber Orchestra and his various quartet and solo commitments over the next ten months. Music by Cooper, Warlock, Howells, Wright and Goossens featured frequently in his programmes, both in Britain and abroad. When the Music Society String Quartet toured Spain in February 1926, for example, Goossens's *By the Tarn* and *Jack O'Lantern* were given in Girona, Vich, Figueras and Palafrugell. Also given on that tour were fantasias by Gibbons and Purcell. Having been in the quartet's repertoire for some time, Gibbons's fantasias were committed to disc by the group in June 1925 followed by Purcell's fantasias seven months later.[27] Considered 'startlingly modern in places', the sound-worlds of these arrangements intrigued *The Musical Times*'s critic. So moved was the journalist by the 'searching yet delicate beauty of some of the music', he found himself compelled to listen to the recordings 'over and over again'.[28]

Criss-crossing Britain for the British National Opera Company from September 1926, Barbirolli had little time for his beloved chamber orchestra. But he never lost touch with it completely during his BNOC years and made his first orchestral recordings with the group in 1927. Billed as the National Gramophonic Society Chamber Orchestra, the group set down Warlock's *Serenade* and Delius's *Summer Night on the River* on 3 January, before documenting Elgar's *Introduction and Allegro for Strings* and Purcell's Suite for Strings (arr. Barbirolli) that October. Built on 'rather loose swaying harmonies of the neo-modal type', the *Serenade* was considered 'a valuable addition to the limited répertoire of modern works for string bands'[29] after it was premiered by Barbirolli in December 1925. It is a little surprising, then, that Barbirolli gave only one further public performance of it after its first hearing.[30] In contrast, the works of Elgar and Delius remained close to his heart for the rest of his long and eventful career and he soon became known as a distinguished interpreter of them.

Although admired by artists such as Sir Henry Wood, Sir Thomas Beecham, Sir Malcolm Sargent, Sir John Pritchard and Sir Mark Elder, Delius's works have often proved divisive. Something of an acquired taste, the composer's music has always struggled to be accepted widely abroad. Take the Vienna Philharmonic, for example. During its 178-year history, the orchestra has given only nine performances of his music, one of which was with Barbirolli at the Salzburg Festival in 1947.[31] With the Boston Symphony Orchestra, the composer's music fared somewhat better, with fifty-six performances being given between 1909 and 2011.[32] Of those, forty were by visiting British conductors, including nine by Barbirolli in 1959 and 1964, the most by any artist with the orchestra. But foreign conductors and ensembles are not alone in their reticence to engage regularly with Delius's unique sound-world: British orchestral players also struggle with it, as Sir Mark Elder has wittily pointed out:

When [Delius's] music appears on the stands of the Hallé in Manchester, there is always a sigh of despondency from the players. But, being British, the players' despondency is always tempered with wit and good humour. We were rehearsing the *Poème* by Chausson, for example, and I asked the players if they knew how the composer died. As the silence was deafening, I filled the void by explaining that it was terribly tragic. Chausson lived in the country and drew inspiration from going on bike-rides almost every day. He would cycle through the countryside using the same route, which he knew by heart and adored. But, on his last, fatal ride, his brakes failed on the way home. He careered down a hill, went straight into a brick wall and died instantly. One player snorted, 'Pity they didn't give a bike to Delius'. When performing *Sea Drift*,[33] the players say that they can't bear how the harmony slithers around like overcooked spaghetti. Even though they often temper their reaction by saying that they enjoy the work, they are not impressed by Delius's music in general.[34]

Had he lived to hear it, Barbirolli probably would have raised a disapproving eyebrow at the Hallé player's response but would hardly have been surprised by it. Undoubtedly, Barbirolli, like Sir Mark, would simply have had the players plug away at these works until they were convinced of their beauty and merit. Barbirolli never lost faith in Delius's sound-world and performed his compositions on no fewer than 684 occasions, with his twenty-one recordings of them representing the alpha and omega of his work in the recording studio.[35]

Little more than a year after making his first commercial discs with his chamber orchestra, Barbirolli was snapped up by the American-born producer, Fred Gaisberg, for HMV. A direct result of a remarkable performance of Elgar's Second Symphony with the London Symphony Orchestra for an indisposed Sir Thomas Beecham on 27 December 1927, Barbirolli's new recording contract should have been an ideal platform from which to proclaim his interest in British composers.[36] HMV was nothing if not commercial, however, and it had no intention of recording works by Warlock, Goossens, van Dieren and Vaughan Williams with him. True, Gaisberg was not averse to taking financial risks and commissioned the first complete recordings of Beethoven's piano sonatas with Artur Schnabel, Mozart's *Le nozze di Figaro* with Fritz Busch and Bach's *Ouvertüren*, 'Brandenburg' Concertos, Cello Suites and *Das wohltemperierte Klavier* with Adolf Busch, Pablo Casals and Edwin Fischer.[37] But these were masterworks by master composers played by master interpreters whose international cache was already established. The same could not be said for Barbirolli or many of the native composers whom he had championed with his chamber orchestra during the early 1920s. Consequently, the only works by living British composers that Barbirolli set down with HMV during the first of his three periods with the company were his second recording of Elgar's *Introduction and Allegro* with the John Barbirolli Chamber Orchestra, Delius's *A Song Before Sunrise* with the New Symphony Orchestra and Quilter's *A Children's Overture* with the London Philharmonic Orchestra.[38]

After extended stints with the British National Opera Company and the Covent Garden Opera Company, Barbirolli moved to the Scottish Orchestra. As the orchestra's Music Director from 1933, he faced a steep learning curve. Apart from a handful of concerts with the London Symphony, the BBC Symphony and the Royal Philharmonic Society Orchestras,[39] J.B.'s professional encounters with the mainstream symphonic repertory were largely restricted to his experiences as an orchestral cellist. While his work in the opera house and the recording studio was undoubtedly demanding and useful in consolidating his conducting technique, those engagements were either as a staff or guest conductor. To be a successful music director is a completely different ball game and not all conductors are suited to that role. Take Carlos Kleiber, for example. Undoubtedly a remarkable artist and a master interpreter, he felt inhibited by the strictures of tenure and functioned best as a visiting conductor. So, too, did Carlo Maria Giulini. And although he was Music Director of the Los Angeles Philharmonic for a period during the late 1970s and early 1980s, he had little interest in the day-to-day running of the orchestra.[40] Conversely, Barbirolli seems to have thrived on the administrative and planning responsibilities that his new job demanded. Combine these with the prospect of conducting a full diary of orchestral concerts for the first time in his career and it might be assumed that he would have been at least a little fazed by the prospect. But this was not the case and he happily set about preparing a schedule of events over the next three years that involved multiple works by more than 100 composers.

Expected to participate actively in the financial management of the Scottish Orchestra, Barbirolli was aware that he needed to keep a cautious eye on the box-office. Viewed retrospectively, it is obvious that the part-time orchestra experienced something of a golden age under Barbirolli.[41] With a glittering roster of soloists that included Arthur Rubinstein, Artur Schnabel, Vladimir Horowitz, Leopold Godowsky, Bronislaw Hubermann and Adolf Busch, and a repertoire that extended from Purcell to Stravinsky, it is equally obvious that this golden age did not come cheaply. Mindful that audiences were increasingly attracted to radio sets rather than concert halls, and that sponsors were jittery after the Wall Street Crash, Barbirolli had to tread cautiously when it came to programming. The easy option would have been to perform an unending stream of standard classics that pandered to the taste of his populist audiences. But Barbirolli believed that conductors had an educational function and should be proactive in broadening audiences' musical experiences and spiritual horizons. Unafraid to preach that message to anyone who would listen, he made it clear that his 'ideal … for orchestral music in Scotland [was] a high and [a] great one'.[42] Moreover, he argued strongly that 'the regeneration of … an art which has drawn some of the noblest inspiration from all that is best in Life, Literature, and Religion … [is] not merely … a cultural asset, but [is also] a spiritual beacon of hope and comfort in our every-day lives'.[43]

To achieve those lofty aims within a national context, it seemed self-evident to Barbirolli that British music had to play its part. But given the box-office's reliance on the works from the Austro-German and Russian canons, it was perhaps inevitable that his compatriots' music would never dominate his orchestra's schedules. Nevertheless, Barbirolli did perform the works of twenty-three British composers with the Scottish Orchestra, of whom fifteen were contemporary.[44] Most frequently heard were the works of Delius and Elgar and least familiar were those of Bax, Walton and Vaughan Williams.[45] Virtually absent from Barbirolli's programmes was Scottish music. Aside from Mackenzie's Overture to *The Cricket on the Hearth*, *Benedictus* and the Funeral March from *Coriolanus*, the only other work by a Scotsman was Hamish MacCunn's 'The Land of the Mountain and the Flood' Overture. But these were compositions by artists who had studied in London and who had spent the greater part of their lives south of the border. Barbirolli did, however, give six performances of the now-forgotten *Scottish Fantasia* by his Sicilian-born brother-in-law, Alfonso Gibilaro. Based on traditional Scottish folksongs, the *Fantasia* always proved popular with local audiences, but is more of a musical postcard than a true expression of Celtic culture.[46]

Adamant that British works should be heard within an international context, Barbirolli nearly always presented them alongside established Continental masterpieces at his Scottish concerts.[47] The exception to that rule occurred on 19 and 20 November 1934 when he conducted an all-English programme that was comprised solely of works by Elgar, Delius and Holst.[48] All three had died earlier that year and all three had appeared in Barbirolli's programmes from the beginning of his career. Left artistically bereft by the loss of three of Britain's greatest creative minds, Barbirolli must have felt that he was witnessing the end of an era. But he was determined that the works of Elgar, Delius and Holst should not sink into obscurity following their deaths. And by generally programming their music side by side with that of other major contemporary figures from abroad, Barbirolli not only did much to secure their place in the pantheon of modern musical masters, but also actively put paid to the myth that Britain was '*Das Land ohne Musik*'.

A KNIGHT AT THE OPERA:
BARBIROLLI AND THE LYRIC THEATRE

Born within a stone's throw of the Royal Opera House, Covent Garden, Sir John Barbirolli was raised by a family besotted with opera. Active musically throughout much of the nineteenth century, the Barbirollis could boast three generations who had distinguished themselves on the Italian operatic scene. With a great-granduncle who had composed an opera for Ferrara's Teatro Apollo in 1837,[49] and a grandfather and father who were members of La Scala's orchestra for the first performance of Verdi's *Otello* on 5 February 1887,[50] Barbirolli must have felt predestined for a life in the theatre. Yet, operatic predestination was not always a given for a young musician growing up in Edwardian and post-Edwardian London, for unlike much of the rest of Western Europe, Britain had something of an uncertain relationship with the lyric stage. Before the Arts Council was established in 1946, opera companies came and went with disarming regularity at Covent Garden, touring troupes were notoriously cash-strapped and managements preferred exotic Continental *maestri* to less-glamorous local conductors.[51] With his foreign-sounding name, his Mediterranean antecedents and his strong familial connection to the Italian operatic canon, Barbirolli's route to the Royal Opera House's podium should have been relatively straightforward. But that route proved more circuitous than either he or his family ever expected, taking him to Aberdeen in the north, Cardiff in the west and Lewisham in the south before it finally reached its Bow Street destination in 1928.

Having started his career as a prodigy cellist, Barbirolli was no stranger to the word '*cantare*'. And what better way to learn 'to sing' on the cello than to play excerpts from well-known operas? Transcriptions of popular arias were big money spinners for artists, publishers and recording companies during the early twentieth century and were often a good means of introducing unknown performers to a wider public. This was certainly the case for Barbirolli, who took his first steps as an operatic musician with his disc of 'O Star of Eve' from Wagner's *Tannhäuser* in 1911.[52] Five years later, he joined the cello section of Henry Wood's Queen's Hall Orchestra before being introduced to professional theatre life as a member of Thomas Beecham's and Carl Rosa's opera bands. After being demobilised from the British army in 1919, he joined the Orchestra of the Royal Opera House, where he took part in the local premiere of Puccini's *Il Trittico*. Supervised by the composer, the rehearsals for the trilogy were a revelation for Barbirolli, and in an article written some thirty-eight years later, he recalled vividly his encounter with the Italian master and the impact that it had on him:

> The first time I ever saw the composer was in 1920, when he was of course world-famous, and when I was at the last desk of the 'cellos in the Covent Garden orchestra. And the occasion was a rehearsal for the first performance in England of his *Trittico* – *Il Tabarro*, *Suor Angelica* and *Gianni Schicchi*. As a young musical enthusiast I had already bought and studied the vocal scores, and these rehearsals, under Gaetano Bavagnoli, who knew the works thoroughly, were a constant source of pleasure for me. This was not so for many of my colleagues in the orchestra, who resented somewhat the conductor's intense application and care for detail. We were rehearsing in the Covent Garden crush-bar foyer, where most preliminary orchestral rehearsals are still held. And I can recall to this day my delight when I looked up and suddenly realised that Puccini himself was standing behind my chair. He was a tall handsome man and we immediately noticed about him one personal idiosyncrasy in dress. He had a passion for English-made striped ties. But when he bought them he was quite unaware that many of them were special ones – either Old School colours or Club ties. And it was rather fun to see him one day masquerading, without knowing it, as an Old Etonian, perhaps the next day as a Carthusian, speculating whether by the next rehearsal he would have "joined" I Zingari![53]

While Puccini's fashion *faux-pas* might well have raised a smugly dismissive eyebrow or two amongst the clannish club-going set of Pall Mall, it was of little lasting importance to Barbirolli, who was more interested in what the composer had to say musically rather than what he did sartorially.

Even though Puccini spoke no English at the rehearsals, it was immediately obvious to Barbirolli that the composer wanted a 'great warmth and subtlety of lyrical expression, allied to an almost constant overall *rubato*' from both the singers and the orchestra. This was achieved in part by 'him singing, to the trombone-players, the big phrase in *Il Tabarro* with a tremendously broad *rubato* on the triplet in the second bar'.[54] But, then, 'in the more purely rhythmical elements of his music, as, for instance, in the opening of *Gianni Schicchi* he sought a tight and sharply accented form of playing'.[55] Barbirolli quickly realised from all this that Puccini was a 'consummate artist … [who did] not write *ff* or even *fff* in unison with voices without a particular tonal concept in mind'. More important still, it was 'the ultimate refinement of his orchestration, and the originality of it'[56] that were amongst the composer's greatest achievements for the aspiring conductor. In particular, it was Puccini's 'beautiful placing of wind chords, and the exquisite and moving quality of his writing for the flute in the lower register'[57] that appealed most to Barbirolli. And then there was the composer's remarkable ability to 'transform thematic material' and to 'give it varied and pregnant meaning'.[58] A case in point for J.B. was the 'four-note figure which opens' *La bohème*. Its transformation from a lively, vital motif into a 'heart-rending' theme by the end of Act 3 truly inspired Barbirolli, who found such things the sure sign of 'an absolute craftsman and [the] master of his particular genre'.[59]

So what did Barbirolli's seminal encounter with Puccini mean for him in the long term and how was that expressed by the conductor in later life? First and foremost, it confirmed for Barbirolli that he possessed a particular affinity with the composer's works and, secondly, that he was uniquely placed to be one of their most active champions. This was certainly borne out statistically, and along with eighty-two excerpts from Puccini's operas that he conducted in the concert hall and the recording studio, Barbirolli gave no fewer than 128 complete performances of *Madama Butterfly*, *La bohème*, *Turandot*, *Tosca* and *Gianni Schicchi* in the opera house; no other lyric composer was performed more frequently by him. And then there was the increasingly contemptuous tone that some commentators and musicians adopted when reflecting on Puccini's more popular scores. J.B. had no time for such artistic snobbery and was quick to counter cultural naivety with swift and damning ripostes. When Joseph Kerman famously quipped that *Tosca* was a 'shabby little shocker' in 1956,[60] for example, Barbirolli rode to the work's defence two years later by barking 'that anyone who can dismiss this opera as mere "blood and thunder" should have himself seen to'.[61] Even a 'sadly neglected' score, such as *Manon Lescaut*, was worthy of attention according to Barbirolli, who argued that 'the quality and the abundance of musical material in it [is] enough for most of the composers of today to be able to write a dozen operas'.[62]

Barbirolli's chance to conduct a complete opera for the first time came in 1926 when he was engaged by the British National Opera Company. News of his BNOC appointment spread like wildfire through Britain's close-knit operatic community, with conductors, singers, managers, journalists, audience members and orchestral musicians all quick to speculate about the neophyte's suitability for the post. But Barbirolli knew that all this gossip was simply white noise. He was more concerned about the task itself and where it might take him professionally. Aware that all the conductors whom he admired in his youth had risen through the ranks of the opera-house system, he hoped that his new appointment would at least ensure a firm foot-hold on the bottom rung of the operatic ladder. Yet, it cannot have escaped him that it would have been considerably easier for him to ascend that ladder in the German-speaking countries with their hierarchal and highly organised approach to theatre management, than in Britain with its paucity of lyric stages. Nevertheless, he was determined to learn the operatic ropes from the bottom up, and even though those ropes were marred by musical and theatrical pitfalls of all kinds, he knew instinctively that 'these [were] compiled to equip an artist [to become the] master of his craft'.[63]

When Barbirolli did take his first tentative steps towards becoming the 'master of his craft', it was with Gounod's *Roméo et Juliette* at the Hippodrome Theatre in Newcastle-upon-Tyne on 22 September 1926. Given with little rehearsal, the performance was nothing short of a triumph and was received positively by press and public alike. The critic for the *Newcastle Chronicle* was particularly smitten by what he saw and heard and was thrilled to report that:

> It was a magnificent performance, with many brilliant stage pictures, and a fine co-operation between orchestra and stage, due to the magnetic and alert conductorship of Mr John Barbirolli … The rich and lavish Oriental colour of the music was quite splendidly realized, and the grandeur of the whole opera was at once impressive and pleasing. There was much enthusiasm, but no speeches were delivered.[64]

Undoubtedly pleased and relieved to have triumphed critically at his first attempt at conducting an opera in a theatre, Barbirolli must have been aware that the performance was only the start of a very steep learning curve. For within three days of that reading, he not only took charge of Puccini's *Madama Butterfly*, but also Verdi's *Aïda* on the same day for the company.[65] Reflecting on those challenges in later life, Barbirolli recalled that:

> I was called upon to conduct Gounod's "Romeo and Juliet", Verdi's "Aïda" and Puccini's "Madame Butterfly" – all in the first week with approximately three

hours of rehearsal! Within a year I was conducting in *Covent Garden* in the so-called "Grand" season.[66] During this time, I was acquiring a repertoire. Those were gruelling days. All day rehearsals went on. Evenings were taken up with performances. Then at five the next morning I would get up to study for a few hours before rehearsal. Since my mother was French and my father was Italian, I knew their native languages, and the knowledge helped in the opera house. Any conductor who wishes to conduct operas with sense should know the languages in which they are sung. Opera is not just notes, it is also drama. I am one of the few to have conducted opera in Covent Garden in four languages.[67]

From Newcastle, Barbirolli and the troupe moved on to Glasgow, Edinburgh, Leeds, Birmingham, Manchester – where he was reviewed as 'Mr Barbarello'[68] – and Liverpool.[69] The company then returned to London where J.B. gave *Roméo et Juliette* at the Golders Green Hippodrome on 12 January 1927.[70] Of the performance, *The Daily Mail* chirped 'Mr. John Barbirolli conducted with zest and the audience was enthusiastic',[71] while *The Morning Post* was delighted that 'the B.N.O.C. … did the orchestration real justice'.[72] But it was Barbirolli's conducting that proved most revealing, as he 'achieved a plasticity and expression that [the critic] had frankly not expected to find'.[73] 'Show[ing] admirable theatre sense', it was also clear to the critic that J.B. 'knew the score inside out, and clearly was able to inspire his players with something of his own understanding and enthusiasm. In short, he was, in my opinion, the real success of the evening'.[74] *The Daily Telegraph* was equally impressed by the novice conductor and reported that:

> [The performance was] immensely helped by Mr. John Barbirolli, whose first London appearance this was in control of the B.N.O.C's forces. The playing of the orchestra showed perfect responsiveness on their part to the wishes of a conductor who very evidently knew exactly what he wanted, and how to get it, so that there was not a detail in the orchestral score that was not treated with care and finish. The singers, moreover, were not a little indebted to Mr. Barbirolli for the always alert and sympathetic accompanying.[75]

After its short season at Golders Green, the company headed north again to Bradford and Manchester, where Barbirolli conducted his first performance of

Rossini's *Il barbiere di Siviglia* on 2 February 1927.[76] Clearly a subscriber to the theory that works are better given by artists who share the same ethnicities as their composers, the critic for *The Yorkshire Post* felt that 'the Opera Company is as British in its constitution as its name would imply, but it has in Mr. Barbirolli a conductor with sufficient Italian blood in his veins to enter into the spirit of the music'.[77] At Bradford in February, J.B. gave *Butterfly* and *Aïda* before adding Humperdinck's *Hänsel und Gretel* to his repertoire. Arranged in conjunction with the Bradford Education Committee, the opera was given in front of 1,600 local school children from Bradford, Halifax, Dewsbury, Bingley, Shipley and the Spen Valley on 10 February. Performed at the Alhambra Theatre at specially reduced prices, the *Yorkshire Observer* considered the afternoon to be 'a happy and valuable adjournment to school study with the formation of good taste'.[78] At Birmingham on 19 March, Barbirolli continued to expand his repertoire with *Il trovatore*, but unlike at Newcastle the previous September, speeches were given at the end of the run with Frederic Austin paying tribute to a new local committee that was formed specifically to support the company. A week later, J.B. conducted *Bohème* in Liverpool and gave another schools' performance of *Hänsel und Gretel*, this time in front of some 2,600 young Merseysiders. So popular was the performance and so great was the demand for tickets that another schools' performance was arranged for a further 2,600 children the following Monday afternoon.

With the onset of summer, the company dispersed and Barbirolli returned to his first love: the cello. With his old chum, Edith Bartlett, he took part in a recital at the New Chenil Galleries on 24 June[79] and amongst the audience that night was the mother of another old chum, Mrs Mulholland, the owner of the Wimbledon Theatre and the King's Theatre, Hammersmith.[80] Deciding to chance his arm, Barbirolli suggested a business proposition to the impresaria. As her theatres were dark during the summer months, and as it might be possible for him to re-form the BNOC in July and August, would she be interested in mounting some repertory works at the two venues?[81] Mrs Mulholland loved the idea and, on 25 July, Barbirolli gave the first of seven performances of *Barbiere* over seven nights at Hammersmith, followed by a second series of seven performances over seven nights at Wimbledon.[82] With well-established casts that included Heddle Nash, Miriam Licette, Parry Jones and Robert Radford, and with theatres that had a combined seating capacity of more than 4,700, the chances of financial success were good. The 'little experiment' did indeed succeed financially and Barbirolli was thrilled by 'the enthusiasm of everybody over the presentation of "The Barber" at Hammersmith'.[83] The critics were also impressed by the short season, and thanks to 'the verve and precision of [Barbirolli's] beat', and to a 'strong cast … [that] ensured good singing and clear diction[,] … there was never a dull moment at [the King's Theatre].[84]

Buoyed by the rave reviews of its *Barbiere* performances during the summer, the BNOC returned to the North Country for the start of its 1927–8 season and kicked off the new artistic year at Newcastle before moving on to Glasgow and Edinburgh.[85] At the Scottish cities, Barbirolli led performances of *Barbiere*, *Aïda*, *Butterfly*, *Bohème* and *Die Meistersinger von Nürnberg*, an opera that had formerly been the province of Malcolm Sargent, a conductor now better remembered for his work on the concert platform than in the theatre. Further north still was Aberdeen, where the troupe made its debut in October with *Barbiere* and where it gave the local premiere of *Die Meistersinger* a few days later.[86] The company's visit triggered something of a stir in the town and the local press was awash with stories and articles about it. Wondering whether Aberdonians would be able to cope artistically, one journalist felt the need to ask:

> Will Aberdeen rise to the occasion? Upon this question hangs the future of grand opera here, and our answer during the week will decide whether it is to be the best or (as in the past) merely what the god of chance sends us. The crowded theatre and the intense enthusiasm last night seemed to indicate that the importance of the occasion was being fully realised. Let us hope it is a good augury for the success of this courageous venture.[87]

The local audience *did* rise to the occasion and the performance *did* confirm the importance of opera for the town. Oozing with parochial pride, the *Aberdeen Journal* was then able to crow:

> The performance of "The Mastersingers" last night probably saw the turning point of the opera week, and fortunately the turning was in the right direction. There was a huge audience, and the audience enjoyed itself hugely. Call after call followed each act, with a storm of applause at the close of the opera. There was not a moment's doubt as to the general enjoyment or its cause, for in "The Mastersingers" Wagner deals with a human subject and real personages.[88]

After performances at Dundee in late October and early November, the company travelled south to Leeds, Newcastle and Birmingham, where Barbirolli conducted *Barbiere*, *Bohème* and *Die Meistersinger*, before returning to the Hippodrome in Golders Green for further performances of *Aïda* and *Die Meistersinger* in December. In January 1928, the troupe gave a series of performances at Lewisham, which again included *Die Meistersinger*.[89] As in Aberdeen, the company played to sold-out houses and, as in Aberdeen, the critics waxed lyrical about the standard of the music-making. But by the time of these performances, Barbirolli was largely conducting the same repertoire over and over again at the same venues.[90] There were some exceptions, however. In Manchester, Birmingham and Liverpool, he caused a sensation with Rimsky-Korsakov's *The Golden Cockerel* during the spring of 1928, while in Scotland that autumn, he conducted Verdi's *Falstaff* for the first time.[91] And although Barbirolli continued to conduct for the BNOC throughout the 1928–9 season, he was aware that the writing was on the wall for the troupe. Facing mounting debts and a tax demand of £17,000, the company was failing financially and was finally wound up in 1929.[92]

But waiting in the wings was Colonel Eustace Blois. A commanding figure who also commanded the financial support of the Hungarian-born banker, Frederick Szarvasy, Blois formed the Covent Garden Opera Syndicate in 1928. During its initial six-week season at the Royal Opera House, the new company staged a formidable sixty performances of nineteen operas, including a complete cycle of Wagner's *Der Ring des Nibelungen* under Bruno Walter.[93] Sharing the podium with the Italian *maestro*, Vincenzo Bellezza, for short runs of *Bohème* and *Butterfly*, Barbirolli also took part in the company's first season and made his Bow Street debut with the latter work on 30 June. Trialled as an 'experiment of Saturday night opera at ordinary theatre prices,'[94] the evening saw J.B. conduct what can only be described as the second cast.[95] Nevertheless, the experiment was a success and Barbirolli not only 'added to his reputation' but also 'contributed a considerable share to the success of the performance' by 'obtain[ing] excellent playing from the orchestra', even though he 'hurr[ied] a little in the first act'.[96] As promising as Barbirolli's performance clearly was, it also drew attention to some of his weaknesses, principal amongst which was his lack of experience in the symphonic repertoire. For *The Times*'s critic, it was clear that he was more at home in the opera house than in the concert hall and 'succeeds in obtaining vivid and detailed playing [in the theatre] without sacrificing the flow and unity of the whole as he sometimes does in the concert room'.[97] It seems, then, that Barbirolli still had a great deal to learn.

Sufficiently impressed by Barbirolli's readings of *Bohème* and *Butterfly*, Blois invited J.B. back to Covent Garden the following year. Confident that the conductor had still more to offer musically, Blois decided to allow him to take sole charge of a run of performances of Mozart's *Don Giovanni*, rather than simply taking over an established interpretation from a more experienced senior colleague. Admittedly, the run was short and, admittedly, it only involved three performances, but what it lacked in length it made up for in difficulty. A technical and musical minefield that is notoriously challenging for unsuspecting young *maestri*, Mozart's Prague masterpiece either succeeds or fails depending on the theatrical and interpretative skills of its conductor. With its demanding accompanied recitatives, its difficult multi-movement finales and its complex tempo relationships, the opera sets challenges that even the most experienced of Mozartians find daunting. It cannot have escaped Barbirolli that when it was last heard at Covent Garden it was under the direction of Bruno Walter with a star-studded cast of singers that included Frida Leider, Lotte Lehmann, Elisabeth Schumann and Marianno Stabile.[98] Clearly aware of the big shoes he had to fill, and of the musical complexities that he was about to confront, Barbirolli explained in an interview with the *Daily Express* on the morning of the first performance that:[99]

> I cannot remember ever experiencing so many conflicting emotions. I am thrilled and apprehensive; hopeful and nervous; happy and unhappy; awed and confident. And all at the same time … I want [*Don Giovanni*] to be so fine … I am conscious of the great privilege that is being entrusted to a young Englishman to conduct at the Garden at all and especially at being entrusted with the performance of a work which is notoriously one of the most difficult in the repertoire … I know it is going to be a moving experience to stand in the place where so many illustrious conductors have stood before me … I have literally been living with the score in front of me. I study it the whole time. The great difficulty is to sustain dramatic unity throughout … It has all my waking moments. I dream of it, and sometimes I wake at three or four in the morning and go and turn over the pages. I feel that I must keep in touch.[100]

Barbirolli's 'waking moments' were well spent and all his hard work paid off. The first performance on 27 May 1929 was a resounding success with his natural ability as an orchestral trainer being considered one of his greatest strengths. *The Times* reported that:

> Mr John Barbirolli had a difficult task in combining so heterogeneous a team, and he showed his ability in the result he succeeded in obtaining. Much of the orchestral playing was very fine, notably the delicate wind passages of the ballroom scene and the richly imaginative orchestration of the last scene of all.[101]

Seen as a triumph of musical common sense over operatic snobbery by some members of the press, Barbirolli's successful return to Covent Garden was also considered by *The Gramophone* as something of a turning point for British conductors at the theatre:

> It will be remembered that Mr. Barbirolli conducted twice at the tail end of the Italian season last year, and his re-engagement for this season is proof of the excellent impression that he then made. His brilliant work with the B.N.O.C. has won him this great distinction, and he is probably the only conductor who has never conducted an opera outside England and yet has been chosen for the International Season at Covent Garden. Mr. Albert Coates had won his spurs in Russia before he earned a similar distinction.[102]

With two successful engagements with the Covent Garden Opera Syndicate under his belt, Barbirolli was the obvious choice to lead the company's touring troupe from the autumn of 1929. Starting at Theatre Royal, Halifax, with *Die Meistersinger* on 23 September, Barbirolli took charge of a company that consisted largely of former members of the BNOC. Not only were many of the singers and orchestra familiar to him, so, too, were most of the venues and the majority of the repertoire. But familiarity was no guarantee of excellence, particularly as far as Barbirolli's management of the orchestra was concerned. Unlike at Bow Street, he seemed to have trouble balancing the fifty-strong ensemble and failed to maintain continuity in the opera's overture. Reflecting on *Die Meistersinger* in Halifax, *The Times*'s 'Special Correspondent' grumbled that 'the difficulty of hearing words was increased by the almost uniform loudness of the orchestral playing under Mr. John Barbirolli who rarely gave us a real *pianissimo*. In other respects the conductor held the work together well, though he began badly by chopping the overture into little pieces'.[103] Barbirolli's reading of *Turandot* at Halifax five nights later also failed to impress, prompting the 'Special Correspondent' to bemoan:

> [Barbirolli's] brusque beat, while keeping things lively, chopped the rhythms into little pieces, whereas what Puccini's music needs is a careful welding together to conceal its tendency to be short-breathed. It was, perhaps, not the conductor's fault that the orchestra sounded uniformly too loud, since there is no orchestral pit. It was hardly to be expected that an orchestra of 50 players could present the full elaboration of Puccini's score … The chorus sang well in the first act, but a general hesitation in attack, some serious faults of intonation, and several missed leads showed that more rehearsals are needed before they can sing the music with assurance.[104]

Given Britain's lack of commitment to opera in general, reviews such as these were perhaps inevitable. In a German city of a similar size to Halifax, there would have been a theatre capable of staging a large opera. In fact, a German city of that size would have had an opera company of its own and would have had no need for a visiting company with an undersized orchestra and a sub-standard chorus to introduce Puccini's final operatic masterpiece to them. But with all its faults, this very British way of presenting the score was a relatively effective means of giving provincial audiences a chance to experience opera first hand. And while art should never be used as a job-opportunity scheme, it did provide work for a great many conductors, singers and orchestral players at a time of great financial uncertainty. It also gave Barbirolli the chance to explore works that were new to him, and with either the Covent Garden Opera Company on tour or the Covent Garden Opera Syndicate at the Royal Opera House, he was able to add Johann Strauss II's *Die Fledermaus*, Puccini's *Gianni Schicchi*, Smetana's *The Bartered Bride*, Smyth's *The Wreckers*, Richard Strauss's *Der Rosenkavalier*, Verdi's *Rigoletto* and Wagner's *Tristan und Isolde* to his ever-expanding operatic repertoire.

With Barbirolli's appointment as Music Director of the Scottish Orchestra in 1933, his work in the opera house was temporarily put on hold. Nevertheless, he did continue to perform extracts from operas with his new orchestra with 'bleeding chunks' from Wagner's music dramas being especially popular.[105] From the late-nineteenth century onwards, all-Wagner programmes were particularly common in the English-speaking nations, due, largely, to the relatively small number of opera theatres in those countries. Barbirolli openly embraced that trend and gave at least two such programmes with the Scottish Orchestra. When he was appointed Music Director of the New York Philharmonic-Symphony Orchestra in 1937, he continued to programme all-Wagner concerts and went on to give a further ten during his six seasons with the orchestra, the last of which was at Carnegie Hall on 5 April 1942.[106] At best, the critical reaction to that performance was mixed with *The New York Times* being less than impressed by Barbirolli's pacing of the programme:

> The idea of moving from the devotional pages of "Parsifal" to the festive music from the third act of "Die Meistersinger" was a good one and would have been the more effective had the "Meistersinger" excerpts been more knowingly interpreted. That Mr. Barbirolli invested the excerpts from "Meistersinger" with more life and vigor than the rest was inevitable because of the nature of the score. But otherwise it could not be called an improvement on what had preceded.[107]

When Barbirolli returned to Britain in 1943 as Permanent Conductor of the Hallé Orchestra, operatic excerpts were also heard regularly at his concerts, but as Music Director of the Houston Symphony Orchestra from 1961, they all but disappeared.[108] Yet, given the regularity with which this type of concert appeared in his programmes over the years, there can be little doubt that Barbirolli felt committed to it and perhaps even considered it a form of compensation for not being able to spend more time in the theatre. Of course, some performances had greater personal significance for him than others, and three on which he lavished particular care were his reading of Act 2 from Wagner's *Tristan und Isolde* at the Royal Albert Hall, London, in 1954 and his performances of Puccini's *Madama Butterfly* and Verdi's *Otello* at the Free Trade Hall, Manchester, in 1966 and 1968 respectively.[109]

After conducting the first performance of *Tristan* at Munich in 1865,[110] Hans von Bülow rhapsodised that it was 'as beautiful as the most beautiful of dreams … [and] simply indescribable … [because of the] dreadful fascination it exerts[;] … an experience beyond time and place'.[111] With two outstanding Wagnerians - Wolfgang Windgassen and Martha Mödl – in the title roles, and with an extremely musical contralto – Constance Shacklock – as Brangäne, Barbirolli might well have hoped for a similar transcendental response after his London performance of Act 2. But any hopes of that kind were largely dashed when Windgassen let the team down by his apparent lack of preparation and his very obvious vocal difficulties. Having failed to memorise the score, and having been overwhelmed by the orchestral accompaniment at the performance, the tenor elicited a less-than-enthusiastic reception from the critics with *The Times* reporting that:

> Mr. Wolfgang Windgassen seemed more dependent on this occasion on his printed score, and was thus less able to fling his whole heart into his passion—which sounded lukewarm. His tone was a little thin and his voice not always audible above the orchestra in climaxes.[112]

All was not lost, however, and it was generally felt that the real star of the evening was Barbirolli. It seems that his years in the opera house had paid dividends and had equipped him with the necessary tools to tackle even the most difficult of jobs. Looking to the orchestra to compensate, at least in part, for Windgassen's very noticeable vocal shortcomings, Barbirolli drew playing from the Hallé which 'offer[ed] beautifully mellowed tones … and much finely wrought pliable phrasing throughout'.[113]

With the prospect of recording *Madama Butterfly* in Rome for HMV during the summer of 1966, Barbirolli decided to reacquaint himself with the score by conducting two concert performances of it at the Free Trade Hall.[114] In an attempt to breathe some extra dramatic life into the proceedings, J.B. opted for a semi-staged approach with the singers performing in full concert dress. A serious miscalculation that provoked the ire of the local critics, the partial staging was considered a clumsy distraction that came close to derailing the whole performance:

> With the singers in concert evening dress doing some sketchy acting on a slightly raised platform behind the audience [*sic*][,] I think I would have rather seen them stiffly lined in front of the orchestra, in oratorio style, for this was the sort of compromise that ran pretty close to disaster. How close it was could be seen when the singers with less stage experience than those in the most important parts attempted the same stylized movements and looked most uncomfortable in doing so.[115]

But Barbirolli's years of experience with the score shone through. Paced expertly so that the climactic structure of the work was clearly evident to performers and listeners alike, J.B.'s architectonically sensitive reading was the undoubted highlight of the evening. And while *The Guardian*'s critic was eager to point this out, he could not quite let go of his misgivings about the staging even at the very end of the review:

> As for Sir John Barbirolli's conducting, it was even better than I (who have never heard him conduct an opera before) had hoped. It was never lacking in drama, but it was also a beautifully detailed performance in the orchestra and there was a sensible restraint in the early stages that made the climax of the final scene all the more effective, musically. What a pity that the platform arrangements allowed the dramatic climax to escape and leave the impression of a not very advanced stage in an opera house rehearsal.[116]

Only too aware of its central place in his family's history, *Otello* was something of an artistic holy relic for Barbirolli. To be treated with the greatest awe and respect, Verdi's late masterpiece was only ever going to be performed by him under the best possible conditions, and perhaps this is why he never conducted it with the BNOC or the Covent Garden Opera Syndicate. With their minimal budgets, their paucity of rehearsal time and their diminutive orchestras, these companies offered conditions that were far from optimal when preparing and performing a work of such great personal significance. By May 1968, however, Barbirolli had shaped the Hallé in his own musical image and had assembled a cast that he felt sure would meet the vocal challenges that Verdi's mature masterpiece presented.[117] And it seems that he was right to have waited. *The Guardian*'s critic was delighted by what he heard at the first of the two performances and reported that: 'the fourth act began marvellously … for here there were two scenes which depended to a large extent on the singing of Elizabeth Vaughan … They depended, too, on Sir John Barbirolli's lyrical sensitivity, and it was his sympathy for the fate of Desdemona that distinguished this performance above all'.[118] But what was Barbirolli's own response to those performances, did they meet his high expectations and were they worth waiting for? He was, in fact, overwhelmed by the whole thing and later confided to his engagement book: 'My first Otello. Triumphant reception and nobly served by all concerned. Feel humbly grateful that this has been vouchsafed me, on this great occasion of my 25 years with [the] Hallé [Orchestra]'.[119]

When the Royal Opera House reopened for business after the Second World War, the first operatic sounds heard there were not produced by local singers and musicians, but by members of the Teatro di San Carlo, Naples, who were in London to perform two short seasons of Italian masterworks.[120] But by the time of those seasons in September and November 1946, plans were already well underway for a permanent British opera company to be based at the theatre and to be funded partially by the newly established Arts Council. Yet, when the new troupe finally did take to the stage for the first time in 1947, it was not with a British music director at its helm, but with an Austrian, Karl Rankl. Viewed with some political suspicion at the time,[121] Rankl's tenure was relatively short, and when it was announced that he was to give up his post in 1950, it was hoped that Barbirolli would be his replacement. Discussions were had and arguments were made, but after much toing and froing, J.B. decided that the job was not for him and opted to remain with the Hallé Orchestra instead. Nevertheless, he did conduct multiple performances of *Turandot*, *Aïda*, *Bohème*, *Butterfly*, *Tristan* and *Orfeo ed Euridice* with the company between 1951 and 1953. Considered transformational at the time, Barbirolli's masterfully paced performances with the troupe then went on to become treasured musical memories for many of those who were lucky enough to be present. The opera historian, Harold Rosenthal, was one such person and later recalled affectionately that 'Barbirolli was warmly welcomed by the audience, and he treated them to some of the finest playing heard in Italian opera … since before the war; the strings glowed and throbbed and the woodwind were sonorous'.[122]

With those Covent Garden performances at an end, Barbirolli's career in the lyric theatre had nearly come full circle. But there was still one final theatrical ambition that he had yet to achieve: to conduct an Italian opera at a leading Italian opera house. With very few exceptions, Barbirolli's years in the theatre were largely spent in the British Isles. True, he had conducted *Aïda* twice with the Vienna Staatsoper at the Theater an der Wien in 1947, but extended visits to foreign opera houses were largely out of the question due to his unswerving devotion to the Hallé Orchestra. Thanks to the remarkable success of his HMV recording of *Butterfly* with the musical resources of the Teatro dell'Opera at Rome in 1966, however, J.B.'s dream finally came true. Impressed by his idiomatic understanding of the score, and inspired by his deep commitment to Italian opera in general, the company's management was determined to lure him back to the theatre and set about pursuing him with vigour.[123] But with the chance of conducting his beloved *Aïda* with a stellar cast that included Gwyneth Jones, Gianfranco Cecchele and Fiorenza Cossotto, Barbirolli needed little convincing. And it must have been with a sense of great pride that he mounted the podium on 14 April 1969 to perform a complete opera in the land of his forefathers for the first time.[124] A fitting operatic farewell for an artist who placed great store by tradition, Barbirolli's time in Rome was not only special to him, but to all of those who took part in the production. Indelibly etched on the memories of his fellow artists, J.B's reading of Verdi's opera that spring took on a near legendary status in the decades that followed and it was Gwyneth Jones who best captured the spirit of that remarkable period when she wrote some fifty years later:

> The time I spent in Rome with Sir John and his lovely wife, Evelyn Rothwell, whilst doing a new production of Aïda, six performances at the Rome Opera in the spring of 1969, was very special. Sir John always wore a very large hat, of which he was very proud, as it was a gift from Toscanini. When we walked through the streets to have lunch in our favourite trattoria after the rehearsals heads were constantly turning to take a second look at this very special little man with the enormous hat. Everyone adored him![125]

IN DEFENCE OF THE REALM: BARBIROLLI AND BRITISH MUSIC (PART TWO) – FROM NEW YORK TO MANCHESTER

When the charismatic Hungarian conductor, Arthur Nikisch, was asked for programming ideas for his tour of the United States with the London Symphony Orchestra in 1912, he immediately thought of Elgar's 'Enigma' Variations and First Symphony. He had no doubt that 'the greatest symphony of modern times, written by the greatest modern composer'[126] would have New Yorkers queuing in their thousands for tickets. But the tour's sceptical American sponsors thought otherwise. Petrified that Elgar's works would prove fatal at the box-office, they rejected them out of hand in favour of more popular pieces by Beethoven, Tchaikovsky, Weber, Strauss, Liszt and Wagner.[127] Yet, by the time of Nikisch's tour, Elgar's music was already familiar to American audiences thanks to the pioneering work of Walter Damrosch, Fritz Steinbach and Gustav Mahler. So, too, were the works of Delius, Bax, Ireland, Goossens, Vaughan Williams, Walton, Bliss and Anthony Collins by the time of Barbirolli's appointment as Music Director of the New York Philharmonic-Symphony Orchestra in 1937. But being familiar was some way from being besotted. For most Americans, British music was best left to British audiences. Determined to change American musical hearts and minds, Barbirolli decided that a different approach was necessary if the music of his fellow countrymen was ever to be given a fair hearing in the United States. Perhaps a world premiere or two might do the trick? And who better to prick the curiosity of his conservative Knickerbocker audience than Britain's newest rising musical star, the young Benjamin Britten.

A college friend of Barbirolli's second wife, the oboist Evelyn Rothwell, Britten left England for North America in April 1939.[128] A particularly productive period for the composer, Britten's stay in the United States resulted in the world premieres of his Violin Concerto and *Sinfonia da Requiem* being given by Barbirolli and the Philharmonic-Symphony Orchestra in 1940 and 1941 respectively. Performed first by its dedicatee, the Spanish violinist, Antonio Brosa, the Violin Concerto was an instant and unqualified critical success, with the city's reviewers rapturous in their praise of both the performance and the work itself.[129] Writing in the *New York*

World-Telegram, Louis Biancolli probably summed up the critics' delight best when he wrote 'Mr. Britten's concerto is the last word in musical sophistication [and] bubbles over with tart wit and cleverness'.[130] But critics can be fickle and were left bewildered after attending the premiere of the *Sinfonia da Requiem* the following year.[131] Completely unimpressed by the composer's new sound-world, Noel Straus pulled no punches in *The New York Times* when he wrote:

> From start to finish, the shrilly, dissonant score … favored [*sic*] a type of sound heavy above and below, with little or nothing in the middle … its themes were neither symphonic in essence nor symphonically developed in any real sense … The pronounced weakness of the entire composition was its pitiful lack of emotional warmth … [The] "Lachrymosa" failed … because nothing more was suggested than merely the wailing and shrieking of instruments … [and the] "Dies Irae" was simply wild and noisy … Piling up climaxes was the chief form of procedure in both movements, climaxes just for their own sake. The "Requiem Aeternam" … at times verged on real emotional utterance, but never achieved it.[132]

For the overly sensitive Britten, the critical response to his new work must have come as a great blow, probably made worse by the reviewers' near-universal praise of Barbirolli's spirited reading of it. Conducting 'with the zeal of an evangelist',[133] the young British *maestro* was 'congratulated for two reasons: first because he presented the *Sinfonia* and second because he presented it so well'.[134] And from a private recording of the second performance's broadcast, it is immediately obvious why it was felt that J.B. 'conducted with authority and imagination'.[135]

With tempi that were considerably more extreme in the second and third movements than those indicated in the printed score, Barbirolli not only risked musical life and limb but put a very personal stamp on the reading as a whole. And while J.B.'s markedly quicker speed in the *Dies Irae* and the decidedly slower tempo in the *Requiem Aeternam* might well have added a certain frisson and poignancy to the performance, they were clearly at odds with the composer's published intentions.[136] Britten never forgave Barbirolli for these interpretative indiscretions and harboured a grudge against the conductor for the rest of his life. Writing many years later, Barbirolli's wife, Evelyn, recalled that 'these performances were crucially important for Ben at this stage of his career and I know that John was hurt that Ben never acknowledged them in later years'.[137] Even though Barbirolli was one of the first of Britten's famous 'corpses', an artistic mortuary that would later include Eric Crozier, Lord Harewood, Sir John Pritchard and Sir Charles Mackerras, he remained committed to the composer's music to the end of his life. Aware that great art should always transcend petty insecurities, Barbirolli went on to give a further seventy-five performances of Britten's works after leaving New York, ten of which were of the Violin Concerto and twenty-nine were of the *Sinfonia da Requiem*.

By the time of the Britten premieres, war was raging in Europe and Barbirolli longed to return home. Eager to help in any way that he could, he courageously crossed the Atlantic by convoy in April 1942 in order to give concerts with England's beleaguered orchestras that summer. Shocked by both the level of devastation that he witnessed and the degree of misery that was being endured by the British public, he was determined to return permanently to his homeland and to stand shoulder to shoulder with his fellow countrymen. After returning to North America in August for guest appearances in Los Angeles, San Francisco, Seattle, Vancouver and Chicago, he arrived back in New York in February 1943. Within days of resuming his duties with the Philharmonic-Symphony Orchestra, a telegram arrived inviting him to become the Permanent Conductor of Manchester's Hallé Orchestra. He leapt at the chance and set sail for Britain that summer. As a musical patriot, it seemed only natural that he should champion the works of his fellow countrymen with his new band and that the music of Britain's greatest living composer should be at the heart of his programming policy.

Barbirolli first encountered the works of Ralph Vaughan Williams as a student at the Royal Academy of Music. Quickly attracted to the composer's unique sound-world, J.B. performed and recorded Vaughan Williams's pieces as a chamber musician, both at home and abroad. As a young conductor, Barbirolli then led an early performance of the *Concerto Accademico* with his Chenil Chamber Orchestra in 1928,[138] before giving the *Fantasia on Sussex Folk-Songs*, the Suite from *Job*, the *Fantasia on a Theme by Thomas Tallis*, *Toward the Unknown Region* and the *Fantasia on Christmas Carols* with the Royal Philharmonic Society and Scottish Orchestras during the 1930s.[139] But it was not until he was appointed Music Director of the New York Philharmonic-Symphony Orchestra that J.B. conducted one of Vaughan Williams's symphonies for the first time. Eager to share his enthusiasm for the composer's music with his American audiences, he gave the haunting Third Symphony on 16 February 1938.[140] Unaware that the work is actually a deeply moving elegiac commentary on the futility of war, the American critics' responses were largely shaped by their misunderstanding of the work's Arcadian title, 'A Pastoral Symphony'. Misunderstanding or not, they were impressed by the composition as a whole, with *The New York Times*'s Noel Straus predicting that Vaughan Williams's 'intensely personal and poetic creation [would] outlive most of the other symphonies of the present time'.[141] *The Sun*'s Irving Kolodin was also impressed by the work and was quick to praise Barbirolli's 'devoted and understanding treatment of [it]' which he felt was handled with 'particular finesse and sympathy'.[142]

Two years then passed before the conductor was able to perform another of Vaughan Williams's symphonies for his New York audience. Again a personal first for Barbirolli, his reading of the composer's Second Symphony ('A London Symphony') on 8 February 1940 was considered so compelling that Kolodin concluded:[143]

> Mr. Barbirolli's sympathy for the music of his countrymen has been among the strongest of the inclinations he has manifested here. It found an eloquent outlet in the poetic score of Vaughan Williams, which, if not the strikingly original utterance it once seemed, is nevertheless music of warm spirit and enduring craftsmanship. The performance rounded out an evening of excellent playing by the orchestra.[144]

But it was only after being made Permanent Conductor of the Hallé Orchestra in 1943 that Barbirolli began to perform and record Vaughan Williams's symphonies frequently. Before taking up his post at Manchester, J.B. had only given twenty-six performances of ten works by the composer, a tally that grew exponentially over the next twenty-seven years to a formidable 531 performances of twenty-nine works. From a closer analysis of these statistics, it seems that three compositions were of particular importance to Barbirolli and were given most frequently by him: *Fantasia on a Theme by Thomas Tallis* and the Sixth and Eighth Symphonies. Of the first, he gave a remarkable 119 performances and, of the second and third, he gave a-not-inconsiderable sixty-nine and seventy-nine performances respectively.

With its luxuriant string writing and its modal nod to England's glorious musical past, the *Fantasia* appealed to Barbirolli's instincts as a virtuoso string player and his passion for British history. Conversely, the Sixth Symphony was very much of its time and was a work that awakened in him memories of the privation and loss that so many had suffered during the Second World War. With its challenging harmonies, its recurring rhythmic figures and its unsettling *pianissimo* last movement, Barbirolli saw the symphony as a telling commentary on man's inhumanity to man and a stark reminder of the pointlessness of armed conflict.[145] Having performed close to the front line for Allied servicemen during 1944, Barbirolli identified immediately with the work's perceived anti-war message and gave it for the first time on 2 July 1948. Following that performance with the Hallé Orchestra at the Cheltenham Music Festival, he conducted it throughout the length and breadth of Great Britain and Ireland over the next two years before taking it to Lisbon, Sydney, Melbourne, Houston, New York, Washington, Boston and Munich.[146]

After a particularly 'beautifully played'[147] performance of the Sixth Symphony at Oxford's Sheldonian Theatre on 2 June 1949, a deep and intimate friendship developed between Barbirolli and Vaughan Williams. Over the next three years, the conductor performed the composer's symphonies regularly, culminating in all six existing symphonies being given during the Hallé Orchestra's first season in the newly re-opened Free Trade Hall in 1951.[148] Encouraged by Barbirolli's undoubted commitment to his music, the ageing Vaughan Williams then entrusted the conductor with a series of premieres of which the *Sinfonia antartica* was the first.[149] Then came the Tuba Concerto, followed shortly by the Eighth Symphony.[150] Overwhelmed and overjoyed by the conductor's reading of the *Sinfonia antartica*, Vaughan Williams famously wrote on Barbirolli's copy of the programme: 'For glorious John, the glorious conductor of a glorious orchestra'.[151] Equally delighted by Barbirolli's reading of his 'robust [and] buccaneering' Tuba Concerto,[152] the composer then decided to express his gratitude more permanently by dedicating the Eighth Symphony to the conductor. But little more than two years after inscribing 'For Glorious John, with love and admiration from Ralph' on the first page of the manuscript score, Vaughan Williams was dead. On learning of the loss of his beloved friend, colleague and hero, Barbirolli wrote movingly:

> Early on the morning of 26 August [1958] there passed from us one of the greatest and most beloved figures in British musical history. I have been privileged to have had his intimate musical and personal friendship for many years; years that were to become more and more precious as they passed. He was one of the most 'complete' (if I may use the word) men I have ever known. He loved life, he loved work, and his interest in all music was unquenchable and insatiable. Only a few weeks ago in Cheltenham at the Festival of British

Contemporary Music, he was in his place at ten o'clock every morning to hear us rehearse the efforts of his youngest, sometimes even obscure, contemporaries, and we all marvelled at him. It is given to few men to touch the hearts and minds of his fellows in such degree as he has done; and only to the anointed is given the genius that can span such opposites as the lovely little 'Linden Lea' and the tremendous Fourth Symphony. Dear Ralph: we shall always honour, admire and be grateful to you; but above all we shall always feel blessed that we walked the same earth with you.[153]

Aside from Elgar and Delius, Vaughan Williams was undoubtedly the British composer with whom Barbirolli identified most closely and whose music he performed most frequently during his Manchester years. Along with his critically acclaimed concert performances of the composer's works, he also made iconic recordings of *Fantasia on a Theme by Thomas Tallis*, *Fantasia on 'Greensleeves'*, the Overture to *The Wasps* and *Five Variants of Dives and Lazarus* with various orchestras during that period. But what of the symphonies and why did Barbirolli record only four of them?[154] With all nine firmly in his repertoire, the absence of *A Sea Symphony*, 'The Pastoral Symphony' and the Fourth, Sixth and Ninth Symphonies from his discography is puzzling. Perhaps there were scheduling problems or perhaps EMI and Pye[155] felt that Sir Adrian Boult and Sir Malcolm Sargent had stronger claims to these works.[156] The answer might never be known. But what is certain is that the failure of the recording companies to document all nine symphonies with one of their most gifted and committed interpreters was neglectful musically and short-sighted historically.

And who amongst the other living British composers did Barbirolli champion during his Manchester tenure and how committed was he to them? For those commentators and listeners who mistakenly assume that J.B. was something of a musical reactionary whose symphonic interests began and ended with the works of Brahms, Bruckner, Mahler, Elgar and Delius, they might be surprised to learn that he performed pieces by no fewer than fifty-five contemporary British composers during his Hallé years. Along with works by Vaughan Williams, he frequently conducted the music of Walton, Britten, Bax, Rubbra, Alwyn, Rawsthorne, Moeran, Arnold and Berkeley. Given less often were the compositions of McCabe, Simpson, Racine Fricker, Hoddinott, Stanley Bate, Iain Hamilton and John Veale. Noticeably absent from these lists is Michael Tippett. Barbirolli struggled to come to terms with the composer's challenging sound-world and abandoned the Second Symphony during rehearsals, arguing that it was 'not worth the effort involved'.[157] But Barbirolli's antipathy to Tippett's music seems to have been the exception rather than the rule and it was during his annual visits to the Cheltenham Music Festival that J.B. made his greatest contribution to the music of his own time.

Having started conservatively with two programmes of established masterworks at both the 1945 and 1946 festivals, Barbirolli upped the new-music ante from 1947. Performing annually at Cheltenham until 1958, he conducted seventy-four works by forty-two contemporary British composers.[158] After returning to the festival with more conventional programmes in 1962 and 1964, he then went on to perform Rawsthorne's 'Street Corner' Overture and Racine Fricker's First Symphony in 1965, before devoting a complete programme to twentieth-century composers in 1966.[159] At that performance, Barbirolli and the Hallé Orchestra gave the world premiere of John McCabe's First Symphony ('Elegy'). Dedicated to both conductor and orchestra, the 'sombre' symphony was dismissed as 'nothing really worth thinking about' by *The Times*'s 'Special Correspondent'.[160] But Barbirolli knew only too well from the reviews of Britten's *Sinfonia da Requiem* in New York that critics can often miss the musical point and can be unnecessarily harsh when confronted by the unfamiliar. He was also aware that little can be gained by dismissing out of hand the early works of young composers. Both Britten and McCabe were only in their late twenties at the time of their premieres and had their artistic lives in front of them. While posterity has favoured Britten's work, Barbirolli was determined that McCabe's symphony should have a fair hearing. Consequently, he programmed it on six further occasions in the nine months following its first performance.

In 1958, Barbirolli returned to North America for the first time since 1943 for an extensive tour.[161] Nothing short of a festival of British music, the tour started with the Winnipeg Symphony Orchestra on 4 December before moving south to the United States for two concerts with the Detroit Symphony Orchestra. J.B. then visited the Boston Symphony, Los Angeles Philharmonic, San Francisco Symphony and Vancouver Symphony Orchestras before ending the tour with sixteen concerts with the New York Philharmonic at the beginning of the New Year.[162] Trumpeted by the *New York Journal-American* as a 'homecoming for Sir John',[163] his return to the Big Apple was greeted warmly by musicians, audiences and critics alike. Hailed in the local press as an ambassador for British music, J.B. conducted twenty performances of seven works by six of his fellow countrymen with the Philharmonic, including the local premieres of Vaughan Williams's Eighth Symphony, Arnold's 'Tam O'Shanter' Overture and Walton's Violin Concerto.[164] But without question the highlight of his New York concerts, and arguably the tour as a whole, were his four Carnegie Hall performances of Elgar's *The Dream of Gerontius*.[165] Given only once before by the orchestra under Nicholas Elsenheimer in 1913, the work was greeted warmly by the press and public and so, too, was Barbirolli's reading of it. Writing in *The New York Times*, Howard Taubman was particularly impressed by the conductor's approach to the oratorio and argued that 'it is not often that one encounters so comprehending an interpretation of a large-scale work'.[166] But it was *Musical America* that probably summed up the response of the critics best when it stated simply: 'To Sir John, the orchestra, the soloists and the chorus one can offer congratulations for an ideal performance'.[167]

The American critics were equally impressed by Barbirolli's performances of his own *An Elizabethan Suite*. An indefatigable arranger of music by masters from the past, J.B. was something of a child of his time in this regard and unashamedly reworked the music of others to meet his own specific performance needs. Ranging chronologically from Purcell to Bax, Barbirolli edited, transcribed and arranged the music of at least twenty composers during his career. Challenging both technically and interpretatively, *An Elizabethan Suite* is a sumptuous modern arrangement of works by four Tudor composers for strings and four horns.[168] Based on music by John Bull, the work's last movement is particularly effective and is a taxing exploration of string technique that even the most virtuosic of orchestras find demanding. Given for the first time in Los Angeles in 1941, the suite then became something of a musical calling-card for Barbirolli and he performed it at fifteen of his sixteen concerts during his 1958–9 tour of North America.[169] Invariably given as a 'tasteful, atmospheric curtain raiser',[170] the suite charmed the New York critics. Unconcerned that it was 'no more Elizabethan than a subway', they were delighted that it was 'a handsome … tonic to the ear … [that] was played … with a golden lustre absent from the Philharmonic's string section for fully fifteen years'.[171]

An undoubted triumph, Barbirolli's 1958–9 tour of North America confirmed for him the musical and financial benefits of international guest conducting. Determined to build on the success of that tour, he returned to North America at the beginning of 1960 for concerts in St. Louis, Houston, San Antonio, Toronto, Atlanta, Chicago and Oklahoma. British music once again took pride of place in his programmes with eighteen of the tour's twenty concerts containing a work by one or more of his fellow countrymen.[172] Concerts with the Czech Philharmonic, the Hungarian State Symphony Orchestra and the Israel Philharmonic quickly followed, before short tours of Iberia, Switzerland, Scandinavia, Italy and Eastern Europe over the next few years. Between these relatively brief visits, J.B. made more extended excursions to Central America, South America and the Caribbean with the Philharmonia, New Philharmonia and Hallé Orchestras in 1963, 1965 and 1968 respectively. Aware of his continuing role as a cultural ambassador during these tours, Barbirolli was adamant that the works of Elgar, Delius, Vaughan Williams, Britten, Walton and Rawsthorne should be given centre stage, an ambition that was finally realised fully during the Hallé's 1968 tour, where British compositions were heard at twenty-two of the twenty-three concerts given.[173]

Along with his ongoing work with the Hallé Orchestra, Barbirolli's engagements as a regular guest conductor with the Berlin Philharmonic from 1961 were also of importance to him. While it might be something of a stretch to suggest that German-speaking musicians and audiences were, and to a large extent still are, antipathetic to British music, it is probably fair to say that English works have never been high on most Teutonic artistic agendas. When, for example, the renowned British conductor, Sir John Pritchard, began a rehearsal of a work by Elgar with a distinguished German orchestra in the 1980s, it was quite clear that it was alien to the players. Asked by Pritchard whether they had ever played a work by Elgar before, they looked perplexed and shook their heads vigorously. Then asked whether they had ever heard a work by Elgar before, they gave an equally perplexed look and continued to shake their heads with vigour. But a hand *did* rise hesitantly from near the back of the cello section which piqued Sir John's interest. Keen to chat more to the young player to whom the hand belonged, Pritchard tracked him down at the rehearsal break and quizzed him about his encounter with Elgar's music. Slightly overwhelmed by the conductor's interest, the cellist vaguely recalled having heard the composer's Cello Concerto some time earlier but didn't particularly like it and hadn't bother to investigate it further.[174] And if Arthur Nikisch's, Wilhelm Furtwängler's and Herbert von Karajan's programmes with the Berlin Philharmonic are anything to go by, they, too, found British music largely unappealing. True, Nikisch had performed works by Ethel Smyth, George Dyson, Adam von Ahne Carse, Joseph Holbrooke, Arthur Somervell and Edward Elgar at nine of his concerts with the London Symphony Orchestra between 1908 and 1914, but his interest in these composers quickly evaporated after he returned to

Germany. Furtwängler and Karajan *did* perform Vaughan Williams's *Fantasia on a Theme by Thomas Tallis* with the Philharmonic, but British music was again largely absent from their programmes.[175] It appears, then, that Barbirolli was presented with something of an artistic open goal when it came to the music of his compatriots in Berlin. But he was reluctant to take the shot and played it safe by conducting only a handful of established British compositions with the Philharmonic.[176]

And what of Barbirolli's commitment to new works as Music Director of the Houston Symphony Orchestra? Aware that his charismatic, British-born predecessor, Leopold Stokowski, had tried and failed to convert his Texan audiences to the music of their contemporaries through audacious programming, Barbirolli was careful to avoid pushing the artistic envelope too far when it came to the pieces of his fellow countrymen. Take his first season with the orchestra, for example. During 1961 and 1962, he conducted twenty-eight concerts at which British music was heard at ten. But, as in Berlin, the works were far from challenging and were all well-known compositions by Delius, Walton and Arnold.[177] Benjamin Britten was the only other living Englishman that Barbirolli performed with his American orchestra, but even his music was restricted to the much performed *The Young Person's Guide to the Orchestra*. If consolidation was the name of the game in Berlin, conservatism dominated the field of play at Houston. With a British repertoire largely revolving around the music of historical figures, such as Elgar, Delius, Butterworth, Vaughan Williams, Finzi and Locke, Barbirolli seemed to be taking an artistic step back. But for a musician who was spending increasingly large amounts of time in the air and on the road, this was probably more an act of necessity rather than a statement of cultural intent.

So had Barbirolli turned his back completely on contemporary British music or was he simply trading national pride for box-office returns? The answers to these questions are far from straightforward. During his Houston tenure, he never completely lost touch with new music and performed works by at least thirteen living American composers with his Texan players.[178] While it could be argued that these were given at the expense of Britons from the same period, their inclusion was simply a natural extension of Barbirolli's role as a music director of a major American symphony orchestra. And, of course, as one of Britain's elder musical statesmen by the 1960s, the public increasingly associated him with works that were composed during the glory days of the country's imperial past. But perception and reality are often two very different things. His commitment to Britten's music never waned during his twilight years and he continued to programme the *Sinfonia da Requiem* with remarkable regularity. He was no less committed to the works of Walton and gave a formidable thirty-one performances of his *Partita* between 1958 and 1969. But it was the compositions of Delius, Vaughan Williams and Elgar that continued to speak to Barbirolli with greatest intensity and it was to those works that he turned increasingly during the final period of his career.[179]

A LIFE RECORDED:
BARBIROLLI AND THE GRAMOPHONE

At a time of increasingly generic music-making, Sir John Barbirolli's recorded legacy stands as a powerful reminder of conducting's golden past. Artists such as Willem Mengelberg, Sir Thomas Beecham, Wilhelm Furtwängler, Carlo Maria Giulini, Herbert von Karajan, Sir Georg Solti and Leonard Bernstein all gave concerts that excited, stimulated and provoked listeners and all made recordings that thrilled, moved and intrigued critics. No less eagerly anticipated or highly regarded were the performances and recordings of the charismatic Sir John Barbirolli. Small in stature, but big in personality, he took on a near-legendary status during his lifetime.[180] While it would be easy to remember him simply as the man who saved Manchester's Hallé Orchestra from near extinction during the dark days of the Second World War, he was also indefatigable as a champion of opera in Britain during the late 1920s, was fiercely defensive of live music broadcasting in the early 1930s, was defiant in his stance against critical bias in New York in the 1940s, was passionate in his advocacy of the works of Gustav Mahler and Anton Bruckner from the 1950s, was revelatory at his concerts with the Houston Symphony Orchestra in the 1960s and was missionary-like in his promotion of British music throughout his career. But for those listeners who were unable to experience these great achievements at first hand, it is surely his formidable discography of no fewer than 452 commercial recordings for at least thirty-two labels over a period of nearly sixty years that has secured his place in their personal pantheon of great conductors.

Born twenty-two years after Thomas Edison's earliest experiments in sound reproduction, Sir John Barbirolli was literally a child of the recording age.[181] Having begun musical life as a violinist, he transferred to the cello at the age of six. A precociously gifted child who quickly impressed as a student at Trinity College of Music from 1910, he entered a recording studio for the first time the following year to record works arranged for cello and piano by van Biene, Wagner, Thomé and Pergolesi with his sister, Rosa.[182] After enrolling at the Royal Academy of Music in 1912, Barbirolli was taken under the wing of Herbert Walenn, Britain's leading cello pedagogue and founder of the London Violoncello School,[183] before giving an early performance of Elgar's Cello Concerto with Dan Godfrey and the Bournemouth Municipal Orchestra in 1921.[184] A committed chamber musician throughout these years, Barbirolli was also a member of a number of leading string quartets, including the Kutcher and Music Society String Quartets, with which he made a series of critically acclaimed acoustic recordings of music by Mozart, Gibbons, Goossens, McEwen, Vaughan Williams and Purcell for Vocalion and the National Gramophonic Society during the mid-1920s. With playing that is focussed and vivid, these discs are good examples of British string style during the early twentieth century and offer a fascinating insight into the true foundations of the 'Barbirolli sound'. Unlike his earlier discs with his sister, those that J.B. made with his quartet partners are of real musical interest and are not simply historical curiosities. But by the time of his quartet recordings, Barbirolli had already set his sights firmly on the conductor's podium and had founded his own chamber orchestra.

Known variously as The Guild of Singers and Players Chamber Orchestra, The Chenil Chamber Orchestra, the National Gramophonic Society Chamber Orchestra and the John Barbirolli Chamber Orchestra, J.B.'s hand-picked ensemble of young virtuosi made its discographic debut when it recorded works by Corelli, Warlock, Delius and Debussy for the National Gramophonic Society on 3 January 1927. Encouraged by the high standard of the playing on those discs, the Society then set down Elgar's *Introduction and Allegro for Strings* with Barbirolli and his players that October. The work soon became a signature piece for the conductor, who went on to document it on five further occasions for either HMV or Pye. The composer's music then became something of a red thread that wove its way through the fabric of Barbirolli's studio activities. Proud of his heritage as an Edwardian Londoner, J.B. always felt a great affinity with Elgar's music. The heady mix of panache, devotion and grandeur with which Barbirolli approached these pieces not only produced recordings that impressed the composer himself, but were also quickly recognised as benchmark interpretations by critics and fellow musicians. Of the thirty-seven commercial recordings that Barbirolli made of Elgar's works, perhaps the one of greatest personal importance to him was his reading of *The Dream of Gerontius* from 1964 with Richard Lewis, Janet Baker, Kim Borg and the Hallé Orchestra. A devout Roman Catholic who identified closely with the oratorio's spiritual message, J.B. gave a remarkable forty-eight performances of the work in the concert hall, and his intensely moving studio recording of it for HMV is both a true reflection of his long relationship with the score and an enduring reminder of his deep commitment to it.

While Barbirolli's early sessions with Edison Bell, Vocalion and the National Gramophonic Society are fascinating insights into the response of a young musician to the rapidly developing recording industry, it is really his work for HMV from 1928 that represents the start of his career as a mature recording artist. The direct result of a concert that Barbirolli conducted for an indisposed Sir Thomas Beecham at the Queen's Hall in 1927, his debut with the company was nothing short of career-changing. Recalling those events later in life, J.B. said: '[the HMV producer] Fred Gaisberg, that immortal character in the history of EMI, was standing amongst the first fiddles [at the end of the concert] and as I walked off after one of the calls said: "My name's Gaisberg, don't sign any contracts, I'll phone you in the morning"'. True to his word, the producer did telephone the young *maestro* in the morning and did sign him for the company. Set to work almost immediately, Barbirolli documented Haydn's 104th Symphony with his own chamber orchestra at the Small Queen's Hall on 27 January 1928, before committing to disc no fewer than twenty-nine works by sixteen composers within the first year of his contract.

Although many of Barbirolli's early sessions for HMV were given over to accompanying leading singers with the orchestra of the Royal Opera House, Covent Garden, his flexible stick technique and his chamber musician's ear for ensemble playing meant that he was also ideally suited to concerto recordings. Reading like a *Who's Who* of great soloists, his emerging discography soon included performances with Guilhermina Suggia, Mischa Elman, Yvonne Arnaud, Jascha Heifetz, Fritz Kreisler, Gregor Piatigorsky, Edwin Fischer, Alfred Cortot, Wilhelm Backhaus and Arthur Rubinstein.[185] Of these now-legendary figures, the one with whom Barbirolli had the greatest personal and professional affinity was Rubinstein. Even though they made no further recordings together after their famous concerto discs of Mozart, Tchaikovsky and Chopin from that period, they later performed as a partnership on thirty-one occasions in Edinburgh, Glasgow, Manchester, Houston, Los Angeles, New York and London. Yet, despite their undoubted musical affinity and the critical success that they enjoyed with their recordings of Chopin and Tchaikovsky, their 1931 discs of Mozart's 23rd Piano Concerto were poorly received.[186] *The Times* was particularly scathing about Rubinstein's and Barbirolli's qualities as Mozartians and was even less impressed by the standard of the orchestral accompaniment:

Unfortunately neither Mr. Arthur Rubinstein nor Mr. John Barbirolli is an ideal interpreter of Mozart. Mr. Rubinstein's tone sounds unsympathetic on the gramophone and his rhythm in the statement of the beautiful theme of the slow movement is wooden. The second subject of the first movement, too, is far more shapely than Mr. Barbirolli makes it, and it is only in the Rondo that the pianist's brilliance and the conductor's vitality find a suitable outlet. The orchestral playing is ragged in places.[187]

The Manchester Guardian was more favourably disposed towards the discs but bizarrely dismissed Mozart's orchestration of the *Adagio*'s central section as 'trivial wood-wind tootlings'. Nevertheless, the critic did feel that 'Arthur Rubinstein play[ed] nimbly and well, and [that] the piano tone [was] on the whole reproduced in the H.MV.'s best manner'.[188] Barbirolli once again fared less well with a 'tempo [that was] not steady enough for Mozart' and by presiding over playing which was only just 'good enough'.[189] As an experienced orchestral conductor, was 'good enough' ever likely to be good enough for Barbirolli? The short answer to that question is 'no'. But as a pragmatist who knew that time was money in the recording studio, he probably realised that he had to pick his battles and that he was in no position to win that particular conflict with a clock-watching producer.

After being appointed Music Director of the New York Philharmonic-Symphony Orchestra in 1937, Barbirolli began to record for Victor and Columbia. First to be documented with his new orchestra was his own arrangement of Purcell's Suite for Strings, Four Horns, Flute and Cor Anglais.[190] Over the next five years, twenty-five works by fifteen composers were recorded by Barbirolli with his American orchestra, including symphonies by Mozart, Schubert, Brahms and Sibelius. Of these, his discs of Brahms's Second Symphony for Columbia in 1940 proved particularly contentious. As the symphony had been performed on multiple occasions by the orchestra under leading Brahmsians, such as Seidl, Steinbach, Mengelberg, Toscanini, Furtwängler, Walter and Klemperer, it was perhaps inevitable that the young Englishman's reading of it would attract the interest of the critics. Released at the same time as Eugene Ormandy's recording of the work with the Philadelphia Orchestra for Victor, Barbirolli's discs faced stiff opposition and received some very mixed reviews. Taking a positive stance, the critic for the *New York World-Telegram* argued that the 'symphony [was] performed with [an] emphasis on clarity, lyricism and polish'.[191] Less impressed was Harold Taubman of *The New York* Times, who thought that the 'conception [was] solid, straightforward and unpretentious',[192] while Henry W. Simon of *PM's Weekly* simply dismissed the recording, as the conductor was 'not a distinguished baton … [who gave a] performance [that was] stiff and in many places too fast'.[193] For a work that was central to Barbirolli's performance aesthetic, and one that he would give on at least 228 occasions during the course of his career, this must have been far from the ringing endorsement that he had hoped for. And as the recording was also his first of a large-scale Romantic symphony, the critics' response must have been doubly disappointing.

Barbirolli's thrilling, but divisive, New York tenure ended in the summer of 1943 when he was offered the post of Permanent Conductor of the Hallé Orchestra. Excited to 'do his bit' for wartime Britain, Barbirolli's enthusiasm turned quickly to horror when he realised that he had been misled by the orchestra's management. As if the contrast between war-torn Manchester and neon-lit New York was not unsettling enough, the realisation that the once great Hallé Orchestra was a shadow of its former artistic self sent Barbirolli into a personal and professional tailspin. With barely half the players necessary to meet the needs of the concerts already booked, he faced what seemed like an insurmountable challenge. But he was made of stern stuff and was determined to restore the orchestra's fortunes: a formidable task under normal circumstances let alone during wartime. With his musical sleeves well and truly rolled up, he set to work and auditioned all comers for three weeks. Players were found and contracts were offered. The re-formed orchestra then began rehearsals on 28 June and gave its first concert at the Prince's Theatre, Bradford, on 5 July. A miracle had occurred in Manchester with conductor and orchestra being virtually inseparable thereafter.[194]

Crucial to the development of the newly refurbished orchestra was recording. Barbirolli was very aware that recordings not only worked as great publicity but also served to raise standards and to provide extra income for the players. After re-establishing his link with HMV shortly after his return from America in 1943, J.B. documented Bax's Third Symphony that December and Vaughan Williams's Fifth Symphony the following February. While these works might seem unlikely commercial choices for a conductor who was about to rekindle his relationship with his former recording company, or one keen to establish a new audience base for a struggling orchestra, they were, in fact, savvy for at least two reasons. First, they flew the flag for British culture at a time of national crisis and, second, they re-affirmed Barbirolli's credentials as a champion of new music. They were also a boon critically for the conductor and the players, with Barbirolli being described as having 'musical wisdom and force' in the Bax recording.[195] Over the years, his interest in the works of his compatriots never waned and it is easy to forget that fifteen of the twenty-two fellow countrymen whom he committed to disc were direct contemporaries.

Barbirolli might well have been one of the supreme interpreters of the great Austro-German canon, but he was also a staunch advocate of the music of his own time.

In 1955, Barbirolli left HMV for Pye, a move that he later regretted. Keen to make recordings available to as wide an audience as possible at a price that was as affordable as possible, J.B. thought that Pye's mass appeal would achieve these objectives. With popular artists such as Lonnie Donegan and Petula Clark on its books, Pye was a label with cross-cultural and cross-generational appeal. That said, Barbirolli had no intention of lowering his musical standards or sacrificing his artistic principals on the altar of commercialism. This was strikingly clear from the composition with which he made his company debut: Vaughan Williams's Eighth Symphony. Having given the work's first performance on 2 May 1956, and having been named its dedicatee, J.B. recorded it on 19 June. Within days of that historic session, he then set down music by Butterworth, Bax, Delius, Purcell, Elgar, Johann Strauss I and Johann Strauss II before tackling symphonies by Dvořák, Berlioz and Tchaikovsky over the next three years. While these are undoubtedly compelling readings of great masterpieces, perhaps more important historically are the works of composers that Barbirolli secured for Pye that he performed regularly in the concert hall but were largely absent from his existing discography.

A passionate and indefatigable interpreter of Mozart's compositions from an early age – he conducted a breathtaking 1,276 performances and recordings of the composer's works during his career – he had only recorded one Mozart symphony before moving to Pye.[196] In a clear attempt to remedy that situation, and in a bid to raise his profile as a Mozartian on disc, he recorded the 29th and 41st Symphonies for his new company in December 1956. Greeted positively by the critics, the 'Jupiter' received 'a brilliant full-bodied performance' according to *The Gramophone*. Barbirolli's 'firm but affectionate reading' also benefitted from the 'care given to phrasing of individual melodies … [that] never … detract[ed] from the onward drive of the music'.[197] That said, the critic was not completely convinced by the tempo of the second movement, which he found more akin to an *Adagio* than that of an *Andante cantabile*. But when Barbirolli's speed (♪ = 62) is compared with those of Sir Thomas Beecham with the Royal Philharmonic Orchestra from 1957 (♪ = 69) and Bruno Walter with the Columbia Symphony Orchestra from 1960 (♪ = 69),[198] it is clear that his tempo is largely in keeping with contemporary trends. If, on the other hand, the critic had a longer memory and had in mind Strauss's speed with the Berlin Staatskapelle from 1926 (♪ = 80),[199] Barbirolli's tempo would have seemed disturbingly slow. The critic did, however, recognise that 'andante in later Mozart is a tricky marking' and went on to pronounce the disc 'excellent in every way'.[200] As the readings are superbly paced, it is hard to disagree with that view and, as such, they also act as a fascinating foil to Barbirolli's more-robust and better-known discs of Haydn's 83rd, 88th, 96th and 104th Symphonies that he made for HMV between 1928 and 1953.

By 1959, it had become obvious to Barbirolli that his musical objectives were no longer in step with Pye's financial and artistic aims, and after documenting Brahms's Fourth Symphony for the firm that September, they parted ways. But, having turned his back on Pye, Barbirolli found himself without a permanent recording company for the first time since childhood. The gap was filled briefly by Concert Hall (UK), Electrecord (Romania) and Supraphon when they made discs of Mendelssohn's 'Italian' Symphony, Rimsky-Korsakov's *Capriccio espagnol*, Schubert's Fifth Symphony and Franck's Symphony in D minor with him in 1961 and 1962.[201] But within weeks of the 1962 sessions, Barbirolli had returned to the HMV fold and was back in the studio for the company that May. Over the next few months, his busy studio schedule produced a series of recordings devoted to the compositions of Vaughan Williams and Elgar. With those sessions in the can, Barbirolli then turned his attention to the music of Mahler, Brahms and Sibelius and committed to disc a string of iconic recordings of their works that are amongst his most famous and most contentious.

Now considered one of the great Mahler interpreters of the late twentieth century, Barbirolli was slow to appreciate the composer's worth. Over-blown and poorly orchestrated were only two of the criticisms that he levelled against the Fourth Symphony in 1930.[202] In contrast, he had no such concerns about the works of Mahler's great friend and contemporary, Richard Strauss, whose music he performed and recorded on 548 occasions between 1931 and 1969. A devoted Straussian for much of his early and middle career, Barbirolli remained largely unconvinced by Mahler's symphonies until the critic, Neville Cardus, encouraged him to study and to perform the Ninth Symphony with the Hallé Orchestra in 1954. That was the beginning of a love affair with Mahler's music that continued to the end of his life. As a recording artist, however, J.B. documented Mahler's works only selectively during the last thirteen years of his career, a situation that was not self-imposed but the result of caution on the part of the record companies.

Having set down the First Symphony for Pye without any professional preconditions in 1957, Barbirolli was not so lucky when it came to EMI. They already had a leading Mahler interpreter – Otto Klemperer – recording for them, and to appease the ageing German, and to benefit commercially from his relationship with the composer, the company gave him first choice when it came to Mahler's works. While there was an overlap with the Ninth Symphony, Barbirolli generally recorded compositions that had little appeal for Klemperer. Consequently, J.B. only documented the Fifth, Sixth and Ninth Symphonies, the *Lieder eines fahrenden Gesellen*, the *Rückert-Lieder* and the *Kindertotenlieder* for EMI.[2034] While these recordings are now generally considered landmarks in the history of Mahler performance, some of them left contemporary critics shaking their heads in disapproval when they were first released. Particularly contentious were Barbirolli's broad tempi in the Sixth Symphony and his dogged insistence on retaining *portamento* as an essential expressive device in the Ninth. Considered a thing of the past, audible sliding was increasingly frowned upon by mid-twentieth-century audiences, critics and musicians, prompting one reviewer to write in 1964: 'the only stylistic criticisms I have to offer [of the Ninth Symphony] are of the Barbirolli characteristic string portamento, which I find a little excessive'.[204] Sadly for that particular critic, performance practice and performance history were firmly on Barbirolli's side, as he knew only too well that Mahler's music was first heard at a time when *portamenti* were frequently added by the players and that the composer often notated string slides as an expressive gesture in his printed texts.

A committed Brahms interpreter from near the beginning of his career, Barbirolli began his discographic exploration of that composer's works with 'Ye that now are sorrowful' from *Ein deutsches Requiem* with Florence Austral in 1928. He then went on to record all of Brahms's concertos with Fritz Kreisler, Alfredo Campoli, André Navarra and Daniel Barenboim between 1936 and 1967 and the Second, Third and Fourth Symphonies and the 'Academic Festival' Overture with the New York Philharmonic-Symphony and Hallé Orchestras between 1940 and 1959. While these discs left listeners in no doubt that Barbirolli was a Brahmsian of the front rank, he was keen to record a more comprehensive and unified overview of the composer's orchestral works with a single leading orchestra. It was hardly surprising, then, that when EMI asked him to document Brahms's major symphonic works with the Vienna Philharmonic in 1966 and 1967 he jumped at the opportunity.[205] For tradition-loving Barbirolli, the chance to record the Second and Third Symphonies with the orchestra that had given their premieres was to be nothing short of a musical pilgrimage. Reverence quickly turned to concern, however, when the sessions proved difficult from the start. With sound-worlds that could not have been more different, battle-lines were quickly drawn between conductor and orchestra with neither party prepared to give way. Barbirolli eventually left Vienna disenchanted with the players, the recordings and the experience as a whole. He felt that only the disc of the Third Symphony reflected his high interpretative standards.[206] But when heard today, it is clear that he was being overly critical. At worst, the readings are magisterial and, at best, they are nothing short of revelatory.

Another composer close to Barbirolli's heart was Jean Sibelius. After performing the 'Karelia' Suite for the first time in 1932, he went on to conduct the Finn's music on a further 637 occasions over the next thirty-eight years. Unlike conductors from the German-speaking countries, those from Great Britain always had a particular affinity with Sibelius's works. Sir Henry Wood and Sir Thomas Beecham were early advocates of his compositions and conducted complete cycles of the symphonies. No less committed was Barbirolli, who not only performed all the symphonies, but was the first of the three to record them as a unit. Having added the First and Second Symphonies to his discography in the early 1940s, he then recorded the First, Second, Fifth and Seventh Symphonies, *Pohjola's Daughter*, *The Swan of Tuonela* and *Valse Triste* for HMV, Pye and *Reader's Digest* between 1949 and 1962.[207] But it was while recording for EMI in the late 1960s that his passion for the composer's works reached its peak. And with the aid of three of the company's most eminent producers, Christopher Bishop, Ronald Kinloch Anderson and Victor Olof, Barbirolli committed to disc a comprehensive overview of the composer's music that included all seven symphonies and ten of the shorter orchestral works.[208] Made over a four-year period with the Hallé Orchestra, and completed only weeks before his death,[209] Barbirolli's cycle is not only a powerful reminder of the special affinity that existed between conductor and composer, but also a searing expression of the artistic truths that so dominated their professional lives.

No discussion about Sir John Barbirolli on disc would, or should, be complete without mentioning his work as an opera conductor. As a member of the Covent Garden orchestra's cello section in 1920, the young Barbirolli was able to observe Puccini at work during the preparation period for the London premiere of *Il trittico*. The corrections and suggestions that the composer made during the rehearsals were soon indelibly etched in Barbirolli's memory and were later fundamental to his approach to Puccini's operas as a whole. When J.B. returned to the Royal Opera eleven years later to lead three performances of the composer's *Turandot*, memories of Puccini must have come flooding back. And when Barbirolli returned to the theatre for a second run of the opera in 1937 with Eva Turner in the title role, HMV was on hand to document two of the performances.[210] Yet, with the exception of Purcell's *Dido and Aeneas* with Victoria de los Angeles, Peter Glossop and the English Chamber Orchestra in 1965, Barbirolli made no further operatic recordings until he set down Puccini's *Madama Butterfly* with Renata Scotto, Carlo Bergonzi and the orchestra and chorus of the Teatro dell'Opera, Rome, in August 1966.

Something of a landmark in Barbirolli's discography, his recording of *Butterfly* was the first, and only, sound-document that he made of a complete opera that he had previously given in the theatre. But as he hadn't performed it publicly since 1953, he wisely decided to reconnect with the score by giving two concert performances of the opera with the Hallé Orchestra in the months leading up to the recording.[211] The dividends of this approach were quickly apparent, with the discs being hailed critically after their release in 1967. Considering that Scotto, Bergonzi, the orchestra and the chorus were all unfamiliar to him, Barbirolli's reading is remarkable for its sense of ensemble and for the linear continuity that underpins both the singing and the orchestral playing. *The Gramophone* certainly thought so and argued that 'Barbirolli conveys an unexpected "inner" tension, to make most of his rivals on disc, even Serafin, sound trivial and even stodgy'.[212] Quick to recognise that the discs were not simply a vehicle for vocal display, the critic also went on to point out that 'it was [Barbirolli's] individuality rather than that of the singers' which 'struck [him] at [his] initial hearings'.[213] And in contrast to 'most Italian opera recordings dominated by the conductor[,] … the singers … [were] positively encouraged into their best form' rather than being 'put off-balance by [their] decreased importance'.[214]

As significant as Barbirolli's *Butterfly* recording surely was, it was his reading of Verdi's *Otello* for HMV that was the jewel in his discographic crown. Given the sheer number of operatic performances that he conducted during his career, and given the pride that he felt knowing that his father and grandfather had played in the first performance of the work in Milan under the composer's direct supervision, it is curious that Barbirolli never performed Verdi's late masterpiece in the theatre. But he was very aware of the artistic and logistical limitations of the various opera troupes that he conducted during his early years and felt that they were simply not up to the mark. That was certainly not the case when it came to the performers that HMV had assembled for his much-anticipated recording of the opera in 1968.[215] Acutely conscious that he had never performed *Otello* in the opera house, and equally conscious that he lacked the necessary hands-on experience to do the score justice, J.B. again decided to give two concert performances of the opera with the Hallé Orchestra in the months preceding the recording sessions.[216] With his father's and grandfather's memories of Verdi's 1887 comments, suggestions and corrections still ringing in his ears, and with his own ideas shaped and distilled by his preparatory performances in Manchester, Barbirolli then went on to create a recording of *Otello* that is as remarkable for its breadth and excitement as it is for its poise and beauty.

Why, then, was Sir John Barbirolli so unique and so important as a recording artist? Having spent his mature years shaping the Hallé Orchestra in his own artistic image, he created a sound-world on disc that was both distinctive and immediately recognisable. As an outstanding cellist, J.B. littered his conducting scores with bowing marks and detailed instructions for the strings. Carefully crafted and lovingly realised, these annotations created a body of sound on record that was as bold as it was delicate. Tempo was also central to his approach in the studio, and while some commentators might have raised an eyebrow or two at his often-broad speeds, he never allowed tension to wane or architecture to suffer. Aware that musical performances never operate in isolation, he actively set out to shape the cultural lives of three generations of musicians and listeners through his work with the gramophone. Adamant that a great conductor is also a great teacher, he was indefatigable in broadening artistic hearts and minds. Even today it is still common to hear in Manchester, London and Houston that 'I learned my music from Sir John Barbirolli'. And thanks to the thousands of hours that J.B. spent in the studio, listeners around the globe can continue to learn their music from him and can continue to marvel at the famous 'Barbirolli sound'.

A COCKNEY DOWN UNDER:
SIR JOHN BARBIROLLI IN AUSTRALIA

For much of the first half of the twentieth century, Australia played host to a string of international conductors. Perhaps for financial reasons, perhaps to avoid the yoke of fascism, perhaps to escape the privations of post- and pre-war austerity, or perhaps simply out of curiosity, leading artists, such as Eugene Ormandy, Otto Klemperer, Rafael Kubelik, George Szell, Sir Thomas Beecham and Sir Malcolm Sargent, travelled to Australia, thrilled its audiences, elevated its musicians and dazzled its critics. These men did much to shape the cultural perception and reception of the country abroad and often actively encouraged their European and North American colleagues to explore the musical possibilities Australia had to offer. Admittedly, antipodean orchestras were unable to compete technically with those of Berlin, London, Vienna or New York, but they did offer extended rehearsal periods and did boast some outstanding individual players. For a conductor such as Sir John Barbirolli this must have been an intriguing prospect and one that would have appealed to his sense of adventure. He adored tackling the musical unknown and famously quipped 'I like to be given the impossible to do, it rather suits me'.[217] So when the Australian Broadcasting Commission (ABC) came calling in the mid-1940s, the lure of 'Down Under' would have been difficult for Barbirolli to resist.

But having accepted the permanent conductorship of the near-moribund Hallé Orchestra in 1943, Barbirolli was determined to restore its flagging musical and financial fortunes before even considering such an invitation. By the end of that decade, however, the orchestra was well on its way to artistic and fiscal stability and J.B. felt better able to explore the cultural and monetary benefits that longer guest-conducting stints abroad had to offer. It is no exaggeration to say that his achievements with the Hallé had taken on a near-legendary status by the time of the ABC's initial approach with orchestras and opera houses around the world champing at the bit for his services. But nothing, no matter how tempting financially, would shift him permanently from his devoted Hallé players and his even-more-devoted Mancunian fans. It is little short of remarkable, then, that his first major trip abroad as a guest conductor after taking charge of the Hallé was for an extended period to far-off Australia at the end of 1950 for the Australian Broadcasting Commission.[218]

Yet, it was not as a guest conductor that Barbirolli first discussed the possibility of performing in Australia; rather, it was as part of a tour that would also involve the Hallé Orchestra. It seems that as early as 1946, Barbirolli had suggested to the ABC that he would like to bring the Hallé to Australia and had raised the matter again in January 1947.[219] The General Manager of the ABC, Charles Moses, felt that the time wasn't right for such a tour but was keen to have Barbirolli by himself that year for twenty-five concerts at a fee of £175 (Australian) per performance.[220] Nothing came of the offer and another attempt was made to tempt him for 1949. Eager to show cultural support for a proposed visit by members of the Royal Family that year,[221] the ABC had first approached Sir Thomas Beecham to perform during the tour but turned to Barbirolli in the spring of 1948 after Beecham rejected the offer. With a fee of £150 sterling per concert for sixteen performances, and with all travel costs covered, the proposal must have been tempting. But Barbirolli again failed to take the bait, even though he had hinted that he might be interested.[222]

The Australian management team was nothing if not persistent, however, and they contacted J.B. again later that year with a renewed offer.[223] The conductor didn't reject the idea out of hand but did stress that any visit would have to be 'in [the] December, January and February [of] either 1949–50 or the following year'.[224] 'One of the main stumbling blocks … [for this plan was] the orchestral holiday'[225] that was traditionally taken by the players during the Australian summer. A possible solution was for the Victorian Symphony Orchestra (VSO) to take its break from 20 January, thus allowing Barbirolli to work with it from the beginning of the month.[226] By 7 February 1949 matters had become urgent and the Commission's management team was desperate not to let the conductor slip through its fingers. They were aware that they were 'most fortunate in obtaining him at considerably less than his B.B.C. fee (£125 as opposed to £175) and [that] he would be entitled to raise the bid if we began negotiations again at a later date'.[227] Moreover, as 'he is quite the most sought-after conductor in Britain he may be tempted to accept other more lucrative offers from people on the spot unless we have a firm arrangement with him'.[228]

Unwilling to take 'no' for an answer, the ABC had done its homework and knew that if anything would attract Barbirolli to Australia it would be the siren call of leather on willow. With that firmly in mind, the management pulled out all the stops and 'remind[ed] him that he'll be here for the next Test [cricket] series and we'll see he's an honoured guest at a match or two'.[229] The Commission had confirmed its 'offer to Barbirolli for a tour during the early part of 1951 … at a fee of £125 [sterling] per concert' by the first week of March but had yet to hear the conductor's response.[230] Even though Barbirolli seems to have agreed by June, the proposed tour was briefly threatened by his increasingly poor health, as he was advised by his doctors in August 'to cancel all guest engagements for a year or so'. 'Disregard[ing] [their] orders', he decided 'to have another medical in a fortnight's time after which he [would make] his final decision'.[231] The matter was settled in December when the Commission received a cable from its London office informing them that Barbirolli was happy with his fees and was applying for release from the Hallé Orchestra for the period of the tour.[232]

Barbirolli was scheduled to conduct a total of fifteen broadcast concerts with the Sydney, Melbourne, Adelaide and Brisbane orchestras between 28 December 1950 and 12 February 1951. Concerned about their individual standards, he contacted the ABC in early July 1950, prompting the Commission to send him a detailed and very honest appraisal of each band later that month:

Quality of the Orchestras:

Sydney: High general level and efficiency throughout the orchestra, which can cope with practically anything in the classical or modern repertoire.

Melbourne: An experienced orchestra with good key players. Under expert leadership is capable of fine performances of almost any type of music.

Adelaide: A less experienced orchestra but most enthusiastic and promising. Strings and woodwind generally good quality and reliable; horns and brass fair; excellent percussion; no harp. This orchestra can be counted on to give good performances of any except the most difficult works in the standard repertoire.

Brisbane: Is the weakest of the four orchestras but generally rises to the occasion. It has given some very good performances under visiting conductors such as [Rafael] Kubelik, [Paul] Klecki[233] [sic] and [Alceo] Galliera. The strings are of a fair standard; oboes and bassoons rather weak, other woodwind fair; brass and percussion generally fair. [Moreover,] it may be a useful guide to Sir John to know that Kubelik, returning to Brisbane on his second visit and knowing the capabilities of this orchestra, performed with success such works as "Fidelio" Overture, Mozart "Prague" Symphony, Dvorak 4th Symphony, "Hebrides" Overture, Beethoven 1st Symphony, Suk's "Fairytale" Suite, Dvorak Slavonic Dances. Works of this type can safely be programmed, but not those requiring virtuoso technique or extreme finesse.[234]

Barbirolli was also concerned about soloists. Although he had been a highly successful cello prodigy, and had given one of the first performances of Elgar's Cello Concerto, he was sceptical of engaging soloists as a matter of course. When he took over the Hallé Orchestra in 1943, for example, he immediately reduced the number of soloists, arguing rightly that performing a series of concertos might have been good for box-office receipts but did little to improve the standards of the orchestra. Moses was aware of this and raised the matter at the beginning of August 1950. He mentioned to Barbirolli that:

> It is our normal practice to include an instrumentalist or vocalist in the majority of our symphony concerts and we are always particularly pleased to be able to give local artists of real excellence the opportunity of performing under distinguished conductors from overseas … [But] as we understand that you would prefer not to have a soloist as a normal practice we are arranging that at least two of your concerts in Sydney, two in Melbourne, one in Adelaide and one in Brisbane would be entirely orchestral (i.e. without soloist).[235]

Barbirolli recognised the importance of Moses's argument and replied:

> It is quite true that I do not care to have soloists as a normal practice in so short a visit, but I shall certainly be glad to make the acquaintance of the young Australian artists you mention, as I have always been interested in fostering young talent, and it is the more self-satisfied and complacent virtuosi that I seek to avoid![236]

In the months leading up to Barbirolli's visit, preparations went into overdrive. Although he was fairly easy going personally, he did have a number of quirks and passions. His management in Manchester was keen to ensure that these were met and sent out a detailed list of his idiosyncrasies to Australia in advance:

> (a) He has a love of tradition and all things ancient. A preference for chandeliers rather than modern strip lighting and for gas lamps rather than neon!
>
> (b) His feeding arrangements are unusual. He never takes breakfast or lunch

and will not dine in any circumstances before a concert. Apart from literally <u>one</u> sandwich at lunchtime he eats nothing all day until dinner, when he likes to sit down comfortably and eat a good meal. It does not worry him if his evening meal does not commence until 11 p.m., so long as he can take it in comfort. As to preference of food, the general answer is "anything from the grill". He realises that it is necessary on occasions for him to attend special luncheons and is quite willing to do so provided that it is realised in advance that he will only nibble a sandwich.

(c) Rehearsals: He likes to work to a methodically arranged rehearsal schedule, which include sectional rehearsals, and his only request is that they commence punctually so that he can make use of every minute available to him.

(d) In spare moments he likes to have a quiet look for himself at shops and market places etc., without the formality of a "conducted tour".[237]

Originally booked to fly from London with B.O.A.C. on 18 December 1950,[238] Barbirolli and his wife, the oboist Evelyn Rothwell, had to rearrange their plans at the eleventh hour as the airline was on strike. Eventually, the couple secured seats with Pan American Airways and arrived in Sydney on 23 December, a day later than originally planned. Today, it takes the best part of twenty-one hours to fly directly to the New South Wales capital from Britain but, in those days, it could take up to five days to make the trip by air. For J.B., the tediously long journey was certainly worth it, as the local press greeted him on arrival as if he were visiting royalty. The papers were awash with articles, stories and anecdotes about him. His colourful Continental antecedents,[239] his love of all things Edwardian, his passionate advocacy of an orchestral exchange between the Sydney Symphony and the Hallé Orchestras[240] and his penchant for being considered a cockney all captured the public's imagination. He was even described by Sydney's *Daily Telegraph* – along with Pope Pius XII – as one of the 'world's 10 most attractive men',[241] a description that was as fanciful as it was curious.

But the euphoria that greeted him on arrival was quickly eclipsed when the local and national presses went into a frenzy after the orchestral parts for the first concert with the Sydney Symphony Orchestra (SSO) were stolen from their stands following the final rehearsal. Having returned to the Town Hall for the performance, the management discovered that the orchestral material had been pilfered and a search of the building was started. When it was clear that it was unlikely to be found, J.B. and the orchestra's principal conductor, Sir Eugene Goossens, decided to go quickly to the New South Wales State Conservatorium of Music (now Sydney Conservatorium of Music), of which he was also Director, to try to replace the parts. Scrambling over the Conservatorium's fence in the dark – the caretaker was nowhere to be found – Sir Eugene was only able to put his hands on Wagner's Prelude to *Die Meistersinger von Nürnberg* and Brahms's Second Symphony.[242] After the concert was given in much reduced form, an anonymous caller telephoned the *Daily Telegraph* with the whereabouts of the missing material and explained that 'he had acted because he admired Sir John Barbirolli [and that he] wanted Sir John always to remember his visit to Sydney'.[243] The press and the public were outraged and flogging was considered too good for the culprit. Luckily for him, he was never caught and the whole episode was later simply dismissed by the conductor as an example of antipodean high-spirits.

During the Sydney phase of the tour, Barbirolli performed six pairs of concerts with the SSO at the city's Town Hall. The programme planned for 28 and 29 December was Rossini's Overture to *La gazza ladra*, Vaughan Williams's Sixth Symphony, Sibelius's *The Swan of Tuonela* and Brahms's Second Symphony, but because of the missing parts, the full programme was only heard at the second concert. Perhaps unsurprisingly, these works were all standard fare for Barbirolli, who gave at least 187 performances of the Rossini, 228 of the Brahms, eighty-two of the Sibelius and sixty-nine of the Vaughan Williams during his career. First performed under Sir Adrian Boult and the BBC Symphony Orchestra in 1948, Vaughan Williams's symphony had in excess of 100 performances during its first year. Even though the work had been heard in Melbourne in October 1948, Barbirolli decided that it needed some pre-performance marketing and explained to the *Daily Telegraph* that '[it] is just two years old … [and] it is [already] one of my favourite symphonies'. Keen to underline its international appeal, he continued by saying that 'I have played it in … Continental centres, and its reception by European audiences [has] amazed me. Latin audiences, who do not usually respond to British music, loved it'. Apparently, the 'delicate, lovely, muted last movement – *pianissimo* for 12½ minutes – thrilled the Latins with an electrical kind of excitement … [and] I am sure that Australian audiences, who are among the most appreciative in the world, will love the Sixth Symphony, too'.[244] As it happened, Barbirolli had nothing to worry about. His Sydney audience instantly warmed to the work and the critics were overwhelmed by his reading of it. The *Daily Telegraph* reported that the '6th Symphony of Vaughan Williams … makes an immediate and terrific impact with its powerful opening notes',[245] while the *Sydney Morning Herald* felt that it was 'a powerful and richly argued performance'.[246]

With the New Year celebrations behind him, Barbirolli led a second pair of concerts on 5 and 6 January with the SSO at the Town Hall, the first of which was Sydney's official Jubilee Concert marking the fiftieth anniversary of Australia as a federation. The programmes were typical of Barbirolli and were reflective of his approach with the Hallé Orchestra. They consisted of Berlioz's '*Le carnaval romain*' Overture, Vaughan Williams's *Serenade to Music*, Mendelssohn's Violin Concerto, with the orchestra's leader Ernest Llewellyn as soloist, and Tchaikovsky's Fourth Symphony. In keeping with his normal practice, J.B. performed the *Serenade to Music* in the version without voices. Composed to mark Sir Henry Wood's golden jubilee as a conductor in 1938, the *Serenade* was originally written for sixteen solo voices and orchestra but was then arranged for orchestra alone in 1940. Barbirolli gave his first performance of the orchestral version in 1947 and went on to conduct a further thirty-four performances of it. His reading of the work in Sydney was generally well received unlike Llewellyn's performance of the concerto, which proved divisive. While the *Telegraph*'s critic looked on the bright side and remarked that the violinist had given 'a most brilliant yet thoughtful interpretation',[247] the *Herald*'s critic experienced 'a somewhat plain account of the Mendelssohn violin concerto … [where] the rare luminosity of great lyrical tone and the feeling for supremely beautiful curve in melody [seemed] to elude Mr. Llewellyn'.[248] The *Daily Mirror*'s critic was also unimpressed and opined that:

> As a conductor Barbirolli gives a lot, but … for all his coaxing and drive …
> he was unable to get more than a very safe and unspectacular performance
> of the Mendelssohn violin concerto … [as] Mr. Llewellyn refused to budge
> from his usual quite pleasant, but rather stolid style, and maintained a
> Hassett-Archer[249] attitude towards Sir John's invitation to brighten things up
> a bit – even in the final enticing allegro.[250]

All the critics agreed, however, that Barbirolli's readings of the Berlioz overture and the Tchaikovsky symphony were nothing short of breathtaking and that the latter was given with 'such [an] astonishingly high emotional voltage [that] has not been heard in Sydney for a good many years'.[251]

Barbirolli's sojourn in Sydney came to an end with his final pair of concerts on 10 and 11 January. Again with the SSO at the Town Hall, he performed works by Weber, Haydn, Roussel and Elgar. Weber's Overture to *Der Freischütz* was a firm favourite of Barbirolli and was given by him no fewer than 142 times during his career. While Elgar's Second Symphony was performed somewhat less frequently by him – 103 performances in all – it held a special place in his affections and was the work with which he felt the greatest affinity as an Edwardian Londoner. Haydn's 83rd Symphony ('*La poule*') and Roussel's Second Suite from *Bacchus et Ariane* had only been taken up by J.B. in 1948 but quickly became central to his repertoire. Neither the Haydn nor the Roussel had been heard in Sydney before, prompting *Truth* to run the banner headline 'Barbirolli to premiere two works in final concerts'.[252] Understandably, the majority of the reviews were given over to the Elgar symphony but Haydn's and Roussel's works also caught the critics' attention with one commentator arguing that 'the 83rd Symphony of Haydn contained far more serious content than one is accustomed to from his lighthearted pen'. And that 'without too much sparkle [it] might have become dull if the performance had not been so beautifully accomplished'.[253] Roussel's composition also appealed to the critics, who found it 'a vivid and highly dramatic piece with modern tendencies of a not-too-disturbing nature [that] needs – and had – brilliant orchestral playing'.[254]

Flying with Trans Australia Airlines (TAA), Barbirolli left Sydney for Brisbane the day after his final Town Hall concert. With the Queensland Symphony Orchestra at City Hall, he was scheduled to give two performances, the first on 15 January,[255] Brisbane's Jubilee Concert, and, the second, five days later.[256] With the exception of Wagner's Prelude to *Die Meistersinger*, all the works given were new to his Australian repertoire. That said, they were far from unfamiliar to him and the shape and content of the programmes once again followed the Hallé model. Given the ABC's warning about the standard of the northern orchestra, the works performed by Barbirolli were not straightforward technically and all presented challenges that even the most experienced orchestras of the time would have found demanding. The programmes were not particularly short and each would have required considerable rehearsal. But if the local press is to be believed, nothing short of a musical miracle happened in Queensland that January. The Brisbane critics were thrilled by the orchestra's performance and the local audience snapped up every available ticket. *The Courier-Mail* reported after the first concert that 'a superb blending of dynamic energy and poetic refinement was revealed by the distinguished international conductor Sir John Barbirolli at the City Hall last night … which was attended by a capacity audience [with] many people [having to stand] throughout the performance'.[257] While the critics were less than impressed by the orchestra's reading of the 'Enigma' Variations at the second concert, it was again oversubscribed, prompting the headlines to crow paradoxically that the 'Best Was Kept to the Last'[258] and 'Triumph to Barbirolli'.[259]

Buoyed by the public success of his Brisbane concerts, Barbirolli flew to Melbourne with TAA on 21 January. With the Victorian Symphony Orchestra, his schedule included two concerts at the Town Hall on the twenty-sixth[260] and twenty-seventh,[261] the second of which was the city's official Jubilee Concert, and an open-air concert, yet another Jubilee event, at the Royal Botanic Gardens on the twenty-eighth.[262] Unlike in Sydney and Brisbane, much of the repertoire heard at the three concerts had already been given by Barbirolli in Australia and the only new material was his own *An Elizabethan Suite*, Johann Strauss II's *Kaiser-Walzer*, Rimsky-Korsakov's *Capriccio espagnol* and a suite from *L'Arlésienne* by Bizet. Having been given advice by the ABC about the differences in standards between the various orchestras, he seems to have taken the Commission at its word and programmed accordingly. As the Victorian orchestra had been given the technical thumbs-up by the ABC's management, he included his own suite at his Melbourne concerts. Comprised of five movements based on music by William Byrd, Giles Farnaby, John Bull and an anonymous composer, Barbirolli's arrangements are demanding for strings and horns alike. The last movement, based on 'The King's Hunt' by Bull, is nothing short of a virtuosic *tour de force* that explores every facet of advanced string technique. Sadly, the local band was not up to the task and gave a performance in which the 'virtuoso passages [in] the string playing was often scratchy and the horns uncertain'.[263]

From Melbourne, Barbirolli made a side-trip to Adelaide for two concerts with the South Australian Symphony Orchestra on 1 and 7 February before returning to the Victorian capital for his final two concerts of the tour. In Adelaide, the main talking point was Barbirolli's arrangement of an oboe concerto by Corelli played by his wife, Evelyn. By the time of the concert, the oboist was no stranger to Australian audiences, having already performed the first of four planned broadcast recitals over the ABC's national network on 24 January.[264] Given as part of Adelaide's official Jubilee Concert at the Town Hall on 1 February, Corelli's concerto was heard in a programme that included Berlioz's '*Le carnaval romain*' Overture, Mozart's 'Jupiter'

Symphony and Brahms's First Symphony. The two latter works were new to J.B.'s Australian repertoire, as were all the works given at his second Adelaide concert – Beethoven's Overture to *Egmont*, Elgar's *Serenade for Strings*, Schumann's Piano Concerto, with the Australian pianist Raymond O'Connell, and Schubert's Ninth Symphony – a tough challenge for 'a less [than] experienced orchestra'.

On returning to Melbourne, Barbirolli performed the first real novelty of the tour – Rubbra's Fifth Symphony – at a pair of concerts with the Victorian Symphony Orchestra on 10 and 12 February.[265] Rubbra's work was perhaps the most demanding of the visit and the least familiar to Australian audiences. Having received its premiere under Sir Adrian Boult and the BBC Symphony Orchestra in 1949, it was recorded for the first time by Barbirolli and the Hallé Orchestra on 14 and 15 December 1950, only two weeks before J.B.'s first Australian concert. Its reception in Melbourne was mixed and was best summed up by the critic in *The Age* who wrote 'the structure of the Rubbra symphony is strong and well-defined with embellishments that are interesting, colorful [*sic*] and at times dramatic. There is [a] considerable range of mood and expression [and] the work has exciting, but not startling, moments'.[266]

For the ABC, Barbirolli's visit could not have been more successful. Audiences, musicians and critics took to him instantly and the balance sheet reflected his popularity. The tour's financial report released in mid-1951 must have a brought a smile to the ABC administrators' faces, particularly as 'the series of public concerts conducted by Sir John Barbirolli resulted in a profit in all states concerned except South Australia [with] the total net profit being £4015.12.1, an average of £287 per concert',[267] a tidy sum in 1951. It is little wonder, then, that the Commission was keen to have him back as soon as possible. Negotiations began almost immediately and the urgency of them is evident from the ABC's telegram to its London office on 12 September 1951:

> Concert season 1953 stop anxious <u>Barbirolli</u> august [*sic*] october [*sic*] ten weeks longer if possible please offer minimum 20 concerts ten weeks stop if Barbirolli accepts interested <u>Sylvia Fisher</u> <u>Kathleen Ferrier</u> same period couldst [*sic*] institute preliminary enquiries their availability etadvise [*sic*] appropriate fees … if artists available other periods 1953 please advise as useful in planning season stop all offers subject commission confirmation.[268]

Following that cable, the ABC tried to contact the conductor's representatives several times by telephone but were told 'that he had been far too busy to give the matter his consideration'.[269] Eventually, they were able to pin Barbirolli down and a tour was agreed for mid-1953. He was to arrive in Sydney towards the end of July and was to head home at the end of September. A contract was sent to J.B. on 14 May 1952 and it was hoped that the matter was well and truly settled.[270] But he had a few stipulations and central to these were choral works. In replying to the Commission, his management asked 'whether he [could] have the following undertakings':

(a) That he gives the following major choral performances: Verdi Requim [sic], Dream of Gerontius, Messiah, and Das Lied von der Erde of Mahler …
(b) That a furnished flat can be found for him in each of the towns. He had a most miserable time on his last visit to Australia (as it was his first visit he did not want your Australian colleagues to think he was being temperamental and therefore did not mention it very strongly!) as he finds it impossible to eat until after his concert, and does not like to have to eat in a night club and such places! If he could be provided with a furnished apartment all he would require would be a cleaner, and he could do the shopping and cooking himself. Although this matter has its humorous side, as far as Sir John is concerned it is quite serious.[271]

For many of the European artists who visited Australia at that time, local hotels often proved disappointing, if not wholly unacceptable.[272] Their lack of refinement and their inability to compete gastronomically with those abroad often left touring musicians disturbed and annoyed. But it was Barbirolli's insistence on what was effectively a choral festival that was the nail in the 1953 tour's coffin. He was adamant that without these works the visit was in doubt and the Commission was equally adamant that such a series was not possible. The trip failed to materialize and Australian audiences had to wait until 1955 before they saw the conductor again.

In the months leading up to the 1955 tour, letters, telegrams and memos ping-ponged between Sydney, London and Manchester. Perhaps unsurprisingly the main topic of discussion was not programming but accommodation. The Commission was determined to show that Australian hospitality was second to none, even though the country's hotels were far from the world's best. Where possible private accommodation was to be provided in each city visited and, if available, detailed descriptions of that accommodation were to be sent to the conductor and his wife in advance. No effort was spared and no request was too extreme. In Sydney, the ABC reserved an apartment at 'Cherwood' in King's Cross, only a short walk from the orchestra's rehearsal rooms, for the Barbirollis at £17/17/- per week;[273] in Adelaide, a large, private flat on the sea-front at Glenelg had been booked for them at 12 Guineas per week; in Melbourne, a two-storey maisonette in fashionable South Yarra was put at their disposal by a female fan, again at 12 Guineas per week;[274] in Brisbane, they were allocated a suite at Lennon's Hotel at £5 per day, while, in Perth, Colonial Mutual Life Insurance offered them their company apartment at 'Lawson' on The Esplanade free of cost.[275] These arrangements were both time-consuming and galling for the ABC. So Charles Moses and his colleagues must have breathed a huge corporate sigh of relief when Evelyn Barbirolli wrote 'we are delighted to read about the arrangements for our accommodation and it all looks extremely satisfactory'.[276]

The razzamatazz that trumpeted Barbirolli's impending arrival in 1955 was certainly impressive but actually getting to Australia once again proved problematic. Intercontinental travel was far from straightforward in the 1950s and delays, cancellations and air disasters were commonplace. After their scheduled flight with Qantas had been cancelled, they were forced to fly a day earlier, landing in Sydney on 5 May. Within hours of setting foot on Australian soil, Barbirolli quickly became the darling of the popular press and used that popularity to raise once again the thorny issue of an exchange between the Hallé and Sydney Symphony Orchestras. His tour consisted of twenty concerts in Sydney, Adelaide, Melbourne, Brisbane and Perth and was distinguished by its adventurous programming. All twenty performances contained works by British composers of which nineteen featured pieces by his contemporaries, including seven Australian premieres.[277] Of the works heard during his first visit, only eight were given again but these were performed in different cities, thus ensuring healthy box-office receipts for the ABC.[278] Soloists continued to be something of a *bête-noir* for J.B. with only six of his twenty performances being given with orchestra alone.[279]

Barbirolli again kicked off his tour in Sydney with seven performances between 11 and 21 May, all with the Sydney Symphony Orchestra and all at the Town Hall. His first pair of concerts on 11 and 12 May contained works by Kabalevsky, Wagner, Bate and Brahms.[280] Of these, the least familiar was Bate's Third Symphony, which prompted the *Sydney Morning Herald* to opine '[it is] a resourceful and earnest work which spins attractively on the Shostakovich-Vaughan Williams axis [and] is the writing of a young Englishman whose certainty in musical structure, in mood change, and in apt instrumentation is wholly remarkable'.[281] The next tranche of Sydney concerts were on 14, 16 and 17 May and involved music by Geoffrey Bush, Delius, Strauss, Wagner and Sibelius[282] and were followed two days later by a programme of works by Elgar, Haydn, Stravinsky and Rubbra.[283] Barbirolli then bid farewell to Sydney on 21 May with an evening of music by Moeran, Castelnuovo-Tedesco and Beethoven.[284] His reading of Beethoven's Third Symphony at that concert was certainly provocative and ignited a heated critical debate that burned for days. Bowled over by J.B.'s approach, the critic for *The Bulletin* wrote that 'Beethoven strode [through the programme] like a colossus … [and] the Symphony was the best Beethoven heard from the orchestra for a long time'.[285] The critic for the *Sydney Morning Herald* was less enthusiastic, however, and reported that 'there were some magnificent episodes in the "Eroica" … but, in sum, the work seemed diffuse and scattered, with something of its epic distinction as a human document surrendered to immediately vivid dramatic effects'.[286]

After Sydney, the Barbirolli roadshow moved on to Adelaide where he performed music by Wagner, Mozart, Moeran, Elgar and his own *An Elizabethan Suite* with the South Australian Symphony Orchestra at the Town Hall on 26, 27 and 28 May.[287] Then, on 1 and 2 June 1955, he gave Beethoven's Overture to *Coriolan*, Vaughan Williams's *Sinfonia antartica* and Brahms's First Symphony at Melbourne's Town Hall with the Victorian Symphony Orchestra, Elsa Haas and the Oriana Madrigal Choir. These were followed by a second pair of concerts with the VSO at the Town Hall on 4 and 6 June at which he performed music by Purcell, Finzi, Ibert and Dvořák.[288] J.B. then made a five-day side trip to Brisbane where he conducted the Queensland Symphony Orchestra at City Hall on 10 and 11 June.[289] Three days later, he was back at Melbourne's Town Hall with the VSO for a programme of music by Rossini, Butterworth, Haydn, Wagner and Stravinsky[290] before conducting the highlight of the tour – Elgar's *The Dream of Gerontius* with Joan Jones, Ronald Dowd, Morris Williams, the Choir of the Royal Melbourne Philharmonic Society and the VSO – on 16 June. This was the first of thirty-nine performances Barbirolli gave with Ronald Dowd in Britain, Ireland and Australia and was the beginning of a working partnership that continued until the conductor's death in 1970.[291] Barbirolli then moved on to Perth for a pair of concerts with the West Australian Symphony Orchestra at the Capitol Theatre on 24 and 25 June[292] before setting off for Britain from Sydney later that month.

The success of Barbirolli's second tour was apparent to all concerned. The ABC was desperate to lure him back to Australia as soon as possible and even approached him in May 1959 to take over the permanent conductorship of the Victorian Symphony Orchestra.[293] As J.B.'s time commitment to the Hallé Orchestra had been reduced considerably after he resigned as its Permanent Conductor to become its Conductor-in-Chief in 1958, the ABC must have thought that it was in with a chance. But Barbirolli had bigger fish to fry. From the late 1950s, the musical world was at J.B.'s feet and many of the great orchestras of North America and Europe were falling over themselves to engage him. From 1961, he was a regular guest conductor with the Berlin Philharmonic and was appointed Music Director of the Houston Symphony Orchestra the same year. Manchester, Houston and Berlin quickly became the axis around which his schedule revolved and extended trips to Australia would have been impractical, both musically and financially. That said, money was never the primary motivating factor for Barbirolli, but he was a workaholic who needed his daily fix of world-class music-making. The sheer amount of time involved in travelling to Australia meant that he would be away from his beloved Manchester, Berlin and Houston orchestras for far too long and this was unthinkable. It seems, then, that the tyranny of distance had claimed yet another victim.

FROM THE CRADLE TO THE GRAVE: BARBIROLLI, ELGAR AND *IN THE SOUTH (ALASSIO)*

Ever since I can remember – and my memories go back over 40 years now – I was regularly taken to the Henry Wood "Proms" and Sunday Concerts and from the age of ten onwards the music of Edward Elgar has meant more to me than I can say. I never argue about him with people who try to point out his faults to me – if full-bloodedness, grandeur and nobility of melodic invention, can be termed "faults". He has sometimes been called "vulgar" – and if there be any vulgarity in his music, it is of the kind that belongs to the greatest of artists, and you can find it in the same way at times in Verdi and Wagner. [294]

Written during the centenary of Elgar's birth in 1957, Barbirolli's lovingly crafted words sum up a lifetime's relationship with a composer whose works he revered above all others. While Delius might have been the alpha and omega of Barbirolli's career in the recording studio, Elgar was the beating heart of his work in the concert hall.[295] With each passing year, the composer's music took on a greater significance for the conductor, with Barbirolli's name becoming virtually synonymous with that of Elgar's by the end of his long and eventful life. Of course, other British artists, such as Sir Henry Wood, Sir Landon Ronald, Sir Malcolm Sargent, Sir Adrian Boult and Albert Coates, could also lay claim to the composer's music, but it was Barbirolli alone who acted as Elgar's greatest touring advocate. Whether it was in Manchester or Mexico City, Bulawayo or Brisbane, Los Angeles or Leningrad, the conductor programmed his hero's compositions whenever and wherever possible and gave no fewer than 869 spirited readings of thirty-one of the composer's works between 1921 and 1970.

Given Barbirolli's early enthusiasm for Elgar's music, it is somewhat surprising that the young J.B. never played the composer's String Quartet or Piano Quintet as a professional chamber musician.[296] But he was quick to recognise the importance of the Cello Concerto and was one of the earliest and most passionate interpreters of it. Having played works for cello and orchestra by Goltermann, Saint-Saëns and

Bruch as a boy at the Queen's Hall between 1911 and 1914,[297] Barbirolli played no other concertos in public until he was engaged to perform Tchaikovsky's *Variations on a Rococo Theme* with Dan Godfrey and the Bournemouth Municipal Orchestra in March 1920. Impressed by the young Londoner's very obvious musicianship, Godfrey then invited him to return the following year to give a performance of Elgar's Cello Concerto with his Bournemouth band,[298] the start of Barbirolli's lifelong love affair with the concerto and his first professional encounter with the composer's music. The success of that concert encouraged J.B. to explore the concerto still further and to include it in a recital that he gave with the pianist, Harold Craxton, at the Aeolian Hall on 12 June 1923. While no longer common today, public performances of concertos accompanied by piano were an everyday part of concert life during the late nineteenth and early twentieth centuries[299] and neither the critics nor the public were particularly disturbed by hearing Elgar's work in a reduced format that night.[300]

Five years after being demobilised from the British Army in 1919, Barbirolli formed a chamber orchestra at his own expense. Yet, it was not until 1925 that he conducted a work by Elgar with it for the first time. Heard at the New Chenil Galleries, Chelsea, on 16 October that year, the composer's *Elegy for Strings* was part of a wide-ranging programme that also included works by Vivaldi, Mozart, Rameau and Debussy.[301] 'Composed of a small number of expert string players',[302] the Chenil Chamber Orchestra impressed with its 'precision' and 'keen, refreshing tone', which *The Times*'s critic considered 'the special charm of [Barbirolli's] small string band'.[303] But with his professional life becoming increasingly peripatetic after being appointed a conductor with the British National Opera Company in September 1926, J.B. was forced to reduce the number of concerts that he gave with his remarkable troupe of young players. Nevertheless, he never lost touch with the band completely and conducted Elgar's *Introduction and Allegro for Strings* with it on 19 October 1926, the first of a remarkable 121 performances of the work that he gave during his career. Speaking directly to his sensibilities as a string player and as an Edwardian Londoner, the composition quickly became one of Barbirolli's favourite pieces and he recorded it for the first time with the National Gramophonic Society Chamber Orchestra the following year.

Founded in 1923 by the novelist and critic, Compton Mackenzie, the National Gramophonic Society produced recordings of works that were either new or had been neglected by some of the bigger companies. While the *Introduction and Allegro for Strings* was hardly fresh from the composer's pen, it was not particularly familiar to the general public and had never recovered fully from the lukewarm reception that it received after its first performance in 1905. Aware that his enthusiasm for the work was not shared universally, Barbirolli understood that his discs might need some added publicity if they were to ignite the interest of the record-buying public. So when Mackenzie invited him to write about them in *The Gramophone*, he seized the chance.[304] Keen to sing the work's praises, and equally keen to explain the ways in which the new electrical recording method enhanced the listening experience, the conductor wrote:

> The Elgar work … is without doubt the finest modern work written for string orchestra, and a superb example of Elgar's genius. I cannot conceive any musical person failing to be thrilled by the spaciousness and loftiness of these lovely tunes, and as to the mastery of the writing that almost leaves one breathless. Though it is not for me to pass judgment favourable or otherwise on these records, there is one feature which I am sure will attract especial notice, and that is a remarkable advance made in the reproduction of the double bass. I shall not easily forget my surprise and delight when I heard for the first time the third part of the Elgar record, to find a real balance in the fugue section and also the typical thickness of the bass tone.[305]

The recording also came to the attention of Elgar, who had been sent a copy of the discs by Mackenzie. Responding quickly to the editor, the composer opined:

> Mr Barbirolli here and there makes a pause somewhat longer than the composer (the composer was six feet when the composition was written) but as he, owing to age and general decrepitude (I don't think) has become shorter there must be a sort of inverse ratio-complex (put that, because it shews [*sic*] we read things). I do not know how long the pause is, but I know that Mr Barbirolli is an extremely able youth and, very properly, has ideas of his own, added to which he is a remarkably able conductor, but if I talk critically of what I do not understand – such things as records, music and tempi – it follows that what I say in an appreciative way may be construed to be equally incorrect.[306]

Although written with tongue firmly in cheek, Elgar did like the discs and later said to J.B. that he 'had no idea it was such a big piece'.[307] Hot on the heels of that recording, and nestled between his discs of excerpts from *Caractacus* with Peter Dawson and two of the *Sea Pictures* with Maartje Offers, Barbirolli documented the *Introduction and Allegro* for a second time in January 1929.[308] He then went on to record it on four further occasions for either HMV or Pye between 1947 and 1962 before including it in his penultimate concert with the Hallé Orchestra at the King's Lynn Festival on 24 July 1970.[309] Subsequently released on the BBC Legends label, that performance was part of an all-Elgar concert that also included the *Sea Pictures* with Kerstin Meyer and the First Symphony.

So what did Barbirolli's performances of the *Introduction and Allegro* mean musically and how representative were they interpretatively and technically? Perhaps the most striking aspect of J.B.'s relationship with the piece was his seamless transformation of it from a work for virtuoso chamber ensemble into one for large symphony orchestra. But as different as those instrumental formats were, his underlying interpretative skeleton remained largely the same. This was particularly true of his approach to tempo, which displayed a remarkable consistency over the half century that he performed the work. That said, his recordings of the piece also acted as a kind of barometer for technical change during the middle of the twentieth century and reflected the shifting trends in string technique and string technology during that period. It should be remembered that string players largely abandoned their earthy-sounding gut strings for sturdier, more-brilliant-sounding metal-on-gut strings during the late 1930s and the early 1940s, increased their use of *vibrato* and reduced their reliance on *portamento* as an expressive gesture. As some of these trends can be heard clearly on Barbirolli's discs of the *Introduction and Allegro*, the recordings are, therefore, a useful guide to the ways in which string technique and string technology changed during his lifetime.

Barbirolli's passionate advocacy of the *Introduction and Allegro* would not have been possible had it not been for a career-changing engagement that took place at the Queen's Hall on 12 December 1927 with the London Symphony Orchestra. Suffering from a severe arm injury, Sir Thomas Beecham had to withdraw from the performance that night, leaving the concert's promoters scrabbling around for a replacement *maestro*. Concerned that some aspects of the programme might prove tricky, many of the more-established conductors were understandably wary of putting their hard-won reputations on the line by accepting the engagement.[310] The principal stumbling block was the main work in the concert – Elgar's Second

Symphony – which was far from standard musical fare at the time. With no obvious replacement in sight, the directors of the self-governing orchestra were facing the very real possibility of having to cancel the concert. Remembering that their former back-desk colleague, John Barbirolli, had been doing some good things with the BNOC and was a committed Elgarian, it occurred to them that he might be up for the challenge. Explaining what happened next, J.B. later recalled that:

> When Sir Tommy had to give up the concert owing to indisposition, the orchestra, remembering that I had in fact played with them many times, said, "Why not give old John a chance?" I was therefore rung up on Friday afternoon. Haydn symphonies I knew inside out; well at least some of them, for there are too many! The Haydn Cello Concerto I had, of course, played many times so this work presented no difficulties. I had played the Elgar No. 2 but had never seen the full score, and when I was asked whether I would conduct the concert I was all for saying no: Friday afternoon – Sunday, first rehearsal – Monday, second rehearsal – Monday evening, concert. I remember my dear old Italian father standing by the phone (we had one of those old fashioned ones in the hall) and whilst I was saying no, he said to me: "Don't be a fool! It is not every day that you will get as opportunity like this!" I therefore capitulated and learnt the Symphony between Friday night and Sunday morning (in less than 48 hours).[311]

The prospect of taking on Elgar's technically difficult and interpretatively challenging Second Symphony at such short notice must have been daunting for Barbirolli. But encouragement was soon forthcoming from the orchestra's leader, W. H. Reed, who could see that the young conductor was equal to the task:

> A great man in many ways, [Reed was] a violinist and … composer as well as a great personality. He was *the* great Elgarian by way of his experience of having played under the composer on many occasions. During the rehearsals he was so kind and such a great help, even though by then I had formed my own ideas about the Symphony. When some of the LSO boys very kindly tried to help me, Bill [Reed] said "Leave him alone! He already knows what he wants to do. You know, Elgar might even like it!" This was, therefore, my introduction to the Elgar Second.[312]

87

Any lingering doubts that Barbirolli might have had quickly evaporated and he gave a performance of the symphony that was as memorable as it was remarkable. Eric Blom of *The Manchester Guardian* was certainly impressed by what he heard and was compelled to write that the conductor had 'made himself so fully conversant with this extraordinarily complex score that he had a safe margin of energy left to expend on technicalities … No liberties were taken which could not be justified by the addition of that something to the printed notes without which no music can come to life'.[313] Elgar's friend, Frank Schuster, was also in the audience and reported that the work had been played 'as it is written and, what's more, as it is felt. No point-making and no exaggeration but very cohesive and round and rich'.[314]

As Music Director of the Scottish Orchestra from 1933, Barbirolli had his first real opportunity to explore Elgar's symphonic works in detail. But programming the composer's music could be risky for music directors at that time, as it was often considered challenging for musicians and audiences alike. Box-office revenues were an ever-present consideration for the orchestra's management and attractive programmes were a must. These concerns did little to dissuade Barbirolli from spreading a veritable feast of Elgar's music before his Glasgow and Edinburgh publics, however, and after introducing himself to Scotland as an Elgarian with a reading of his beloved *Introduction and Allegro for Strings* on 16 January 1933, he led his first performance of the 'Enigma' Variations on 20 November that year.[315] A week later, he upped the musical ante considerably by giving the Violin Concerto with Adolf Busch in both Glasgow and Edinburgh.[316] Of all Elgar's works, the Violin Concerto has often proved most problematic for promoters and performers and is one of the few major orchestral works by the composer that Barbirolli never recorded commercially. His interest in it never wavered, however, and he performed it again twice the following year with the Scottish Orchestra's leader, David McCallum, in a programme that also included the Funeral March from *Grania and Diarmid*.[317]

Building on his Queen's Hall success in 1927, Barbirolli then gave the Second Symphony three times with his Glasgow-based band but conducted the First Symphony only once. Something of a Cinderella work during J.B.'s Scottish period, the First Symphony never displaced the Second in the conductor's affections, and the ratio of three performances to one in Scotland was representative of Barbirolli's programming of the two works in general.[318] Curiously, Barbirolli never conducted the Cello Concerto with the Scottish Orchestra. Given that he had worked with leading cellists, such as Pablo Casals and Guilhermina Suggia, during the late 1920s, and given the importance that work held for him personally, it is a mystery as to why it was missing from his Caledonian schedules, a mystery made even more puzzling when the breadth of his Elgar repertoire with the orchestra is taken into account as a whole. During his four years with the band, he gave forty-three complete performances of fourteen works by Elgar, including the rarely heard *Romance* for bassoon and orchestra and the Prelude to *The Light of Life*.[319] Of the works given, the 'Enigma' Variations and 'Pomp and Circumstance' March No. 1 were clear audience favourites, with eleven and nine performances respectively.

As a guest conductor with the London Philharmonic and Hallé Orchestras during his Scottish tenure, Barbirolli was also quick to programme Elgar's music.[320] Of those engagements, perhaps the one of greatest historical and personal significance to him was his concert with the Hallé Orchestra at Manchester's Free Trade Hall on 15 February 1934. Deputising for an indisposed Sir Edward Elgar that night, Barbirolli conducted a programme that included *Froissart*, the 'Enigma' Variations, *Cockaigne (In London Town)* and the Violin Concerto.[321] Smitten by the reading of the Variations, *The Manchester Guardian*'s critic was positively glowing when he wrote that Barbirolli 'gave us one of the best pieces of conducting of the season … [and] a testimony to [his] love of Elgar and his technical resource'.[322] But J.B.'s 'considerable [personal] success' was not extended to the programme itself, which proved something of a sticking point for the journalist. Unconvinced by a concert given over solely to the works of Britain's most distinguished composer, the critic grumbled that 'a whole evening devoted to the music of Elgar is a doubtful enterprise'.[323] Unable to match Wagner's 'dramatic range' or Beethoven's 'variety of form and power', Elgar was only 'great' when he kept 'within the limitations of his temperament'.[324] Nevertheless, the reviewer did concede that the concert did prove Elgar's genius and that England could 'take pride' in having 'produced him'.[325]

When Barbirolli stepped into the great man's shoes that February evening, he must have experienced a sense of great personal satisfaction. But satisfaction quickly turned to sorrow when he learned of his hero's death less than a week later.[326] The pain of that loss never fully left Barbirolli, and when he looked back on those events many years later, he 'wondered':

why I, a Cockney-born Londoner of purely Latin blood, have such an affinity with what some call a purely English composer … [I]t may arise from the fact that I was born just at the end of the Victorian era and was brought up during the Edwardian period which, of course, Elgar expresses so ardently and admirably. Having begun to play in public at the age of eleven, and started to earn my living at fourteen, I suppose I matured rather more quickly than most children of that age, and I have very conscious memories of the splendour of that era. For me it is a London, which, with its horse-buses (on which I went to school), four-wheelers and hackney cabs – providing the main excitement of holiday trips to the sea-side – I have seen disappearing with deep pangs of regret, reactionary as this may seem … I had the melancholy privilege of spending an unforgettable few hours alone with Elgar a few months before his death, and he spoke more about his music and himself than I had ever known him do before. Despite all the official honours that had come to him there were dark passages in his remembrances, one of which was the occasion of his 70th birthday concert at the Old Queen's Hall … It had been half empty. May I beg of you to redress this wrong?[327]

And with his appointment as Music Director of the New York Philharmonic-Symphony Orchestra from the start of the 1937–8 season, Barbirolli did indeed intend to 'redress this wrong'. But that intention proved harder to realise than he ever imagined, and even though older British contemporaries, such as Thomas Beecham, Adrian Boult and Albert Coates, had already laboured tirelessly on the composer's behalf in North America, Elgar's sound-world was still something of an acquired taste for local audiences, critics and players.

Having wisely tested the artistic waters with the ever-popular 'Enigma' Variations at his third and fourth concerts as a guest conductor with the Philharmonic-Symphony Orchestra in 1936,[328] Barbirolli went on to conduct his first work by Elgar as the band's Music Director the following year. But if he had hoped to make an immediate and decisive impact as an Elgarian with his beloved *Introduction and Allegro for Strings* on 4 November 1937,[329] he was sadly mistaken. Writing in *The New York Times*, Olin Downes grumbled:

The "Introduction and Allegro" [under Barbirolli] became not a work of merely classic counterpoint and form, with a pound or two of the good roast beef of old England thrown in for good measure, as the score had often appeared, but something of a fanciful and motivated improvisation. Must a little fly be put in these honeyed words? The orchestra did not help Mr.

Barbirolli's interpretation by the acme of precision in following his beat. The conception merited more finished execution.[330]

Speaking more directly in *The Sun*, Oscar Thompson complained that the orchestra's 'famous strings had some ragged attacks in the British work',[331] while the *New York Post*'s Samuel Chotzinoff simply dismissed the piece as 'one of the less exciting inspirations of the British master'.[332] Determined that local audiences and critics should come to terms with the *Introduction and Allegro*, J.B. then decided to drip-feed his Knickerbocker audience with a further ten performances of the work over the next six years, a strategy that was as fruitless as it was futile.

Barbirolli seems to have fared much better with the 'Enigma' Variations, however. Given on twenty-one occasions with the orchestra at Carnegie Hall and on tour, the work proved popular with local audiences, a response that no doubt pleased the conductor, as it was the composition that he conducted most frequently during his career.[333] But interest in Elgar's music remained decidedly tepid during J.B.'s six seasons with the orchestra, resulting in him giving only forty-five performances of seven works by the composer.[334] Amongst this relatively meagre tally were his first two performances of the Cello Concerto as a conductor, the first of which was an arrangement of the work for viola and orchestra by the distinguished British violist, Lionel Tertis. Given by Zoltan Kurthy on 27 November 1938 at Carnegie Hall, Tertis's version did little to excite the curiosity of the critics and passed relatively unnoticed. Conversely, Gregor Piatigorsky's performances of the work in its original form on 9 and 10 November 1940 sparked a veritable wildfire of pre-concert interest. Public interest does not always translate into critical success, however. And even though the reviewer for the *New York Herald Tribune* was impressed by the soloist's 'sensuous tone, warmth of feeling and technical dexterity', he found the work to be 'sentimental to the core and recalling [the Irish writer] George Moore's remark about the same composer's "Dream of Gerontius" — "Holy water in a German beer-barrel."'[335]

With his return to Britain as Permanent Conductor of the Hallé Orchestra in 1943, Barbirolli hoped for a more receptive response to Elgar's music. Having spent much of the early part of that summer attempting to re-build the war-ravaged orchestra, he then toured with it throughout parts of northern England, Scotland and the Midlands, before conducting it at Manchester on 15 August.[336] Along with popular works by Wagner, Debussy and Tchaikovsky, Barbirolli treated his new Mancunian audience to the 'Enigma' Variations that evening.[337] Ecstatic about the newly reinvigorated orchestra, the local critics were equally enthusiastic about the conductor's reading of the Variations, which had been given five times on the tour. Although the work then became the mainstay of Barbirolli's Elgar repertoire during his first season with the orchestra, he also gave the *Introduction and Allegro*, the Violin Concerto with Albert Sammons, *Cockaigne* and his first performance of *Falstaff*.[338] It is no exaggeration to say that Elgar's music then played a major role in how both Barbirolli and the Hallé Orchestra were perceived and received over the next twenty-seven years, resulting in Manchester being seen as a centre of Elgarian excellence. But of the vast number of performances of the composer's works that J.B. gave during that time, three were of particular personal and historical significance to him: his broadcast of *Cockaigne* to launch Independent Television in 1955, his performance of *The Dream of Gerontius* before Pope Pius XII in 1958 and his first encounter with *In the South (Alassio)* in 1970.

A strong advocate of broadcasting from near the beginning of his career, Barbirolli was only too aware of the educational and cultural possibilities that the increasingly popular medium of television had to offer art music in the mid-1950s. With captive audiences who could engage with the works of Beethoven, Wagner, Brahms and others from the comfort of their sitting rooms, conductors, soloists and singers quickly became household names. The contemporary artist who benefitted most from this kind of media exposure was Sir Malcolm Sargent, whose work at the Proms was beamed into homes throughout the length and breadth of Great Britain. Transmitted by the BBC, Sargent's televised concerts soon made him a musical superstar, whose public profile was comparable to those of movie stars and sporting heroes. Barbirolli was also eager to benefit from the new medium and was given his chance to enter the televisual market place for the first time when the British government decided to challenge the BBC Television Service's monopoly by awarding Independent Television (ITV) six regional commercial franchises in 1954. After the passing of the Television Act that year, the first of the new franchises to broadcast was Associated-Rediffusion. To launch its service, Barbirolli was invited to conduct Elgar's *Cockaigne* with the Hallé Orchestra from London's Guildhall on 22 September 1955. Looking back from a world that is now awash with the puerilities of social media and the often-trivial content of digital broadcasters, Associated-Rediffusion's decision to kick off its franchise with a great conductor performing a great work with a great orchestra seems almost inconceivable. But broadcasters of the period did not subscribe to the modern misapprehension that art music is elitist. Rather, it was seen as something that should be available to all, an egalitarian art form for an egalitarian age. As Barbirolli was also a passionate believer in the universal importance of music, the prospect of disseminating high culture through the populist appeal of ITV was too good to miss, and over the next four years Barbirolli went on to give a further twenty broadcast concerts for Associated-Rediffusion of which three contained a piece by Elgar.[339]

A work that became increasingly associated with Barbirolli from the late 1940s onwards was *The Dream of Gerontius*. Having conducted Elgar's choral masterpiece for the first time at Sheffield in 1946 with Kathleen Ferrier, Parry Jones and Arthur Reckless, J.B. went on to give a further forty-eight complete performances of the oratorio over the next twenty-four years.[340] Speaking directly to Barbirolli's sense of religiosity, the work's deep-rooted spirituality distilled for him the essence of Roman Catholicism. Over the years, he performed it with a string of leading soloists, including Norma Procter, Bernadette Greevy, Anna Reynolds, Janet Baker, Ronald Dowd, Richard Lewis, Donald Bell, David Ward and Kim Borg, and conducted it throughout the British Isles, North America and Australia. But it was not until 1957 that he was able to conduct the work in Rome for the first time. Recalling that performance with Constance Shacklock, Jon Vickers and Marian Nowakowski in later life, Barbirolli felt that it was:

> The next milestone for me [on my personal journey with *Gerontius* and] was [an] opportunity afforded me, through the enthusiasm and indefatigable efforts of Sir Ashley Clarke (then British Ambassador in Rome) to give the first performance in Italy – incredible though this may seem – in the centenary year of Elgar's birth, with the magnificent collaboration of the orchestra and chorus of the R.A.I. in Rome.[341] Never shall I forget the look of joyful surprise and enthusiasm on the faces of the orchestra and chorus at the first rehearsal, when the wonders of the work unfolded themselves. [And] [i]ncidentally, since Italian and English are mother tongues to me, the voluble comments on the work did not escape me.[342]

Less than a year later, Barbirolli was back in Italy for a performance of Part 1 of *Gerontius* before Pope Pius XII.[343] The event was a truly emotional experience for the conductor and one that left him drained both spiritually and musically. Looking back on that remarkable day years later, J.B. remembered:

Pope Pius XII raised me to my feet [with the words 'Figlio mio, questo e un capolavoro sublime' ('my son, this is a sublime masterpiece')] after I had knelt before him to receive his blessing and thanks for a performance of the first part of "The Dream of Gerontius" given at his summer residence of Castel Gandolfo, by the Choir of Our Lady of Dublin and [David Galliver and Marian Nowakowski]. The treasured memory of these noble and sensitively appreciative words is made all the more poignant when we remember that barely ten days were to elapse before His Holiness was to pass from this world, and that this was the last "live" music he was to hear. I have often wondered what the feelings of Newman and Elgar would be if they could know that the last music he heard had been Elgar's setting of Newman's words "Go forth upon thy journey, Christian soul".[344]

For a conductor whose antecedents were Mediterranean, and for a musician who had been a committed Elgarian from his earliest years, it is nothing short of bewildering that Barbirolli never performed *In the South (Alassio)* publicly until the last months of his life. With its atmospheric orchestration, its strength of form and its engaging melodic and harmonic content, the work is not only one of Elgar's greatest compositions, but one that was ideally suited to J.B.'s temperament and musical sensibilities. Yet, it wasn't until the conductor's friend, the writer Michael Kennedy, encouraged him to study the piece in the mid-1960s that he finally decided to include it in his repertoire. Given first by Barbirolli with the Hallé Orchestra at Manchester on 30 April 1970, *In the South* was the opening item in a programme that also included Bruckner's Eighth Symphony. In a review that positively radiates enthusiasm for Elgar's concert-overture, Gerald Larner of *The Guardian* was astounded that it had flown under Barbirolli's artistic radar for such a long time:

It is strange that an Elgar man like Sir John had never before taken up a work as passionate and as colourful as this one[.] I gather (from that other of Manchester's experts, Michael Kennedy) that we owe this performance to the "gentle chiding" of a "friend." He was a wise friend, for this was a great performance of "In the South." It was a superbly calculated interpretation, every tempo change made for a good structural or expressive reason (usually both). The magnificent opening passage and its several reappearances were alive with such energy that their pulse was still felt to throb even throughout the lyrical and scenic episodes.[345]

Performed again at Sheffield the following night, *In the South* was then given for a third time by Barbirolli and the Hallé at the Royal Festival Hall on 20 May.[346] As the penultimate work of the Royal Philharmonic Society's 158th season, an organisation with which J.B. had been associated for more than fifty years, *In the South* made an instant and profound impact. On hand that night for *The Guardian* was the conductor's long-time friend, Neville Cardus, who reported optimistically that 'fresh from recent conquests in Germany,[347] and obviously recovered in health and constitution … [Barbirolli gave a] vivid performance of … music that [was] entirely after [his] heart'.[348] But, sadly, Barbirolli's own heart had been deteriorating for some time and the Society's concert was the last that he would conduct in London. Luckily for posterity, however, the BBC was also on hand that night to record the event and has since released it commercially on its Legends label.[349]

Equally lucky for posterity is the fact that Barbirolli's marked score of *In the South* is also extant. A richly detailed artefact that documents many of his working practices, it also acted as a kind of musical confessional for the conductor. Much like his great German predecessor and friend, Bruno Walter, whose materials are littered with religious and philosophical aphorisms,[350] Barbirolli often laid bare his musical soul in his scores and confided to them his inner thoughts and ideas. Unlike Walter, however, J.B.'s extra-musical annotations tended to avoid direct Biblical quotes and confined themselves largely to his aesthetic responses to the music itself. As these materials *are* so reflective of artists' thought processes, it is perhaps surprising that until relatively recently they remained largely undisturbed on the archival shelves to which they were first dispatched after the deaths of their owners. Little consideration was given to the possible didactic value of these artefacts and even less was given to the ways in which they could be made available securely and easily to scholars and performers. In many cases, the marked scores and orchestral parts of important executant artists never made it as far as institutional archives and were either misplaced, given away to friends or simply lost by those who had inherited them. Barbirolli's annotated Elgar scores are a case in point, with only a handful of them still in existence.[351]

Like his illustrious and influential predecessor, Sir Henry Wood, Barbirolli was an indefatigable marker of scores and orchestral parts. Although laborious and time consuming, the act of setting out their intentions in advance was an essential practice for British conductors who invariably suffered from a paucity of rehearsal time, due, in no small part, to the stringent financial restraints under which they laboured. Often balancing nightly concerts with daily rehearsals during the 1940s and the 1950s, Barbirolli faced a gruelling schedule that meant he needed to plan his limited preparation time with military precision. Sitting at his desk late into the night with a cigarette in one hand and a pencil in the other, J.B. meticulously marked industrial quantities of scores and parts before dispatching them a few hours later to the Hallé's long-suffering librarian. But, what separates his annotated score of *In the South* from the hundreds of others that preceded it, is the knowledge that it was the last major symphonic work that he prepared in detail and the last substantial work to be added to his repertoire. Acting as a kind of musical roadmap that charts Barbirolli's technical demands, aesthetic observations and emotional responses, his working score of *In the South* contains multiple expression, tempo, beating, balance and bowing instructions. Marked mainly in heavy lead pencil, J.B.'s annotations are written in a mixture of Italian, English and German, a language that appeared increasingly frequently in his marked materials during the last decades of his life.[352]

A particular preoccupation of Barbirolli was the way in which an individual instrumental voice could be best balanced within the greater orchestrational whole. Writing on the blank front endpaper facing the first printed page, he jotted down the *aide-memoire*: 'N.B. Any pencil notes of mine such as "Not heard" etc are notes on <u>previous</u> recordings for our future guidance.'[353] A seemingly innocuous comment that could easily be overlooked, it does, in fact, suggest a number of issues that are fundamental to Barbirolli's working practices. Aside from implying that he intended to record the work at some point in the future, the comment also hints at the ways in which he studied and prepared scores. J.B.'s wife, Evelyn, was adamant that he rarely listened to recordings when studying.[354] Yet, here, it seems obvious that he did at least *refer* to the recordings of others when tackling this work for the first time, a hypothesis that is confirmed by the passages marked 'not heard' in the score itself. The descending triplet figure in the second violins and violas at five bars after Fig. 3, the rising horn arpeggios at two bars before Fig. 9, the viola material at Fig. 11, and, most tellingly, the $_{ppp}$ chords in the harps from two bars after Fig. 34 were all singled out by Barbirolli as being problematic acoustically. It is also tempting to speculate that the '<u>previous</u>' imbalances identified by J.B. refer to Elgar's own pre-electrical discs of the work from the early 1920s with the Royal Albert Hall Orchestra, and from the enigmatic note at the top of the same front endpaper – '(Elgar) 20.40 ? cut of 48''' – it might be assumed that it does. But as Elgar's recording takes sixteen minutes and four seconds, and as the excised material takes considerably longer than forty-eight seconds, any suggestion that the annotation refers to that particular sound-document falls at the first hurdle and, by extension, so, too, the note referring to balance. If, on the other hand, the annotation pertaining to timings refers to one of Elgar's performances of *In the South* with the London Symphony Orchestra at the Queen's Hall that Barbirolli might have heard in either 1912 or 1926, then that comment would make perfect sense.[355]

Of particular importance to any conductor when preparing an interpretation is a clearly defined tempo plan. This was no less true of Barbirolli, whose approach to speed was directly related to his understanding of a work's architectonic structure. His scores of compositions by Mahler and Bruckner, for example, are peppered with well-considered metronome marks that were realised in his recorded performances of those pieces. Yet, in his score of *In the South*, he inserted only one metronome mark: '♩ = 63 ✓' [*sic*].[356] Found on the percussion staves in bar 1, the mark is far from revelatory or contentious, as it simply reinforces Elgar's own printed instruction at the top of the page. When it comes to how particular passages should to be beaten, however, Barbirolli is more forthcoming. In bar 1, for example, he circles the number '3' and writes '1st bar only' above the harp part before circling the number '1' on the percussion lines in bar 2. By beating the opening bar in three rather than in one, J.B. not only ensures that the arpeggiated, anacrustic rising woodwind and string figures found at the end of the first bar are played with rhythmic verve and dynamic certainty, but secures the sweep and swagger necessary to give the first subject its Edwardian character when it appears for the first time in the horns and the lower strings at bar 3.

Sometimes, however, Barbirolli's beating choices are not so clear. Take, for example, the four bars leading up to Fig. 6 with its quintessential Elgarian superscription, *Nobilmente*. Clearly of some strategic importance to Barbirolli, the four-bar passage has a '*Virtuoso*' added to the percussion staves, a four-bar arched bracket with the number '4' inserted above the first violins, a supplementary '*Nobilmente*' pencilled in at the end of the trumpet and trombone lines and an additional '*ff*' marked at the end of the first violins' stave. While these annotations do little to suggest that J.B. did anything other than continue to beat in one to the bar up to and including Fig. 6, his circling of an added number '1' directly before the page turn, and the addition of a second circled '1' immediately before Fig. 6 after the page turn, imply that he beat the preceding four bars differently. When the plethora of annotations in those bars are then taken together with the printed *sforzandi* found on the first and fourth quavers of the first three bars of this passage, partially reinforced by added hairpin accents (>) in lead pencil,[357] there can be little doubt that Barbirolli beat these measures in three rather than in one. By so doing, he not only secured a sharp attack on each successive *sforzando*, but ensured that the passage thrust the musicians and the listeners headlong into the spacious *Nobilmente* at Fig. 6.[358]

Rhythmic direction and tempo manipulation were also central to Barbirolli's reading of *In the South*. Using German to good effect when dealing with these issues, he indicates his intentions clearly at passages that precede moments of particular architectonic importance. Writing in large print between Figs. 18 and 19, J.B. reminded himself first in English that 'From here a gradual *accel*[*erando*] till the "*Grandioso*" at No. 20 (*Meno*) (Don't start it too soon)' was necessary. But as if to drive the point home, he then wrote unequivocally in German '*immer ff und vorwarts* [sic]' ('always *ff* and forwards') eight bars before Fig. 20, one of the work's subsidiary climaxes. In leading up to Fig. 58, another subsidiary climax, Barbirolli played a longer game by inserting '*immer vorwarts* [sic]' ('always forwards') and '*più moto sempre*' ('always more forward motion') five bars after Fig. 55, before demanding an even greater sense of forward motion by adding a further, and more emphatic, '*immer vorwarts* [sic]' at Fig. 56. When combined with the frenzy of phrase-length indicators, instrumental *aides-memoire* and reinforced dynamic instructions that pepper the material following Fig. 55, it is clear that Barbirolli was directing the listeners to the work's one true climax, the final *Grandioso* at Fig. 58.

Often associated with compositions from the Austro-German canon, the concept that major symphonic works have only one true climax is an architectonic phenomenon that Barbirolli subscribed to wholeheartedly. Aware that Elgar was a self-confessed admirer of the music of Schumann and Brahms, Barbirolli clearly saw the influence of various Continental masters on his hero's music. Sometimes compared with the larger tone poems of Richard Strauss, *In the South* seems to have strengthened J.B.'s belief that Elgar's compositional aesthetic gave at least a slight reverential nod to the works of central Europe. This theory is confirmed, at least in part, by Barbirolli's continued use of the German language when expressing both the work's inner content and his responses to it at selected moments in the score. The transitory material eight bars before Fig. 26 is a case in point. With its sparse orchestration, its use of muted horns and its remote tonality, Barbirolli describes the passage as '*schattenhaft*' ('shadowy'), a term that would be more at home in a symphony by Mahler rather than a concert-overture by Elgar. Similarly, when he is dealing with moments of heightened beauty, Barbirolli once again turned to German to express his feelings. In the bars preceding the work's best known passage, Fig. 34, later the basis for the composer's *Canto popolare*, for example, Barbirolli notes '*immer sehr ruhig*' ('always very calm') before describing the section itself as '(*sehr zart*)' ('very sweet'). Continuing in German, J.B. then annotates '*sehr ruhig*' ('very calm') four bars after Fig. 35, '*schön*' ('beautiful') at Fig. 37 and, finally, '*Ruhig*' ('calm') four bars after Fig. 38.

But perhaps what is most striking about Barbirolli's marked score of *In the South* is not what is in it, but what is missing from it. Unlike in many of his other annotated scores of large symphonic works, J.B. was noticeably circumspect when adding extra bowing instructions to the string parts here. Whether out of respect for Elgar as a violinist, whether he felt that the printed bowings were largely adequate for his needs, or whether he simply had insufficient time to mark the work in greater detail, Barbirolli's relatively restrained approach to bowing is something of an enigma, particularly as the way in which he generally fashioned gestural nuances relied heavily on his creative use of the bow. And even where he does add additional instructions of this type, they are largely self-evident and would be obvious to most experienced string players. Of course, he does add some bowing gestures that are characteristic of his methods in general and that reflect his passion for an expressive use of the up-bow in particular. At four bars before Fig. 10, for example, the *pianissimo*, two-bar reminiscence of the first subject in the *divisi* second violins is coloured by taking the whole of the first bar under an up-bow followed by an implied down-bow in the next. The contour of the short phrase is then enriched still further by Barbirolli when he instructs the second violins to play the first bar as a *crescendo* and the second as a *diminuendo*, thus reinforcing dynamically the topography of the phrase through a combination of creative bowing and dynamic innovation.[359]

Barbirolli was also acutely aware that the right choice of string was essential when securing the right effect. At moments where a particularly warm sound was required within either a *piano* or *pianissimo* dynamic, he would invariable opt for the lower option, as, for example, at the four bars directly preceding Fig. 14. Here, he indicates that the first violins' high B flat should be played on the A string ('*sul* A') rather than on the more obvious, and colder sounding, E string. And what of his passion for *flautando* playing, a technique particularly close to Barbirolli's heart? Found frequently in his marked material of other Romantic and

99

Late-Romantic compositions, it appears only once here above the second violins' two-bar, descending triplet figure that starts ten bars before Fig. 40. But even when it does appear, it is inserted in such a shaky, faint hand that it is impossible to judge definitively whether or not he intended it to be implemented at all.

What is certain, however, is that Barbirolli never doubted the importance of Elgar's music to him personally or to humanity generally. Returning time and again to the composer's works throughout his career, J.B. championed them with a missionary's zeal. For him, Elgar's compositions represented the best of what Britain had to offer and he was proud to be their emissary. Having spread the Elgarian gospel to the four corners of the world for nearly half a century, Barbirolli could look back with pride at the efforts he made on his hero's behalf. No challenge was too tough and no audience was too unlikely when it came to the dissemination of Elgar's compositions. Asked in 1968 about the response of Latin-American audiences to the composer's works during the tour of Central and South America that he made with the Hallé Orchestra that year, Barbirolli beamed:

> I was absolutely thrilled beyond words at the understanding, the perception and the enthusiasm – most extraordinary – and they'd never heard a note of an Elgar symphony (and an Elgar symphony takes an hour you know and they're very complex works, even though they sound euphonious) and it was really thrilling.[360] And we played as an encore to that, the *Pomp and Circumstance No. 1* which they'd also never heard. Everywhere we played it, we had to play it twice. But can you imagine the thrill? You see, the connotation of "Land of Hope and Glory" means nothing at all to them except a great tune. It really was wonderful to feel the effect – the electrical effect – on a great audience. [And we] did something that the Foreign Office had not been able to do[:] … [we changed] the image of Britain … overnight, through music.[361]

BRUCKNER 8: SIR JOHN BARBIROLLI'S LONDON SWANSONG

> Another great composer who is beginning to come into his own in this country – or at any rate in Manchester! – [is] Bruckner … [His] sublime virtues [are] what some people like to call faults, for they indulge in what seems to arouse such deep resentment in the breasts of some musical commentators who utter (or rather, write) the word "sequences" as if it were some foul and incurable disease.[362]

When Sir John Barbirolli mounted the Royal Festival Hall podium in 1970 to conduct a work by Bruckner for the last time, he must have sighed inwardly knowing that his withering assessment of the critical millstone that hung around the composer's artistic neck in 1957 was still firmly in place thirteen years later. An often-thankless task that became no easier with time, J.B's advocacy of Bruckner's symphonies was an aesthetic uphill struggle that left many orchestral players, critics, promoters and audiences baffled and bemused. With its constant melodic sequences, its ostinato-like rhythmic repetitions and its vast architectonic structures, the composer's sound-world has often proved challenging technically and draining emotionally. Brass players find his endless *fortissimi* exhausting, string players consider his extended *tremolos* tedious and conductors wither under his formal demands. Yet, there is something transcendental about his symphonies, something completely satisfying about them that makes them the true musical manifestation of Aristotle's famous aphorism, 'the whole is greater than the sum of its parts'. Barbirolli clearly thought this to be true and was adamant that Bruckner's music should be put before the public with the same intensity and energy that was normally reserved for the works of Beethoven, Brahms and Mahler. Indefatigable in realising that aim during the last three decades of his life, J.B's efforts on the composer's behalf did not go unnoticed, and in 1959 he was awarded the Bruckner Society of America's Kilenyi Medal of Honor [*sic*], a distinction reserved for only the most committed of the composer's acolytes.

BRIEF HISTORICAL OVERVIEW

Barbirolli conducted a work by Bruckner for the first time on 10 January 1940. And given the response of the critics to that performance, he probably wished that he had waited even longer. Performed during his third season as Music Director of the New York Philharmonic-Symphony Orchestra, the Seventh Symphony was rejected by press and public alike.[363] Leading the critical charge against the work was the *New York Mirror* with the headline: '**Bruckner's 7ᵗʰ Empties The House**'. No less damning was the main body of the review which reported that:

> Half the hall walked out on a symphony by Anton Bruckner in Carnegie Hall last night. Who says Philharmonic-Symphony audiences aren't intelligent? Bruckner was the German schoolmaster who set out in the middle of the last century, with typical Teutonic patience, method and guileless arrogance to compose nine symphonies and thus prove that anybody who put an echt Deutsches mind to it and had learned to avoid parallel fifths could be another Beethoven … [Bruckner's music] is probably the worst, yet in one way the most fascinating … ever written. Its charm is its unending dullness. It holds you like a Scotch sermon, or as a cricket match holds an English gathering. You have to get away from it early if you hope to get away from it at all.[364]

Adopting a slightly different tone to that of his colleague at the *Mirror*, the critic for the *New York Herald Tribune* briefly put aside his concerns about the work to marvel at the 'nobility of intention … [that] marked Mr. Barbirolli's interpretation' and the 'intent and devot[ion] [which was] often characterized by a high degree of eloquence and emotional persuasiveness'.[365] *The New York Times*'s critic agreed that 'Mr. Barbirolli and his men gave the work an honest and solid performance [and that the] aspiration and integrity of the composer shone through'. Nevertheless, he, too, had serious doubts about the symphony, and while he was prepared to accept that it was 'easy to see why the mind of this composer appeals to some contemporaries', it was 'easier [still] to see why many more people can leave Bruckner alone'. [366]

Having faced a critical and popular brick wall when it came to all things Bruckner in New York, Barbirolli understandably gave no further performances of the composer's works during his time with the Philharmonic-Symphony Orchestra. Determined not to be swayed by the aesthetic prejudices that dogged Bruckner's music in North America, J.B. once again took up the cudgels for the composer after he returned to Britain as Permanent Conductor of the Hallé Orchestra in 1943. But Bruckner's symphonies also had something of a chequered reception history in the United Kingdom. Recalling his performance of the Seventh at the London's Queen's Hall in 1903, Sir Henry Wood wrote some thirty-five years later that 'this was its first and last performance at the Promenades … [as the] public would not have it then; neither will they now'.[367] And with a figurative shrug of the shoulder, he asked forlornly, 'perhaps Bruckner is only appreciated in Austria?'[368] With Wood's experience in mind, and with the Hallé still suffering from the privations of war, Barbirolli rightly withstood the urge to programme Bruckner's technically demanding symphonies with the band until 26 March 1947.[369] But if he had hoped that the Seventh Symphony would be accepted unconditionally that night, he was sadly mistaken. Once again the press carped that Bruckner was simply an 'inspired peasant whose music … was made up of homespun material'.[370] And despite 'its mystic [and] passionate expression[,] … unless listeners [could] remain patient when movements grow cumbersome and repetitive[,] … [or] when a passage or even a section hardens into a cliche [*sic*], Bruckner is not for them'.[371] Yet, it seems that Bruckner *was* for them. Eating his words later in the review, the journalist had to admit reluctantly that 'the audience last night obviously revelled in the work as a whole', due, in no small part, to a performance that was 'one of great power and beauty … [and that] was alive in every detail'.[372]

Encouraged by the response of his Mancunian audience, Barbirolli then began to perform Bruckner's symphonies in earnest and conducted no fewer than seventy-two performances of them between 1947 and 1970. But considering the conductor's commitment to the composer's music, it is somewhat curious that he performed only five of the nine numbered symphonies. The First, Second, Fifth or Sixth Symphonies were never conducted by him and were not amongst the plans he made for future engagements in the months before his death. He did, however, give seven performances of the Third, thirteen of the Fourth, twenty-nine of the Seventh, ten of the Eighth and thirteen of the Ninth. Clearly of greatest importance to him was the Seventh, the symphony with which he introduced himself as a Brucknerian to both New York and Manchester during the 1940s. The piece then became something of a calling-card for Barbirolli, as it was also the work by the composer that he conducted first with the Israel Philharmonic, the Houston Symphony Orchestra and the Berlin Philharmonic.[373] Yet, for what proved to be his final London concert on 20 May 1970, he conducted the Eighth Symphony with the Hallé Orchestra for the Royal Philharmonic Society at the Royal Festival Hall.

Coupled with a performance of Elgar's *In the South*, Barbirolli's reading of the Eighth Symphony that night was the last in a series of three that he gave of the work in Manchester, Sheffield and London between 30 April and 20 May that year. Of the Manchester concert, *The Guardian's* critic wrote:

> The Hallé Orchestra's playing was, as a whole, distinguished by its exceptional clarity in the Elgar [*In the South*], and the same quality was sustained throughout most of the Bruckner symphony. There were some signs of exhaustion, of slipping ensemble, and of a lack of interpretative continuity, in the last movement. But the first was coherently and impressively shaped, the marvellous Scherzo delivered with an inspired vitality, and the great Adagio was beautifully played. The symphony was given, by the way (as it was two years ago) in the Haas edition, which is the right musical thing to do even if, on purely musicological grounds, it is difficult to justify.[374]

After the work was repeated in London, *The Guardian* published a second review, in which the critic, Neville Cardus, argued that:

> … the immense Eighth Symphony of Bruckner … is not, you might guess before the event, exactly on Barbirolli's wave-length. He is more closely attuned to the high tensions of Mahler than to Bruckner's complex of the majestically evocative, the ethically introspective and the simple peasant scherzo galumphings.[375]

As Cardus was aware of Barbirolli's deep commitment to Bruckner's music, and the importance of the composer's works within the conductor's performance history as a whole, these comments are at best curious and at worst disingenuous. Cardus's aesthetic views are also highly suspect and, at times, strangely contradictory:

> Sir John tends to linger overmuch during a soulful, heartfelt phrase, to coax it, fondle it, at the risk of crippling the main onward direction of a movement. It is a refreshing fault nowadays, when so much music is played and conducted dehydratedly, as though performers and conductors had been "fed," like computers, stuffed with the score, the tempi markings, dynamic indications, and all the rest. Frankly, Sir John engaged his heart and

affections so much with Bruckner's persistent sequences that the repetitions and doodlings sounded even more trying to the patience than ever — and I write as a devout, if not moonstruck Brucknerian.[376]

Cardus's remarks are as deceptive as they are equivocal. The notion that 'Sir John engaged his heart and affections' at the partial expense of sound musical judgement fuels the myth that Barbirolli's readings were often led by his heart rather than his head. This was far from true. To understand more fully J.B.'s considered approach to the Eighth Symphony it might be helpful, therefore, to compare his annotated score of the Eighth Symphony with the BBC Legends CD of his 1970 Royal Festival Hall performance of the work.[377]

THE ANNOTATED SCORE

One of the main problems facing scholars and musicians interested in marked performance materials is the exact location and availability of them. Scores belonging to artists such as Wilhelm Furtwängler and Felix Mottl were scattered across the globe, while those of Felix von Weingartner had lain largely undisturbed in suitcases and packing boxes in a Basel basement until they were reassessed in the early 1990s. Many of Barbirolli's marked scores can be accessed easily, however, and are housed at The British Library. Even though the only complete set of symphonies are those by Mahler,[378] Barbirolli's collection of scores and orchestral parts reflects his catholic taste and is unusually comprehensive. While a number of important scores that Barbirolli used regularly are missing,[379] The British Library does hold some that are not generally associated with him, such as Malipiero's Third Symphony.[380] A curiosity in the collection is his marked vocal score of the last movement of Beethoven's Ninth Symphony with Basil Swift's English translation of Schiller's *Ode*.[381] Although unthinkable today, it was relatively common during the late nineteenth and early twentieth centuries for the symphony's finale to be performed in the vernacular in English-speaking countries. The great Hungarian-born conductor, Hans Richter, for example, conducted the movement in English in London in 1884, while Leopold Stokowski famously recorded the symphony with the Philadelphia Orchestra using Henry G. Chapman's translation of the *Ode* some fifty years later.[382]

The only Bruckner scores in The British Library collection are those of the Fourth Symphony (edited by Robert Haas), the Seventh Symphony (edited by

Albert Gutmann) and the Eighth and Ninth Symphonies (edited by Leopold Nowak).[383] An enlarged photocopy of the 1890 *Fassung* that was published by the Musikwissenshaftlicher Verlag der Internationalen Bruckner-Gesellschaft Wien in 1955,[384] Barbirolli's marked score of the Eighth Symphony is cloth-bound in red with the title of the work, the composer's name and the conductor's initials (J.B.) embossed in gold on the front cover. As the score was marked both before and after enlargement, the exact chronology of the annotations cannot be determined from the score itself and it is impossible to tell whether Barbirolli's initial markings were made in lead pencil, blue pencil or ink.[385] After enlargement, the majority of his annotations are in pencil with the use of blue pencil and ink being restricted to some manuscript insertions. In keeping with his other Bruckner scores, that of the Eighth Symphony is heavily marked in a combination of Italian, German and English. While many of J.B.'s technical annotations were designed to meet the rigours of live performance – bracketing orchestral entries and shadowing the printed dynamics in bold letters – others represent his performance style and choice of edition.

Barbirolli altered his Nowak score to correspond to Haas's edition[386] and it was this modified score that was used on 20 May 1970.[387] These adjustments meant that he reinstated material omitted by Nowak. Minor corrections in the *Adagio*, for example, were simply pencilled in,[388] while longer sections in both the *Adagio* and the Finale were reinserted by Barbirolli in manuscript form.[389] In keeping with existing trends, J.B. also made some minor modifications to the tuba parts in the Finale for reasons of balance and doubled the woodwind, brass and harps in loud passages throughout the score.[390] Each of these adjustments generally follow the contour of the dynamics and are marked clearly using brackets, vertical lines or numeric indicators (*a2* or *a4*).[391]

TEMPO

The organisation, manipulation and integration of tempo was central to the interpretations of conductors from the late nineteenth and early twentieth centuries. Artists such as Richard Strauss, Karl Böhm and Bruno Walter regularly juxtaposed and linked the various speeds of individual movements within a greater tempo plan.[392] Typical of the central European school of conducting, this approach was a vital tool in creating a sense of unity within the symphonic micro- and macrocosms. Although Barbirolli regularly worked with German and Austrian orchestras, and was a great admirer of conductors from those countries, he did not apply this

106

highly organised approach fully in the Eighth Symphony, but looked instead to the individual architecture of the four movements when constructing his tempo schemes.

Barbirolli's method is immediately apparent in the first movement's exposition, where the integration of structure and tempo is central to his reading. The *Allegro moderato* presents the performer with a number of difficulties that are unique to Bruckner. His personal approach to sonata form, along with his characteristic use of three thematic groups in the exposition, can affect the movement's symmetry if not handled sensitively in performance. Brucknerians have struggled with this problem in different ways and have had varying degrees of success in trying to solve it. For Barbirolli, however, the solution was clear: he simply terraces the exposition's tempi within a greater symmetrical whole. (see Appendix One, tempo table)

After observing his annotated metronome mark ('$\downarrow$ = 54 circa') at the beginning of the movement, Barbirolli then increases the speed of the second theme at bar 51 to $\downarrow$ = 56, before taking yet another new tempo – $\downarrow$ = 58 – at bar 97, the third theme. While this approach might seem at odds with the printed instructions – *breit und ausdrucksvoll* ('broad and expressive') – at the second theme, it was necessary for two reasons. First, any reduction in speed at this point would have diminished the theme's impact as a *Gesangsperiode* ('song period') and, second, its function as an important upward step towards the third theme would have been impaired. Similarly, by increasing the tempo of the third theme still further, it prevented the theme from being dismissed as a kind of *coda* rather than as an essential milestone on Barbirolli's road to the development. More to the point, both increases in speed were indicative of J.B.'s concern that forward motion should be maintained throughout this movement and the symphony as a whole.[393] Within the exposition, these adjustments and relationships are structurally and musically logical but, if Barbirolli had used them solely within the parameters of that section, the overall symmetry of the movement would have been lost. To prevent that possibility happening, Barbirolli secures the *Allegro moderato*'s proportions by taking the second and third theme groups in the recapitulation at the speeds first heard in the exposition.[394]

Again, symmetry was central to Barbirolli's approach to tempo in the second movement. But here he also takes into account the complex elements of the movement's internal and external architecture. As the *Scherzo* and *Trio* are both ternary structures within a greater three-part whole, he balances his speeds accordingly. At the beginning of the *Scherzo* (*Allegro moderato*), there is no printed metronome mark, the absence of which seems to have been a cause for reflection on the part of Barbirolli. At the top left-hand corner of p. 39 '♩=104' is inserted, but as this annotation was made before the score was enlarged, and was crossed-out in pencil after enlargement, it can be assumed that it refers to an earlier performance. This hypothesis is confirmed by the addition of a second metronome mark in pencil – '♩ = *circa* 120' – the tempo taken by Barbirolli on the CD. This speed, however, is simply his point of departure, as he pushes the tempo forward throughout the *Scherzo*'s opening section before reaching ♩ = 138 at bar 49. From bar 65, the *Scherzo*'s middle section, J.B. applies a *poco meno mosso*, creating, in effect, a slower central section.[395] At the return of the *Scherzo*'s opening material at bar 135, he once again pushes the tempo forward in the manner of the first section. In the slower *Trio* (*Langsam*), he acts similarly by making a sharp reduction in tempo from ♪ = 88–92 at the beginning of the *Trio* to ♪ = 72 at the onset of its middle section, the slowest point in the second movement as a whole. By so doing, the middle section of the *Trio* acts as a kind of fulcrum, balancing not only the tempi of the *Trio*'s first and third sections,[396] but also those heard in the statement and restatement of the *Scherzo*. With this complex scheme, the movement's internal and external symmetries are assured.

While the principle behind these techniques might seem obvious, the exact nature of these tempo relationships was not the result of a quick decision on the part of Barbirolli, but the consequence of careful consideration. Earlier, it was mentioned that some conductors of Barbirolli's generation clarified the architectonics of symphonic micro- and macrostructures by linking and integrating their speeds. By comparing his marked score with the recording, it is clear that Barbirolli was able to choose, maintain and manipulate a tempo at will. It can be assumed, therefore, that his decision *not* to apply existing trends fully was a conscious act, rather than a lack of ability on his part. That being so, his annotations at the beginning of the *Trio* are a fascinating insight into the way he prepared a score. Between the trumpet and contra-bass tuba staves (bars 1 and 2) he writes before enlargement, but later crosses out, '♪ = ♩ of 3/4'. Below this, but above the harps, he notes after enlargement '[beaten in] 4 (♪ *circa* 104 [crossed-out]) 96 ✓'. It is clear that the annotation that links the tempo of both the *Scherzo* and the *Trio* is related to the crossed-out metronome mark at the beginning of the *Scherzo*. Moreover, it appears that when Barbirolli re-studied the symphony, he initially considered directing the third movement at a core tempo of ♩/♪ = 104. Central to this initial process, and cause for greatest deliberation, was the *Trio*, as he opts for [♪ =] '96' having crossed out the '104' in (♪ *circa* 104). It seems, then, that when preparing his annotated materials for performance, his need for architectural definition was greater than that for tempo integration.

In the *Adagio*, Barbirolli's tempo modifications are similar to those heard in the first movement, where he terraced the opening tempi and adjusted the subsequent speeds according to the movement's architectonics. (see Appendix One, tempo table) In the Finale, however, he was faced with an ethical problem that had practical implications. Confronted with printed metronome marks for the first time, Barbirolli had to decide whether he should observe those marks exactly and to consider the effect they would have on his broader tempo plan. Barbirolli's solution to the problem was a judicious compromise. Rather than attempt an exact realization of the printed metronome marks, he simply followed their overall contour. Above the superscription, *Feierlich, nicht schnell*, Bruckner's metronome mark reads ♩ = 69, but at the top left-hand corner of p. 105 Barbirolli inserts the following contradictory marks: '♩ = 80' and '♩ = 69'.[397] As these were made before the score was enlarged, they probably pertain to an earlier performance. Between the trumpet and trombone staves, however, he annotates a third metronome mark: '♩ = 69'. Even though this was inserted in pencil after the score was enlarged, and corresponds to Bruckner's own metronome mark, it was later erased by Barbirolli. In fact, the tempo of the first theme on the recording is ♩ = 84, a speed not annotated at the beginning of the movement, but one that is central to his reading of the Finale as a whole. Clearly at some point during his preparation of the score, J.B. considered directing the movement at Bruckner's recommended speed but eventually chose ♩ = 84 for structural reasons. Similarly, at the second theme, where Bruckner's printed metronome mark is ♩ = 60, Barbirolli inserts '♩ = 66 *circa*', but later had a change of heart and took the theme at ♩ = 58, a speed more in keeping with that of the composer. By adopting ♩ = 84 at the first theme group and ♩ = 58 at the second, Barbirolli not only followed the contour of the printed metronome marks but was better able to underline the melodic, tonal and orchestrational variances between the two thematic groups thanks to his increased tempo differential.[398]

Interpreting conductor's marked scores can present problems for performers and musicologists, as they often contain annotations that cannot be easily reconciled in isolation. In the case of some artists, performance traditions often determined performance habits. But, in the case of Barbirolli, his principles and practices cannot be classified so easily and can often only be interpreted through a comprehensive understanding of practical musicianship. Take the beginning of the *Adagio*, for example, where his tempo and beating instructions appear to be contradictory. Here, he writes 'overall *circa* ♪ = 100' at the top left-hand corner of p. 69 and '[beaten] In 4.' between the harp and percussion staves. The answer to the riddle of these seemingly contradictory annotations lies, at least in part, in his understanding of the movement's superscription, *Feierlich langsam; doch nicht schleppend* ('solemn and slow; but do not drag'). Even though Barbirolli writes <u>Solenne</u> ('solemn') above the first violins' stave, it is the qualification within the superscription — *doch nicht schleppend* — that determines his speed at the beginning of the *Adagio*, where it is obvious from the recording that he beats in four rather than eight. If he had beaten the opening in quavers, a series of unnecessary cross-rhythms would have been created between his physical gestures and the printed rhythmic figuration in the orchestra. Had that occurred, the overall *melos*[399] of the movement might well have been lost, a prospect unthinkable for Barbirolli.

But this is only half the story. The tempo at the beginning of the *Adagio* is ♩ = 46–48, the core speed around which the movement's other speeds revolve. As this is a very broad pulse, Barbirolli, like many other performers, would have mentally sub-divided it into quavers, ensuring the music's forward motion, rather than its stagnation. In other words, while he was beating in four, he was thinking in eight. By mentally sub-dividing the *Adagio*'s broad pulse in this manner, he was better able to control the speed of his initial up-beat. As a former orchestral player, the strategic importance of this signal was not lost on him, particularly in a movement where the initial rhythmic figuration is not as straightforward as it might at first suggest. It seems, then, that Barbirolli's pragmatic approach took into consideration the aesthetic needs of the composer, while at the same time recognising the practical needs of the orchestra.

A fundamental element of Barbirolli's conducting style was the way in which he paced individual movements within the context of the whole. While the internal direction and shape of a movement was of considerable importance to him, he also argued that symphonic works have only one true climax. In realising this thesis, he used tempo to direct the listener to what he considered the work's '*Höhepunkt*' ('climax'). In this symphony, the principal climactic point is in the *Adagio*, but in reaching the musical summit, J.B. took a circuitous route that leads the listener up a series of musical *cul-de-sacs* before finally arriving at the work's *Gipfel* ('peak') at bar 239. Barbirolli begins his ascent at bar 185 by observing Bruckner's *a tempo* (*wie anfangs*) and by returning to the movement's opening speed, ♩ = 46. Then, having noted '*aber nicht schleppend*' ('but do not drag')[400] and '*S.[tesso] T.[empo]* (*non troppo*)'[401] at bars 197 and 198 in the score, he pushes the music forwards towards the first false climax at bar 205, where his speed is ♩ = 66. With rising enthusiasm, Barbirolli continues with a flurry of annotations: '*poco movendo* (*sempre*)✓' ('always moving a little') at bars 211 and 212, '*muovere*' ('move') at bar 215, '*S.[tesso] T.[empo]*' at bar 218 and '*poco a poco cresc[endo] al f.[orte] e sempre movendo un poco cresc[endo] sempre*' above bars 220 to 226. These annotations complement his tempo as it increases from ♩ = 66 at bar 211 to ♩ = 84 at bar 226. But it is immediately apparent that this, too, is a false climax. At bar 227, he returns to ♩ = 66 noting '12 bars to *Höhepunkt*. (F[ar] too fast)' before qualifying this with '*Ruhig (aber nicht schleppend)*' ('calm but do not drag'). The '*Ruhig*' at bar 227 quickly gives way to an *accelerando*, culminating in a new tempo at bar 236 (♩ = 80). Barbirolli then reduces the tempo by one notch to ♩ = 76 at the third trumpet's fanfare-like figure in bar 237 before announcing the onset of the climax in the following bar with a *rallentando* reinforced with hairpin accents in the brass.[402] The true climax is finally reached in bar 239, where the conductor writes, triumphantly, '*Höhepunkt*' (♩ = 60) at the top of p.100.

BARBIROLLI'S STRING SOUND

Like Arturo Toscanini, Barbirolli began his career as a cellist, and even though both conductors used their early experiences as the bases for their bowing, phrasing and articulation marks, their individual sound-worlds could not have been more different. For the brusque, unforgiving Toscanini, clarity and precision were paramount, while, for the more spacious Barbirolli, warmth and depth of sonority took pride of place. In what has since become known as the 'Barbirolli sound', the specific tonal colours, nuances and gestures that were the basis for that 'sound' relied heavily on the way that J.B. used the bow to inflect, shape and balance the phrase. In ensuring that his intentions were closely realised in performance, he bowed his materials in a consistent, considered and detailed manner. His score of Bruckner's Eighth Symphony is no exception and it is rare to find a page that has not been bowed thoroughly. And while some of his annotations are in accord with those of the composer, many are at odds with Bruckner's own printed instructions.

The annotated bowings in Barbirolli's score of the Eighth Symphony can be divided into two main categories: those that are designed to highlight the accentual structure of individual bars and those that are intended to colour whole phrases. While Bruckner's printed bowings are generally practical, they are also often naïve. Where this is the case, Barbirolli either alters, supplements or reverses the composer's suggestions. (see Appendix One, score example 1) In the first movement's opening eight bars, for example, the printed bowing in the lower strings follows the bars' accentual structure with down-bows on the stronger first beats in the first halves of bars 4 and 8. Bruckner's reluctance to bow this passage in greater detail, and the musical *non sequitur* that arises as a consequence of this pattern, allows Barbirolli an opportunity to manipulate the dynamics of these bars more fully through a crafty use of the bow. In bar 2, he indicates that the melodic lower strings should play at the point of the bow ('*Punta*').[403] As the violins' *tremolo* is also marked *pianissimo*, one suspects that they, too, play at the point. J.B. then supplements this annotation by adding the following bowing to the viola, cello and bass parts: down-bow (bar 2, last semiquaver), down-bow (bar 3, last semiquaver), up-bow (bar 4, first half), down-bow (bar 6, last semiquaver), down-bow (bar 7, last semiquaver) and up-bow (bar 8, first half). When the anacrustic semiquavers in bars 2 and 6 are played under down-bows at the point, followed by implied up-bows on the crotchets, also at the point, both the semiquavers and the crotchets are weighted equally. In contrast, the arched phrase in bar 4 is bowed so as to highlight Bruckner's printed *crescendi-diminuendi*. Here, the contour of the printed dynamic is enhanced by the motion of Barbirolli's up-bow in the *crescendo* followed by his implied down-bow in the *diminuendo*. From the recording, his detailed understanding of the symphony's opening is obvious: the *quasi*-mystical tranquillity of the sustained *tremolo* material in the violins is both balanced and contrasted by his manipulation of the more-existential phrasing in the violas, celli and double-basses.

Earlier, it was shown that the seemingly contradictory tempo and beating instructions at the beginning of the *Adagio* were, in fact, complementary, and by directing the opening in four while thinking in eight, Barbirolli avoided the possibility of beating a cross-rhythm against the orchestra. (see Appendix One, score example 2) It will come as no surprise, then, that his bowings in the opening bars of that movement are equally pragmatic. By replacing the composer's awkward instructions in bars 1 and 2 with a simplified pattern, J.B. is better able to realise Bruckner's intentions. Looking to the internal symmetry of the phrase as the basis for his annotations, he alters the printed bowing in the second violin, viola and cello parts in bar 1[404] so that the second half of beat 2 becomes a down-bow, while the first triplet quaver of beat 3 becomes an up-bow.[405] This pattern is then reinforced by having the basses play their repeated quavers on beats 1 and 3 under a down-bow and an up-bow respectively. By bowing the material in this fashion, the sound is affected in three ways: first, by the absence of unnecessary bow changes, the players are better able to realise the bar's accentual structure; second, it divides the bar symmetrically, complementing the first violins' melodic material in bars 3 and 4,[406] and, third, it ensures that Bruckner's printed instruction in bar 3, '*ohne Anschwellung*' ('without swelling'), is observed fully. When this accompanying figure is later repeated during the course of the movement, Barbirolli continues to bow in the manner of bar 1.

In a score that is littered with bowings, one might expect the second theme groups in the first, third and fourth movements to be marked heavily, but by comparison, these structurally important sections are bowed only sparingly. Nevertheless, it is clear from the bowings that are added that they are intended to reinforce the shape of the phrase, to underline the passages' cantabile character, to emphasise the sections' differing tempi and to take into account the themes' reduced orchestrations. (see Appendix One, score example 3) At the first movement's second theme, for example, where Barbirolli's markings are characteristically restrained, he pursues these objectives with determination. The first violins' rising figure in bar 51 begins with an up-bow, followed by a second, implied up-bow joining the last two triplet crotchets. By shadowing the trajectory of the phrase in this way, J.B. was able to secure his own interpretative agenda, while still retaining the fundamental elements of *Gesangsperiode*'s phrasing and printed dynamic. Although Barbirolli's approach to the theme is well-considered, it could be argued that a similar effect might have been achieved by simply following the composer's own printed and implied instructions. If the implied down-bow at the beginning of bar 51 was used, the internal architecture of the phrase would, indeed, resemble Barbirolli's reading. But J.B.'s up-bow at the beginning of the second theme has wider significance. By taking a new and increased tempo at this point, the sweep of the up-bow at the beginning of bar 51 complements this sense of forward motion. And as the second violins' and violas' sustained accompanying material in bars 51 and 52 is played under a single up-bow, then the violins and violas must begin this bar with an up-bow if ensemble is to be achieved fully and if the subtle increase in dynamic is to be realised effectively.

A striking feature of Barbirolli's score of the Eighth Symphony is his creative use of the up-bow. In the examples discussed above, this gesture was considered mainly within the limits of the periodic phrase. While the up-bow's function within this type of musical unit was central to his overall interpretative argument, he also used it to good effect when underlining specific dynamic and tempo gestures in longer passages. Take, for example, the closing bars of the first movement's *coda* (bars 403 to the end), where Barbirolli renders the passage in the manner of an extended *morendo*. (see Appendix One, score example 4) To achieve this effect, he changes the first and second violins' down-bows to up-bows in bars 406 and 408 and the violas' down-bows to up-bows in bars 409, 411, 412 (last pair of semiquavers), 414 and 416. Similarly, between bars 410 and 412, the first violins', celli's and basses' crotchets are all marked with up-bows. By avoiding the repeated down-bows in the violins and the violas, and by playing the crotchets with a series of up-bows at the point, the *morendo* is assured. Similarly, in passages where the tempo is pushed forward from within either an initial *piano* or *pianissimo* dynamic, Barbirolli also uses up-bows to colour his manoeuvre. (see Appendix One, score example 5) From bar 129 in the *Adagio*, for example, where the first and second violins are engaged in a loose form of canonic imitation, he joins the first and second violins' dotted rhythm with a slur.[407] By indicating that each of these dotted figures should be played under a single up-bow at the point, and by instructing the violins to play '*Flautando*' with a noticeable increase in *vibrato*, Barbirolli not only maximises the direction and weight of Bruckner's *poco a poco accel.[erando]* from bar 129, but also emphasises the composer's printed *crescendo* four bars later.

Being both an expert string player and a passionate advocate of tempo modification as a structural tool, Barbirolli took every opportunity to support and to colour shifts in tempo with complementary string effects. This approach is particularly evident in the second movement, where the slower *Trio* benefits from his inimitable approach to sonority. Here, Barbirolli colours his reduced speed of ♪ = 88–92 by exploiting the individual qualities of the violin's four strings. By annotating '*sul D*' (bar 1), '*sul G*' (bar 3, second half), '*sul D*' (bar 5) and '*La [sul A]*' (bar 6, second half) above the first eight bars of the first violins' stave, and by continuing to differentiate between the acoustic qualities of the first violins' four strings from bar 21, where he writes '*sul D*' (bar 21, beat 4[408]) and '*sul La [A]*' (bar 23, beat 4), it is clear that he wants a warm, yet vibrant, sound. Put simply: Barbirolli signals the *Trio's* architectonic importance by combining a judicious choice of string with a speed that avoids stagnation.

So did 'Sir John [simply engage] his heart and affections' when interpreting 'Bruckner's persistent sequences … repetitions and doodlings' as Neville Cardus's review suggests? From the above evidence it is clear that was not the case and that there is an obvious correlation between intent and result. Clarity of vision, intuitive musicianship and technical expertise are but three of the defining characteristics of Barbirolli's carefully crafted reading of the Eighth Symphony. Given these qualities, it seems both naïve and foolhardy to suggest that J.B. merely wore 'his heart and affections' on his sleeve when performing the works of his beloved Bruckner. Yet, it would be equally naïve and foolhardy to suggest that Barbirolli's reading of the Eighth Symphony was anything but a labour of love. And despite the undoubted limitations of Cardus' review, it is hard to disagree with him when he wrote:

> The great thing in performance is spirit and power of communication. Sir John always inspires the Hallé, and all other orchestras, with these creative necessities. All in all, in spite of one or two alien italics, and one or two miscarriages, this was the most impressive Bruckner playing and conducting I have heard in years.[409]

WHAT THE PAPERS SAY:
BARBIROLLI, SIBELIUS AND THE CRITICS

While this might seem facetious, I've always believed that the Germans don't take to Sibelius's music because they don't need him. As they have so many symphony-composers of their own, they are not particularly interested in anyone else's. Theodor Adorno called it 'sauna Beethoven', a dreadful thing to say. As we have so few symphonists, perhaps we are more open to a broader symphonic landscape. The intellectual rigour that Sibelius's symphonies espouse touch a nerve within us [British] and we welcome the journey he takes us on.[410]

Spoken some fifty years after the death of Sir John Barbirolli, Sir Mark Elder's perceptive words concerning the differing national responses to Sibelius's symphonies were no less true in 1970 than they were in 2020. With their craggy melodies, their astringent harmonies, their granite-like orchestrations and their atmospheric portrayals of Finland's myths and legends, the composer's works soon found a second home in Great Britain and quickly caught the attention of English conductors. Unlike many of their continental colleagues, artists such as Sir Thomas Beecham, Sir Henry Wood, Sir Hamilton Harty, Sir Malcolm Sargent and Anthony Collins were amongst the first to grasp the significance of Sibelius's symphonies and were some of the earliest to document them in the recording studio.[411] Each was quick to claim the right to call themself the composer's greatest British champion and each was keen to substantiate that claim either on disc, in print or through the broadcast media. Recalling in 1938 that 'no less a person than Sibelius appeared for the first time at the Promenades' on 26 November 1901,[412] Sir Henry Wood reminded his readers that he was one of the very few conductors to have performed all seven symphonies in one season.[413] Proud 'to have helped popularize the music of this deep and original thinker', Wood was equally proud to have 'devoted whole concerts to [Sibelius's] works … [and to have performed them to] large [and] appreciative audiences'.[414] Inspired by the work of Wood, Beecham and others, Barbirolli also committed himself to the composer's music from early in his career and was soon recognised as yet another distinguished British Sibelius interpreter.

IN THE CONCERT HALL

Having shot to fame largely through his work with chamber orchestras and opera companies, the young John Barbirolli was something of a novice when it came to Sibelius's music. That all changed, however, after being appointed chief conductor of the Scottish Orchestra in 1933. As head of a major symphony orchestra for the first time, he was able to explore the composer's music professionally and to programme works that would later become synonymous with him. Kicking off that exploration with a performance of Sibelius's ever-popular 'Karelia' Suite at Edinburgh's Usher Hall on 30 December 1932, Barbirolli took to the work instantly and conducted it again five nights later at St. Andrew's Hall in Glasgow. Part of a 'special New Year holiday concert … [that was given at] reduced prices', the Glasgow performance 'attracted a good crowd to the cheaper seats' but drew only a 'moderate' audience to the pricier parts of the hall.[415] Other than mentioning that the work had been included in the programme, the local press had little interest in it critically and it slipped by largely unnoticed. *Finlandia*, on the other hand, did prompt a critical response largely thanks to Barbirolli's 'very robust' reading of it at the Usher Hall on 9 January 1933. A clear favourite with the public, the tone poem was given on no fewer than five occasions by Barbirolli with the Scottish Orchestra[416] and was 'obviously thoroughly to the taste of the audience'.[417] And when it was given as part of 'a holiday programme' at the end of the following year,[418] it proved to be a spectacular finale to 'a fine concert' that thrilled Caledonian audiences thanks to the 'brilliance' of the playing.[419]

Nestled between his performances of *Finlandia*, Barbirolli conducted the Second, Fifth and First Symphonies with the Scottish Orchestra. Given at St. Andrew's Hall on 2 January 1933,[420] the Second Symphony was not only a local premiere, but also the first of at least 173 performances that J.B. gave of the work during his career. It is nothing short of baffling, then, that the symphony did little to whet the critical appetite of local music journalists, who simply reported that it was being 'performed for the first time at a Tuesday concert' by the orchestra.[421] When it came to Barbirolli's readings of the Fifth Symphony at the end of the year,[422] however, the Scottish press did take notice and was quick to debate its strengths and weaknesses. Reporting on the conductor's Usher Hall performance, *The Scotsman* opined that:

> While [the Fifth Symphony] exhibits little departure from the characteristic stark massiveness of the composer, [it] is less sombre than other of his

works which have been heard here … In its own rugged way it is beautiful, and its colouring has something of the cold brightness of early spring. The various movements are developed at great length, and the last movement, in particular, is an extraordinary example of spacious design and paucity of materials. The listener is disposed to marvel that a composer should be able to do so much, and do it with so little. Unusual as it is, and austerely devoid of any sensuous appeal, the symphony evidently produced a deep impression upon the audience, for there was enthusiastic applause at its conclusion.[423]

Considering the intensity with which Barbirolli approached this magisterial symphony in later years, he probably would have taken great exception to the idea that the work was 'austerely devoid of any sensuous appeal'. So, too, it seems did the Edinburgh audience, who were clearly moved and excited by the work. When the piece was repeated the following night at St. Andrew's Hall, *The Scotsman*'s Glasgow critic was more concerned by the length of the concert rather than the quality of the performance. With a 'programme [that] proved, unfortunately, too long', 'the first hearing of the symphony' was 'rather spoiled', 'as some of the audience had to leave before its conclusion'. Nevertheless, 'the impression created by it was, on the whole, very favourable'.[424] Hardly a ringing endorsement for either the work or the performance and one that would have done little to lift Barbirolli's spirits after watching great rafts of his audience disappear into the night in search of the last omnibus to Pollockshields.

'Congratulated on the success with which he … combined in his programmes a spirit of enterprise with the legitimate desire to give the greatest pleasure to the greatest possible number' during the 1933–4 season,[425] Barbirolli kicked off the new artistic year with a programme that included Sibelius's First Symphony on 10 November 1934.[426] Having watched his audience flee the hall before the end of the Fifth Symphony the previous December, J.B. must have been chuffed to find 'the hall … crowded' with 'a large audience', the like of which was 'rarely … seen at the opening concert' of the season.[427] 'Completing the orchestral items in part one', the First Symphony received 'an adequate performance and an attentive hearing'.[428] And, 'despite the late hour', 'there was much enthusiasm … at the close, [with] the audience [giving] the conductor insistent recalls'.[429] When the symphony was heard again the following month at Edinburgh, the local critic was also happy to report that 'Mr Barbirolli's rendering of the work was superb' and that the 'symphony provided the concert with a great climax, and excited enthusiastic applause'.[430]

Undoubtedly cheered by the public's response to Sibelius's first essay in symphonic form, Barbirolli must have been equally delighted by the critics' reaction to his reading of the composer's last work in that genre on 1 February 1937:

> Last night's programme at the Usher Hall … was a remarkable programme [that] received a brilliant interpretation from Mr Barbirolli. … The Seventh Symphony of Sibelius is at once very short, and gigantic in its effect. Being in one movement only, it could scarcely be otherwise than relatively brief, but its development conveys a suggestion of something vast. Because it is in one movement, it has been questioned by some whether it is rightly to be accounted a symphony at all. Be the design what it may, the effect, however, is that of a symphony, which is all that matters. For those who are apt to take their opinions of music ready made, it might be instructive to listen to this symphony with a view to noting in how many qualities with which Sibelius is ordinarily credited it is deficient. It is a wonderfully impressive work, but it is grand and impassioned in an elemental way, and there is nothing of the bleakness conventionally ascribed to Sibelius.[431]

After repeating the Seventh Symphony the next night at Glasgow, little more than a week passed before Barbirolli presented his Scottish public with yet more Sibelius. Dubbed as 'unfamiliar' by *The Scotsman*, *The Swan of Tuonela* and *Lemminkäinen's Return* were included in a programme that was otherwise devoted to compositions from the Austro-German canon.[432] But the first of these two tone poems was far from 'unfamiliar' to the orchestra, having already performed the work under Barbirolli at Glasgow in 1934.[433] Nevertheless, J.B's decision to include the works in his Edinburgh schedule certainly paid critical dividends, as it did much to dispel the increasing journalistic misconception that the Finn's works were simply sonic sculptures carved from finest Scandinavian stone. *The Scotsman*'s Edinburgh critic clearly understood this, and rather than drawing upon yet more geological imagery, concerned himself with the breadth of Sibelius's compositional style and the orchestra's ability to realise it:

> We are still at the stage of exploring his music, and there is a good deal which remains to be heard. There was an interest, too, in hearing music which did something to combat the popular snow-and-granite conception

of his art. "The Swan of Tuonela" and "The Return of Lemminkainen" belong to the romantic, as distinguished from what may, for convenience, be styled the classical side of the music of Sibelius. His music, of course, is romantic throughout, to employ that hard-worked term in a broad sense, but compositions such as "The Swan" and "Lemminkainen" have the romantic quality of a Finnish Weber. In their own dark-hued style they are wonderful pieces of orchestral colour. "The Swan" is beautiful music, in which the cor-anglais figures prominently as a solo instrument. The solo part was played in a delightfully artistic fashion last night by Miss M. Trevelyan, who has proved a valuable addition to the Scottish Orchestra this season. Mr Barbirolli gave fine interpretations both of "The Swan" and of the exciting "Lemminkainen".[434]

When the works were played again nine nights later at St. Andrew's Hall as part of a wider-ranging programme that included music by Mozart, Brahms, Delius, Chopin and Ravel, *The Scotsman* sent its Glasgow critic to report on proceedings.[435] Much like his colleague in Edinburgh, the local journalist was also quick to point out the novelty factor of the programme, Sibelius's mastery of orchestral technique and Barbirolli's commitment to it:

> The other orchestral items were the symphonic poem, "In a Summer Garden," by Delius and "Legends for Orchestra," by Sibelius—(a) "The Swan of Tuonela," with Miss M. Trevelyan as Cor Anglais soloist, and (b) "The Return of Lemminkainin," the latter performed for the first time at these concerts. These items abound in rich orchestral colouring, and were warmly received. The last item was rather late for a first performance, but it certainly lacks nothing in volume and boisterous devices, in which the resources of the orchestra are fully employed. Mr Barbirolli and his forces were enthusiastically greeted at the close by the largest audience, with possibly one exception, which has attended this season.[436]

When Barbirolli moved to North America in 1937, he was eager to build on his Scottish experiences as a Sibelius interpreter. But, from the composer's chequered history with the New York Philharmonic-Symphony Orchestra, that was not as easy as he might have hoped. Had he taken a moment to glance quickly at the

121

programming statistics for the Finn's symphonies with the orchestra before his first guest engagement, he would have realised that he was facing something of an uphill struggle when it came to the composer's oeuvre as a whole. True, the orchestra gave the tone poems with remarkable regularity, but when it came to the symphonies, the orchestra and its management were ambivalent at best. Of the meagre forty-three performances that the orchestra gave of the symphonies before Barbirolli's North American debut,[437] fourteen were of the Second Symphony. The First and Fourth were heard on nine occasions each, the Fifth and Third were given only eight and three performances respectively, while the Sixth and Seventh were overlooked at Carnegie Hall completely.[438]

It is understandable, then, that Sibelius's works were not amongst the first that Barbirolli conducted as a guest conductor with the Philharmonic-Symphony Orchestra.[439] But after quickly gaining the band's trust and respect,[440] he went on to give the Violin Concerto and the First Symphony less than a month after mounting the Carnegie Hall podium for the first time.[441] Then, as Music Director of the orchestra from 1937, J.B. started to perform the composer's music on a regular basis and gave it at no fewer than thirty-eight concerts with his new band. Yet, it is clear from a close examination of those concerts that Barbirolli's ambition to provide his American public with a comprehensive overview of the Finn's oeuvre was never realised fully. Of the composer's seven symphonies, he conducted only the First, Second and Third in North America and, of those, it was the Second that he gave most frequently.[442] Heard at twenty-two of his concerts with the Philharmonic-Symphony Orchestra at Carnegie Hall and on tour, the symphony was also given a further five performances by Barbirolli as a guest conductor with the Chicago Symphony Orchestra and the Philharmonic Orchestra of Los Angeles during his New York residency. Along with the three symphonies, Barbirolli also revisited *The Swan of Tuonela*, *Lemminkäinen's Return* and *Finlandia* before adding *Pelléas et Mélisande* and *Valse triste* to his ever-expanding repertoire.[443]

Having conducted the First Symphony thrice to critical acclaim as a guest conductor in 1936, Barbirolli must have been relieved when Howard Taubman reported in *The New York Times* that 'the orchestra responded to [his] wishes … with brilliancy and pungency of tone and with crispness of attack'[444] when he gave the symphony for the first time as the orchestra's Music Director on 19 December 1937. The critic for the *New York World-Telegram* agreed with Taubman and thought that Barbirolli 'did an admirable job … show[ing] genuine sympathy with the work's often stormy utterance and its curious broken up cantilena'. And even though 'fascinating, interpretative details abounded, and … tumultuous moments were given their due of plangent power', what really caught the critic's eye, if not his ear, was the fact that Barbirolli had become so excited during the *Scherzo* that his 'baton flew out of [his] hand'.[445] Somewhat less dramatic, but no less fascinating, were his performances of the Violin Concerto and the Third Symphony the following spring.[446] But, of the two, it was the Third Symphony that represented the only substantial addition to Barbirolli's Sibelius repertoire during his New York years. J.B.'s first reading of the symphony on 30 March 1938 did much to raise his profile as a Sibelian in the city and to convince the local press of his worth as an interpreter of the composer's music. Even his most severe critic, Olin Downes, was impressed by what he heard and was moved to write in *The New York Times* that:

> Mr. Barbirolli brought to [the Third Symphony] a freshness of feeling and rhythmic vitality that sustained the interest. He interpreted the whole work with breadth, a strength that was not feverish, a genuine simplicity which became the music well, and said more than much ranting. The quality of a performance and the impression given by a composition are more interdependent than every one [*sic*] realizes. Mr. Barbirolli spoke well for Sibelius last night. The Third symphony [*sic*], whatever its relative weaknesses, had seldom been so convincing.[447]

And what of Barbirolli's reading of the Second Symphony later that year and Downes's response to it? Given four times during the previous season by the Philharmonic-Symphony Orchestra under Artur Rodzinski to rave reviews,[448] the symphony had the potential to be something of a critical stumbling block for Barbirolli. A close personal friend of Downes, Rodzinski had coveted the music directorship of the orchestra after the departure of the critic's musical hero, Arturo Toscanini, and felt that Barbirolli was too young and too inexperienced for the job. Supported by Downes, Rodzinski was eventually appointed to the post in 1943 but never forgave Barbirolli for being given the job in 1937.[449] Add to that the impact of Toscanini's first New York reading of the symphony across town at Radio City with the NBC Symphony Orchestra on 15 January 1938 and it must have been with some trepidation that Barbirolli opened the *Times* the morning after his first New York performance of the work on 3 November 1938. But to his undoubted relief Downes was far from dismissive and was encouraged to write that:

This interpretation should grow into one of [the conductor's] best. It was marred last night by some too rapid tempi, by certain exaggerated changes of tempo, by some poorly contrived balances, and certainly some of the finer shades of the score were lost. However, when all that is said, there is something else to remember. The music in most places had in an exceptional degree its native virility, roughness and primitive power. There was the rightful breadth in the preparation of the climax and the berserker spirit. The average performance of this work is too polite in its quality and accent. Such was the case, for example, in accent. The tremendous passages for the strings at the reprise of the first movement projected in epic style; the transition, when power accumulated irresistibly from the scherzo to the finale; the last iteration of the second theme in the same movement, when heavy accompanying instruments, a dance with swords drawn and the growl of trombones and drums, as the strings soar upward to the finale proclamation. The music gains greatly by this unadorned force of statement. In this it was the true expression of Sibelius.[450]

But two pieces still needed to be added to Barbirolli's repertoire before he could call himself a complete Sibelian: the Fourth and Sixth Symphonies. Although a personal favourite of Toscanini when Music Director of the New York Philharmonic-Symphony Orchestra,[451] the Fourth Symphony was one of the composer's least popular works, but one of the most demanding interpretatively. Had Barbirolli wanted to tread in the older conductor's musical footsteps by programming it at Carnegie Hall, comparisons would have been made and reputations might have been lost. Perhaps this is why J.B. delayed performing the work until he was well and truly ensconced as Permanent Conductor of the Hallé Orchestra. Given as part of his first cycle of all seven symphonies at Manchester's Albert Hall on 14 February 1945,[452] the work was certainly considered aesthetically challenging by the local press and in need of some explanation:

There is no doubt that the Fourth Symphony of Sibelius contains much that is enigmatic in expression, though the actual texture of the music is fairly clear … Difficulties begin when Sibelius gets so deeply into an introspective mood that he has to use an expressive method as aloof, seemingly, from worldly experience as are certain passages in the last quartets of Beethoven

… Yet, however elusive such passages may sound, we feel sure that the composer is distilling essential meanings from them and that with patience we shall follow his thoughts with growing enlightenment … So well had the symphony been prepared that the playing last night was often at its finest in these sections, and Mr. Barbirolli showed wonderful skill in directing his forces. There were a few details in the wind parts that did not find their exact place in the scheme, but as a whole the work was splendidly done.[453]

Less than two months later, Barbirolli could finally call himself a complete Sibelian when he conducted the Sixth Symphony for the first time on 11 April 1945. Considered by the Austrian conductor, Herbert von Karajan, to be amongst the greatest and most emotionally draining of the composer's works,[454] the symphony seemed to have little attraction for Barbirolli. Performed by him on only four occasions during his career, Sibelius's penultimate symphony was the only one of the seven that Barbirolli conducted solely with the Hallé Orchestra and solely before his devoted Mancunian audience.[455] Yet, even some of J.B.'s most reverential fans found the symphony's perfunctory melodic style and novel use of form demanding. The critic for *The Manchester Guardian* was aware of this, and in an attempt to help his readers come to terms with the composer's challenging sound-world, while still acknowledging Barbirolli's sterling work in clarifying it, explained:

During the course of his unique performances of the Sibelius symphonies Mr. John Barbirolli has now given us all but the final work of the series … Listeners who have not studied the score of the Sixth may indeed find themselves baffled at first if they try to pick up definite themes and to hear uninterrupted development of them, yet the work is really shaped quite firmly and logically though with the composer's characteristic flouting of traditional procedure … The compelling features of the Sixth Symphony … are its suggestions of elemental forces behind the notes, of some primeval attributes that existed before music was ever born to solace the world of men and women … In its energy and variety of expression and in technical assurance the playing last night showed an excellent understanding of the Sibelius idiom and of the individual timbre of each movement … [The] performance as a whole was superb in its fluency and in its mingled power and delicacy.[456]

125

IN THE RECORDING STUDIO

As an increasingly committed Sibelian from the early 1930s onwards, Barbirolli must have been thrilled when he was asked to document the composer's Second Symphony with the New York Philharmonic Symphony-Orchestra in 1940. The end result of a series of four live performances of the work that he gave with the band during the winter and spring of that year, the symphony was recorded by Columbia at Carnegie Hall on 6 May. Seen as the natural choice for mid-century audiophiles, Barbirolli's discs were considered by *The Sun* to be a step up technically, if not interpretatively, from those already on offer to New York's listening public:

> John Barbirolli and the New York Philharmonic-Symphony [Orchestra's] … version automatically replaces the earlier one by [Robert] Kajanus in the Columbia catalogue, if only for its brightly burnished orchestral reproduction. That it will also replace the superb [Serge] Koussevitzky performance as the phonographic standard is considerably less certain. Barbirolli's approach throughout is measured, considerate, unhysterical—and it has its rewards, especially in the scherzo, which he illuminates unmistakeably. But a telling measure of the raw energy which is one of the disarming elements of the score is sacrificed thereby, without any compensating finesse. The orchestra plays excellently.[457]

Nearly two years then passed before Columbia documented another symphony by Sibelius with Barbirolli and his players. Moving across town to the Liederkranz Hall on East 58th Street, the musicians set down the First Symphony on 11 April 1942 in a session that also included Tchaikovsky's 'Theme and Variations' from Suite No. 3. Released at the same time as a Victor recording of the Seventh Symphony with Vladimir Golschmann and the St. Louis Symphony Orchestra, Barbirolli's discs were once again seen as a replacement for an earlier set by Kajanus, but did little to excite the critics otherwise. For Howard Taubman in *The New York Times*, 'the performance … [was] straightforward and sonorous',[458] while, for the more-populist critic in the *New York World-Telegram*, the 'zing to the playing of the orchestra' and the ardour with which 'those meteor-like flashes so typical of the composer's music' were delivered, were amongst the discs' defining features.[459]

On returning to Britain in 1943, Barbirolli began to explore Sibelius's music in detail and recorded the First, Second and Fifth Symphonies, *The Swan of Tuonela*,

Valse triste and *Pohjola's Daughter* with the Hallé Orchestra for HMV and Pye between 1949 and 1958.[460] Then, in 1962, *Reader's Digest* came calling and invited him to record the Second Symphony with the Royal Philharmonic Orchestra. A powerful reading that balances moments of extreme intensity with periods of passionate lyricism, J.B.'s third recording of the work is arguably one of the finest on disc and one of the most impressive in his discography. The critic for *Gramophone* thought so, and after it was re-released by RCA on its Gold Seal label in 1976, he wrote rhapsodically:

> To be frank, were I to choose any record [of Sibelius's Second Symphony] made in the past two decades to play for pleasure, it would, I think, be this one. This reading has tremendous life and warmth: it radiates all the vitality of a live performance … I found myself sitting on the edge of the chair throughout. Sir John secures playing of the finest quality from all the departments of the RPO, and rather than detail the individual excellences of each movement, I can only urge readers to sample them for themselves.[461]

And when the disc was re-issued on CD in 1991, it continued to impress the critics at *Gramophone*:

> The merits of Sir John's RPO version are very considerable … it is quite gripping and has one on the edge of one's seat – and is even better recorded … And there is Latin warmth, particularly in the slow movement, without any loss of Nordic atmosphere.[462]

As compelling as Barbirolli's 1962 recording of the Second Symphony undoubtedly is, it is his comprehensive set of symphonies, tone poems and shorter orchestral works that he made for EMI between 1966 and 1970 that is his greatest legacy as a Sibelian. Yet, when the set was first released in the late 1960s, it divided the critics. Of the tone poems, *Hi-Fi News* grumbled that 'we could have managed without these additional and not particularly distinguished performances … [which] are all loving ones, with much care for detail, though without a great deal that is fresh to say, and the overall effect produced is of a lack of real impetus'.[463] When it came to the symphonies, *Records and Recordings* took a different stance. Of the Second, it considered Barbirolli's reading to be 'a full-blown, unashamedly romantic view of

Sibelius's most popular symphony, presented with passionate conviction and superb skill by a conductor able to perform near-miracles with an orchestra that is not really of the front rank'.[464]

Although divisive critically when first released, Barbirolli's late EMI recordings of Sibelius's works took on a deeper, more personal meaning for many critics, listeners and musicians with the passing of time. Reminders for some of a much-longed-for artistic past, they soon became emblematic of all that was good and noble about the art of music-making. This was definitely true for the British composer and pianist, John McCabe, who wrote poignantly of them in *Records and Recordings* after learning of Barbirolli's death:

> I remember going to show him one part of my symphony between a rehearsal and a concert in Bradford; I arrived in time to hear the rehearsal, and since the evening's programme already had been played elsewhere and thoroughly prepared, they took the opportunity to use the last half-hour of rehearsal to start work on Sibelius'[s] Seventh Symphony. There I sat, in the otherwise deserted and darkened body of the hall, listening to a performance that, despite hesitancies due to its being a first run-through, had a uniquely elemental power. Listening now to his superb recording of Sibelius's Seventh, my mind goes back to the atmosphere of that rehearsal, and I am invariably moved to the depths of my soul.[465]

FROM MYSTERY TO MONUMENT: BARBIROLLI, MAHLER AND THE SECOND SYMPHONY

I heard the rehearsal of the 2nd part of the Mahler symphony and was extremely disappointed.[466] The material is very thin, and as regards orchestral *sound* Berlioz and Wagner have all done it far more convincingly. It seemed to be an impertinence to want all those people to make that particular music, as if *size* had become a morbid obsession with him.[467]

Written in 1930, Barbirolli's scathing words about the Fourth Symphony might seem surprising coming from an artist who would later go on to become one of the greatest Mahlerians of his age. But epiphanies are had and minds are changed. And, in fact, J.B. was only articulating a view of the composer's music that was held commonly for much of the early twentieth century. Unlike the works of his great contemporary, Richard Strauss, those of Gustav Mahler struggled to ignite the passions of either the public, press or fellow musicians during his lifetime and were often critical and financial failures. As for any trend, there were exceptions and conductors such as Willem Mengelberg and Bruno Walter were quick to champion the composer's music on both sides of the Atlantic and were amongst the first to commit his symphonies to disc. British Mahlerians were few and far between during the first decades of the last century, however, and with the obvious exceptions of Sir Henry Wood and Sir Hamilton Harty,[468] most local conductors shied away from his compositions. So, too, did the majority of England's concert managers, who were unprepared to risk their hard-earned money on a composer whose music had little box-office appeal. That all began to change after the Second World War, however, with conductor after conductor making a series of *volte-faces* and with audiences flocking to concert halls to be thrilled and moved by Mahler's works. One such conductor was Barbirolli, who went on to become one of the composer's most ardent supporters from the mid-1950s. With work after work revealing itself to him through careful study, J.B. was soon recognised as a Mahlerian of the front rank with his efforts eventually being acknowledged formally when he was awarded the much-coveted Gustav Mahler Medal of Honor [*sic*] by the Bruckner Society of America in 1965.[469]

PERFORMANCE HISTORY

Having grumbled about Mahler's musical inadequacies in 1930, Barbirolli briefly suspended his aesthetic doubts the following year and conducted the *Kindertotenlieder* with Elena Gerhardt for the Royal Philharmonic Society at the Queen's Hall.[470] A personal hero of Barbirolli, Gerhardt was an artist who had shot to fame thanks to the professional support of yet another hero of Barbirolli, Arthur Nikisch. It seems that the chance to perform with Gerhardt was too good an opportunity to pass up, even if that involved a work by Mahler. Sung beautifully and conducted sensitively, the cycle should have been a critical success, but all it served to do was to alienate the local press. *The Times*'s critic was wholly unimpressed by the work and let it be known that he 'would [rather] have listened to anything [other] than five songs about dead babies'.[471] And, if the truth be told, so, too, would have Barbirolli. It is a tad surprising, then, that he decided to conduct yet another work by Mahler during his second season as Music Director of the Scottish Orchestra.[472] But when J.B. gave the *Adagietto* from the Fifth Symphony that season, it also failed to excite the musical press with *The Scotsman* simply reporting that it was 'well received'.[473] The short movement for strings seems to have appealed to Barbirolli's sensibilities as a cellist, however, and he programmed it again with the New York Philharmonic-Symphony Orchestra six years later.[474] Given four times at Carnegie Hall during his third season as the orchestra's Music Director, the *Adagietto* once again struggled to interest the critics with Olin Downes of *The New York Times* dismissing the movement and its composer as abject failures:

> It was good that Mr. Barbirolli felt able to play one movement from a Mahler symphony instead of the whole work and that movement the simplest part of the composer's Second symphony [*sic*]. The adagio [*sic*] is sentimental, and at the climax "Tristan"-like in the melodic curve. Mahler was prone to sentimentality. Can one find here any of those claims to individuality that his admirers advance for him? The performance was the best of the evening, but it could not make a thing of the music, which it is not. Long movement or short, we seek still for the proof that Gustav Mahler was the man his adherents make him out to be.[475]

Yet, despite Downes's withering words, and despite his own earlier musical misgivings, Barbirolli made a complete musical U-turn after returning to Britain in

1943 and began to perform Mahler's works in earnest. After giving a total of twelve performances of *Das Lied von der Erde* and the *Adagietto* from the Fifth Symphony with the Hallé Orchestra in 1946,[476] he went on to conduct a further seventy-eight readings of the composer's symphonies with the orchestra over the next twenty-three years.[477] In pursuing his new-found interest, Barbirolli generally programmed the symphonies in blocks, with all his performances of the Fourth being given in 1963, the Fifth in 1966, the Sixth in 1965, the Seventh in 1960 and 1961, seven of the Ninth in 1954 and nine of the *Adagio* from the Tenth in 1961 and 1962. This was made necessary not only because of Barbirolli's meticulous approach to study, but also because of the touring commitments of the Hallé Orchestra, where programme repetition was necessary for financial reasons.

As Barbirolli showed little interest in Mahler's music before returning to Britain in 1943, it might seem strange that he tackled the composer's works with such passion and determination from the mid-1950s. But he always valued the advice of those he trusted and after the critic, Neville Cardus, suggested to him that Mahler's music was an ideal vehicle for his musicianship, he began to study it in detail. Of particular interest to Cardus was the Ninth Symphony, which was given its British premiere by Sir Hamilton Harty and the Hallé Orchestra in 1930. Although prepared carefully by Harty, the work failed to capture the imagination of the concert-going public at the time and fell quickly from the repertoire. Cardus was determined to see it performed regularly in Britain, however, and pressed Barbirolli to study it. Consequently, the conductor gave his first performance of the work, his first of a complete symphony by Mahler, with the Hallé Orchestra at Bradford on 19 February 1954. Barbirolli never forgot Cardus's contribution to the establishment of Mahler's works in Britain and later celebrated the critic's efforts by conducting three performances and a radio recording of the Fifth Symphony in his honour in 1966.

When Barbirolli was appointed Leopold Stokowski's successor as Music Director of the Houston Symphony Orchestra in 1961, he again pursued his interest in Mahler's music actively. No longer considered curiosities of extraordinary length that were best avoided at all costs, the composer's works had begun to attract large and curious audiences. Admittedly, they still had some way to go before they achieved the phenomenal box-office pulling power that they enjoyed from the 1970s onwards, but they were now taken seriously and were finally regarded as the products of a great musical mind. Yet, with all that considered, Barbirolli's programming of Mahler's works in Texas was far from comprehensive and consisted of only six of the nine finished symphonies. Unheard were the Sixth and Seventh Symphonies, *Das Lied von der Erde* and the *Adagio* from the Tenth Symphony. Nor were any song cycles or individual songs with orchestra included in his Texan concerts. Of the symphonies given, the First, Third, Fourth and Ninth Symphonies were performed only twice each, while the more familiar Second and Fifth Symphonies were heard on four and five occasions respectively. And what makes Barbirolli's highly selective approach to Mahler's works in Houston even more curious was his partial failure to build on their ever-increasing popular appeal. Take, for example, the critical response to his reading of the Second Symphony in 1962, a local premiere:

> Gustav Mahler's Second Symphony, the "Resurrection," [is] one of the most massive and passionate statements of the faith theme in the music of modern times … Those who heard the … performance were in thrall to a curious genius for an hour and a half. By turns they were shaken, astonished, mystified and perhaps a little repulsed. In the end, however, they were exalted by the force of a vast musical document that strives for superhuman expression—and that will be the remembered effect … Under Sir John's direction, the work has been masterfully organized; the performance is one of sustained passion, conviction and eloquence, and to hear it is a major experience … Sir John's conducting of it all, and the spirit with which his own conviction and passion endow this rendering, are quite beyond ordinary terms of praise.[478]

Clearly there was an emerging market for Mahler's works in Houston and clearly Barbirolli was the right man to meet that demand. But raw statistics can been deceptive and when the total number of Barbirolli's performances of Mahler's works in Texas are considered within a wider context, they are not as slight as they might at first appear. In fact, on average, he gave more than twice as many readings of the composer's works with his American band than he did with the Hallé Orchestra.[479] And when the statistics for both ensembles are taken together, Barbirolli gave a far-from-insignificant ninety-nine performances of Mahler's works between them. But what of his performances of the composer's music elsewhere, and with which orchestras did he perform it most frequently after the Second World War?

By any standard, the speed and intensity with which Barbirolli disseminated Mahler's music from the mid-1950s onwards was nothing short of breathtaking.

Whether it be in Tel Aviv, Los Angeles, Puerto Rico, Prague or Stuttgart, J.B. was indefatigable when it came to spreading the news about the composer. In all, he performed at least seventy-eight performances of Mahler's works with twenty-two orchestras in nine countries between 1958 and 1970. Of those, twenty-four performances were with the Berlin Philharmonic, the most he gave with any ensemble other than with the Hallé Orchestra.[480] With the exceptions of the Seventh Symphony, *Das Lied von der Erde* and the *Adagio* from the Tenth Symphony, Barbirolli performed his complete Mahler symphonic repertoire with the Philharmonic. Consequently, his name was soon linked with that of Mahler in Germany, and it was there that he gave his final performance of a work by the composer on 5 April 1970. Conducting the last of thirty-two performances of the Second Symphony that he gave during his career,[481] J.B. led a reading of the work at Stuttgart that left the critics, public and performers searching for superlatives. Exalted and drained in equal measure, one listener expressed the thoughts of many that evening when he was heard to mutter on leaving the hall that 'the grand old man' had conducted 'as if [he] were shaking the gates of heaven from their hinges'.[482]

THE COMMERCIAL RECORDINGS AND THEIR RECEPTION

With the advent of the long-playing (LP) record, the advances in stereophonic sound reproduction and the growing public interest in the composer's music from the mid-1950s, Mahler's symphonies began to attract the attention of recording companies. Barbirolli was quick to benefit from this new-found interest and recorded the First Symphony with the Hallé Orchestra for Pye in 1957.[483] Having conducted seven performances of the work at Manchester, Bradford, London and Leeds during the preceding eighteen months, J.B. and his players felt that they had come to terms with many of the score's technical difficulties and were confident that they could produce a sound-document of real merit. Jostling for a place in an increasingly competitive market that also included discs of the work by Jascha Horenstein and the Vienna Symphony Orchestra, Raphael Kubelik and the Vienna Philharmonic, Paul Kletzki and the Israel Philharmonic Orchestra and Bruno Walter and the Columbia Symphony Orchestra, the Pye recording largely met the performers' expectations and, to some degree, those of the critics. Particularly impressed by the beauty of the Hallé's playing and Barbirolli's fidelity to the score, the critic for *The Gramophone* was happy to report that 'the performance [was] a singularly sensitive one, with every shade of Mahler's music, and his accompanying instructions, given its full value'.[484] But the critic wondered whether Barbirolli had really come to terms with the work's cultural content and sensed that:

> Sometimes, perhaps, the underlining is even on the strong side. Those two middle movements offer always this same problem: the folk-music is neither fully natural nor fully parodistic, and exactly where in between these limits any performance should lie is an awkward question to ask. A wide variety of answers are reasonable ones; most certainly Barbirolli's is, but the sentiment is, in places, arguably near the limit. Without question, however, it is in keeping with the music; when this changes its character so does the performance – in the body of the finale there is an unflagging impulse, sustained right through to the end.[485]

Yet, the journalist couldn't quite bring himself to give the reading his unconditional seal of approval, as he felt that 'for all its qualities I do not think this new version of the symphony quite ranks with the very fine Columbia version made by Kletzki and the Israel Philharmonic … [and] I have no doubt, in fact, that Kletzki is the safest recommendation of all'.[486] A curious recommendation as it turns out, as Kletzki's recording soon fell from the catalogues and it is Barbirolli, and not Kletzki, who is now widely considered the greater of the two Mahlerians.

Seven years after documenting the First Symphony, Barbirolli returned to the studio to set down the Ninth Symphony with the Berlin Philharmonic for HMV.[487] The direct result of a unique relationship that existed between J.B. and the Berlin press, public and orchestra, the recording was seen as a triumph for British music-making by *The Gramophone*:

> Barbirolli is the first English conductor to be invited to make a recording with the Berlin Philharmonic Orchestra since Beecham's famous *Magic Flute* twenty-six years ago; the invitation came as a result of his concert performance of Mahler's Ninth Symphony with the orchestra last year, which was hailed by the Berlin Press as "the finest Mahler heard in a decade"; Barbirolli himself was called the finest conductor of the orchestra since Furtwängler. These are quite phenomenal encomiums to live up to, but one can easily understand them: he is one of very few remaining conductors who puts not only his head and technique into his performances, but his whole heart and soul.[488]

Barbirolli's ability to balance 'head and technique' with 'heart and soul' was a trope that proved endlessly fascinating to musical commentators and was soon the basis for a wider polemic that also included the ways in which he used tempo as a fundamental interpretative tool. This was certainly the case when it came to the Ninth Symphony, with at least one critic examining J.B.'s use of speed as an important structural indicator:

> Barbirolli has been really absorbing Mahler for some years now; he has the tremendous Ninth firmly in his repertoire, having conducted it with the Hallé Orchestra many times. Of course, his own way with Mahler is not the traditional way … The great first movement of the Ninth is usually taken very broadly … Barbirolli, on the other hand, varies widely between powerful breadth and some really swift accelerations towards the climaxes, full of his own volatile kind of urgency … The tempo of the second movement is a continual subject for argument … I do prefer the more lively tempo Barbirolli uses [to that of Bruno Walter, Jascha Horenstein or Leopold Ludwig] … In the clattering uproar of the Rondo-Burlesque, Barbirolli is entirely at home, again taking a tempo midway between the steady *allegro pesante* of Walter and the *presto* of Ludwig … In the final heart-rending *Adagio*, as may be imagined, Barbirolli digs as deep into the emotion of the music as anyone, and is unique in insisting on a real *pianissimo* in the many places where it is indicated.[489]

What disturbed the reviewer most, however, was the playing of the orchestra. Sensing that it lacked familiarity with Mahler's music, the critic was keen to point out that 'the Berlin Philharmonic … [is] nowhere near as used to Mahler as some of our own orchestras'.[490] And having taken the chauvinistic high-ground, the journalist then hammered the point home by drawing attention to the German orchestra's lack of 'absolute precision and virtuosity' in realising 'this fantastically complex and difficult work'.[491]

When the recording was reissued on CD more than twenty years later, the orchestra's playing was again a cause for concern, prompting one journalist to conclude that 'there [was] no disguising the fact that this fondly remembered 1964 Mahler Ninth is orchestrally inadequate'.[492] And with speeds that seemed 'sluggish', textures that sounded 'foggy' and with 'everyone waiting for someone else to make the next move", it was 'no wonder', the critic argued, that 'the recording soon died the death as a "selected comparison"'.[493] While comments such as these were nothing short of sacrilegious for J.B.'s devoted fans, they do contain more than a grain of truth. Unlike his recording of the First Symphony, Barbirolli's discs of the Ninth were not the beneficiaries of an extended period of interpretative and technical maturation with an ensemble that identified closely with the composer's music. And while it is true that J.B. and the Berlin Philharmonic did perform the work together twelve months earlier,[494] a great deal of water had flown under their respective musical bridges by the time of the recording sessions. This inevitably impacted upon their reading of Mahler's last, and arguably most demanding, symphony and was undoubtedly the main reason for its technical inadequacies.

No less contentious was Barbirolli's 1967 recording of the Sixth Symphony with the New Philharmonia Orchestra for HMV.[495] Again, it was the conductor's highly personal approach to tempo that the critics found most challenging and, again, it was this aspect of his interpretation that dominated the reviews of the recording:

> Having complained at length that I couldn't fully enjoy either [Erich] Leinsdorf's or [Leonard] Bernstein's interpretation of this symphony because they took the first movement and the Scherzo much too quickly, I suppose I shall seem merely perverse if I now complain that Barbirolli takes at least the first movement much too slowly. To criticise tempo is always a dubious business … [and] it becomes even more dubious, since [Mahler] rarely used metronome markings. Nevertheless, if one cannot take to a tempo, one cannot enjoy the performance … The heavy dogged plodding character of Mahler's march-music … is not really achieved by Barbirolli either: at his slow tempo the march loses its grim Mahlerian forward stride, to take on a grandiose Elgarian expansiveness.[496]

Concerns about tempo continued to dog the recording in the decades that followed, and after it was re-released on CD in 1996, one reviewer simply dismissed Barbirolli's reading of the first movement as a 'world-weary trudge'.[497] But unlike their thoughts on J.B.'s approach in the Ninth Symphony, here the critics miss the point. True, the speeds of the various movements are very slow, but this was made necessary because of the detailed nature of the score and the conductor's understanding of it. Perhaps more than in any of his other recordings of Mahler's symphonies, Barbirolli seems

136

to have engaged here in an exhaustive search for the work's inner content. That exploration relied heavily on tempo as a means by which to clarify the symphony's orchestration and to unlock its wider aesthetic meaning. And as for the reading's supposed 'grandiose Elgarian expansiveness', as mentioned by the earlier critic, it is hard to know what this means technically or interpretatively, other than to suggest that the journalist enjoyed writing neatly shaped aphorisms.

After recording *Lieder eines fahrenden Gesellen* and the *Kindertotenlieder* with Janet Baker and the Hallé Orchestra for HMV in 1967, Barbirolli recorded the complete *Rückert-Lieder* and Fifth Symphony with Baker and the New Philharmonia Orchestra for the same company two years later.[498] One of his best-loved and most respected recordings, J.B.'s disc of the Fifth Symphony was greeted enthusiastically after its release. Having performed the symphony publicly the day before the first recording session with the orchestra at London's Royal Festival Hall,[499] Barbirolli was able to draw committed and technically brilliant playing from his musicians. But every silver lining has a black cloud, and in the case of Barbirolli, his particular *sable nebula* was tempo. With each passing year his speeds became broader and more magisterial, and with each new recording the critics became more obsessed with them. So when the critic for *The Gramophone* threw caution to the artistic wind and actually praised J.B.'s spacious speeds in the Fifth Symphony, the conductor must have been more than a little surprised:

> As we know from Barbirolli's earlier Mahler recordings, his style could hardly be more affectionate, and to that he adds a fondness for tempi slower than usual. Sometimes, as in his Berlin recording of the Ninth Symphony, the result has all the inner intensity of a great performance heard live; sometimes as in his more recent version of No. 6, the expansiveness stretches the music too far and the tension wanes. Though in the Fifth … I don't think there is any doubt that in commitment and intensity this interpretation matches and even surpasses the Berlin Ninth … As it happens [the] two outer movements bring the two most sharply controversial tempi. In both Sir John chooses speeds very much slower than we are used to, and dangerous though that of course is (as we found in the Sixth) the performance completely justifies it. [500]

After his death in 1970, Barbirolli soon became a cult figure for record collectors and was quickly recognized as being central to what has often been wrongly called the 'Mahler renaissance'.[501] As a direct consequence of that cult status, live recordings of Barbirolli's interpretations of the composer's symphonies have been released by Arcadia, Testament, EMI, BBC Classics, the New York Philharmonic and The Barbirolli Society amongst others. With the exception of the Eighth Symphony, a work that Barbirolli never conducted, there is now available to listeners a comprehensive discographic overview of his activities as a Mahlerian. In contrast to some of the critiques of his commercial recordings, the reviews of his live performances on disc are largely reverential in tone. While a handful of critics continue to have doubts about some of Barbirolli's tempi, they now accept his speeds as part of his performance style as a whole and are happy to acknowledge his place as one of the leading champions of Mahler's works.

BARBIROLLI AND THE SECOND SYMPHONY

Of all the Mahler symphonies, it was the Second that spoke with greatest intensity to Barbirolli. Much like Elgar's *The Dream of Gerontius*, the symphony reflected J.B.'s own understanding of Christian faith and had a directness and grandeur that appealed to his wider artistic sensibilities. From the sheer number of performances that Barbirolli gave of the work, it is clear that it was of some importance to him. And while it is true that the number of readings that he gave of Elgar's 'Enigma' Variations and Brahms's Second Symphony statistically dwarf the number of performances that he gave of the Second Symphony,[502] those facts should not disguise the true importance of Mahler's work to him. Had the logistics and cost of mounting the symphony not been so great, it is highly probable that Barbirolli's tally of thirty-two performances of the work would have been considerably higher. The challenges that these strictures presented were not lost on J.B. and were brought into sharp relief when *The Manchester Guardian* pointed out in 1958 that:

> This is the most ambitious of [Barbirolli's] Mahlerian undertakings in recent years. The work was to have been played at the final concerts of the 1952–3 season, but was abandoned, partly on account of the enormous cost … In this performance some economies in instruments were made, mostly in accordance with suggestions in the score, which left a mere 106 players, some of whom, from the brass section, were obliged to dance on and off the platform several times to contribute to the off-stage effects … [T]he cost of putting these two performances on … will be in the region of £3,500.[503]

This is no criticism of Sir John Barbirolli or the Hallé Orchestra and Choir, who after a slightly tentative first movement gave a splendid performance, and deserve our gratitude for letting us hear a work so rarely played—even though all we have learned is that it deserves no better.[504]

It is difficult to believe today that the work was so infrequently played by 1958, but £3,500 was a considerable sum at the time and one that would make any impresario or concert society think twice before mounting the symphony. But thanks in no small part to Barbirolli, the work became a box-office success and audiences flocked to hear it in their thousands. As the work was of such importance to J.B., he prepared his performances meticulously and his extant marked score of the work reflects that attention to detail. Used at his final performance of the symphony at Stuttgart in July 1970, that score clarifies many of the performance gestures that were heard both at that concert and the one given by him five years earlier with the Berlin Philharmonic.[505] To understand fully Barbirolli's approach to Mahler's works, it might be instructive, therefore, to compare his marked score of the symphony with the sound-documents from those two German performances.

THE MARKED SCORE

Barbirolli's annotated score of Mahler's Second Symphony is housed at The British Library, has the call number I.348.g and is one of eight full conducting scores of Mahler's symphonies owned by the conductor that are now available for inspection there. Published originally by Joseph Eberle & Co (Wien) in 1897, the edition chosen by Barbirolli was released later through Universal Edition, whose sticker can be found on the front cover. Hard bound in red leatherette and measuring 26 cm X 34 cm, the score was used heavily, resulting in the right-hand bottom corner of many pages being either turned or missing. A number of the pages have been repaired with tape and these repairs were probably made during J.B.'s ownership of the score.

The score has been marked on at least three occasions in lead pencil, blue pencil and blue ink. While the lead and blue pencil markings relate to Barbirolli's performance demands, the annotations in blue ink match the amendments to the revised version of the work that were later published by Universal Edition for the Internationalen Gustav Mahler Gesellschaft, Wien, in 1970. All the bowing marks are in lead and appear to have been inserted on one occasion only. The beating marks are often in blue or blue on lead, and some of the blue markings were reinforced later by Barbirolli. Characteristically, J.B. inserted his instructions in three languages – German, English and Italian – but tends to favour Italian at passages of high emotional intensity. He also inserts terms from *solfège* and often, but not always, refers to some of the stringed instruments' individual strings using this method. At four bars before Fig. 53 in the third movement, for example, he inserts '*sul La*' below the second violins, indicating that their C should be played on the A string. This kind of annotation is common in his other marked scores and is a direct result of his use of *solfège* when preparing his scores for performance. As a number of earlier annotations have been erased, it is probable that the score was used by other conductors before Sir John. But with the exception of some of the blue-ink markings that reflect the changes found in the revised edition, all the annotations in the score are those of Barbirolli. The British Library score can, therefore, be considered a true indication of his intentions.

BOWING, PHRASING AND ARTICULATION MARKS

Barbirolli's score is littered with bow marks and instructions for the strings with only thirty-one of its 209 pages containing no supplementary instruction for that orchestral group. Later known as the 'Barbirolli sound', the conductor's unique sound-world was related directly to the ways in which he manipulated the strings, and the annotations in his scores were part of that process. The markings that he inserted were always practical and were designed to achieve either a desired articulation, a heightened awareness of the architectonic content or a specific dynamic effect. Unlike Sir Thomas Beecham, who regularly revised his bowing, phrasing and articulation demands during rehearsal before settling on a fixed reading, Barbirolli's interpretative gestures were generally determined in advance. The score acted, therefore, as a kind of template of his intentions to be sent, if necessary, to orchestral librarians before his first rehearsal.

Although Barbirolli was keen to realise composers' intentions where possible, he had no qualms about altering their printed bowing or articulation marks when they were at odds with his own interpretation. At the beginning of the second movement, for example, (see Appendix Two, score example 1) he alters Mahler's bowing of the first beat of the second bar from an up-bow to a down-bow. Although in some ways obvious, this alteration is made necessary because of the topography of the phrase and Barbirolli's concern that the first beat of each bar of this *Ländler*-like passage is weighted according to the demands of the melodic content. By inserting an up-bow above the second semi-quaver of the second beat of the first bar, he is highlighting the upward trajectory of the melodic material, and by inserting a down-bow and an up-bow on the first and third beats of bar 2 respectively, he underlines the relative strengths of those beats within the bar. By applying the bowing in this manner, J.B. was able to ensure that the simple melodic character of the passage is matched by an equally naïve bowing pattern.

In the third movement, Barbirolli again alters the bowing at key moments. This is particularly noticeable from Fig. 36, (see Appendix Two, score example 2a) where he changes the bowing of the second and third quavers in the lower strings from printed down-bows to up-bows, and the second and third bars before Fig. 37 (the double-bar), (see Appendix Two, score example 2b) where he plays the five-note quaver passage under a continuous *portato* up-bow. The change at Fig. 36 is clearly designed to avoid the possibility of weighting the second and third quavers too heavily if played by down-bows and the effect that that extra weight would have on the articulation and forward rhythmic direction of the passage as a whole. It also ensures that the quavers are played lightly and that the semi-quavers are articulated more robustly. Similarly, the change in the measures directly preceding the double-bar is also designed to secure its function. The eight bars before Fig. 37 are marked *pianissimo* by Mahler and are intended to act as a foil to the sudden *fortissimo* that follows. By altering the bowing before the double-bar, Barbirolli ensures that the violins and violas articulate the quavers in a quiet, even fashion and that the bowing pattern is unified with that of Fig. 36.

The 'Barbirolli sound' is probably the reason for his need to indicate overtly the bowing for passages such as that from four bars after Fig. 17 in the first movement. (see Appendix Two, score example 3) Here, Barbirolli indicates that the staccato quaver and semiquaver of each rhythmic figure should be played under the same bow, a practice that he applies in both quiet and loud passages. While 'tucking in' is common in Britain and Australia, some Central European orchestras use the 'reverse shoe-shine' method in loud passages. This is where the longer note is played under an up-bow, while the shorter note is played under a down-bow. The 'reverse shoe-shine' creates a slightly mellower sound by avoiding the bite of the down-bow on the longer note. As Barbirolli performed this symphony with both the Berlin Philharmonic and the Radio-Symphonieorchester Stuttgart, he might well have been pre-empting their possible use of the 'reverse shoe-shine' in loud passages by having his preferred bowing inserted into their string parts in advance. As a British-trained string player, Barbirolli would also have preferred to tuck this type of rhythm figure in and would have incorporated that technique into his method as a whole. This approach would also have been favoured by the players of the Hallé Orchestra and would have been the natural choice of the orchestra's celebrated leader, Martin Milner.

Barbirolli's interpretations were often distinguished by his creative use of the up-bow. Although he does not supplement his up-bow markings in his marked score of the Second Symphony with some of his customary instructions, such as *flautando*, he does use the up-bow creatively and to good use in passages of dynamic importance. (see Appendix Two, score example 4) In the bars that directly precede the sustained off-stage passage at Fig. 29 in the last movement, for example, Barbirolli ensures the shape of the diminishing dynamic by inserting a series of up-bows, presumably at the point. By bowing the passage in this manner, he not only guarantees a true realisation of the written dynamic, but also ensures that each successive chord dovetails neatly into the next. This is the most sustained use of the up-bow in the symphony and his insistence that such passages should be played lightly at the point resulted in him being given the affectionate nickname '*Herr Spitze*' ('Mr Point') by the strings of the Berlin Philharmonic.

Of course, Barbirolli was equally conscious of the power of the down-bow and used it to great effect in the Second Symphony. A particularly sustained use of that stroke occurs in the last movement from Fig. 14. (see Appendix Two, score example 5) In the bars directly following the double-bar, and in keeping with Mahler's *Maestoso* and somewhat sinister use of F minor, Barbirolli unsurprisingly has the lower strings articulate the staccato quavers and the tied minim under a series of down-bows. The stroke is then used increasingly in the bars that follow until he plays each of the accented minims in the first violins at Fig. 15 under repeated down-bows. This adds weight to the melodic content and ensures that the minims are articulated cleanly and with the separation necessary to underline Mahler's marked accents. From bar 216, Barbirolli indulges in a veritable frenzy of down-bows. The melodic content of this passage is based on the motif first heard in the first violins at Fig. 15 and, for consistency, it is obvious that down-bows should be used again when the motif reappears in diminished form. With the arrival of F major at bar 220, Mahler wants the material to be given greater weight and instructs the string players to play *martellato* on the G string. Keen to stress the martial quality of this passage, Barbirolli inserts a series of down-bows and reduces the tempo from ♩ = 132 to ♩ = 126.

In general, and in keeping with other conductors with an understanding of string playing, Barbirolli bows to sustain the sound while continuing to observe the golden rule of bowing, which dictates that the strong beats should be played with down-bows and that the weak beats should be played with up-bows. There are a few exceptions, however, such as at Fig. 3 in the first movement, (see Appendix Two, score example 6) where he inserts an up-bow in the violins at the beginning of bar 48, presumably. But this was done for obvious musical reasons, so that his bowing reflects the topography of the phrase and so that its climax at bar 50 is played under a down-bow.

Barbirolli was also particular about the way in which important passages were fingered and the manner in which *glissandi* were played. (see Appendix Two, score example 7) For some rising *glissandi* of an interval of a third or more, such as in bars 22 and 23 in the second movement, he specifies that the slide should be made with the third finger. Although trained as a string player during the early years of the twentieth century, J.B. seems to have objected little to the demise of random *portamenti*, a technique common to all orchestras until the late 1930s, and mentions the change in style only briefly in his writings and interviews. While he might well have been happy to move with the musical times, he was still aware of the expressive potential offered by *portamenti* and occasionally inserted one where not marked by the composer. This was certainly true in the second movement of the Second Symphony, where he indicates that the first violins should slide on the third finger from the anacrustic E flat in bar 272 to the first beat B flat in bar 273.

As a string player, Barbirolli understandably marked the woodwind and brass parts comparatively sparingly. But he was not exceptional in this, as conductors such as Clemens Krauss, Sir John Pritchard and Sir Thomas Beecham also annotated the woodwind and brass material only minimally in their marked scores. In his score of the Second Symphony, J.B. inserts no additional phrase or articulation marks in the woodwind, brass and percussion parts and only adds a handful of breath-marks to the chorus and the solo soprano parts.[506] Again in keeping with the practice of the conductors mentioned above, Barbirolli often indicated phrase lengths by inserting slurs and numbers below, above or on the stave. These marks acted as a study tool and served as an *aide-memoire* in performance.

TEXTUAL FIDELITY

Otto Klemperer famously reported that Mahler once said that 'if, after my death, something doesn't sound right, then change it. You have not only the right but the duty to do so'.[507] But Barbirolli was not convinced fully by Mahler's advice and had mixed feelings about altering the text of scores in general. When he heard Toscanini perform Brahms's First Symphony in 1937, for example, he wrote to his future wife, Evelyn, that 'he [Toscanini] has added *timpani* parts here and there to help the climaxes. That I would not have believed of him'.[508] Although shocked by Toscanini's alterations, Barbirolli's position had shifted by the 1960s, and when he came to interpret symphonies by Bruckner and Mahler during the last years of his life, he altered the text when either preparing or reinforcing climaxes. In Bruckner's Eighth Symphony, for example, he added a tuba from bar 652 in the last movement, while, in Mahler's Second Symphony, he inserted pedal notes on the organ in the bars directly preceding Fig. 51 in the last movement.

BALANCE AND THE OFF-STAGE BANDS

An issue of crucial importance when performing the Second Symphony is balance. This is particularly true of the last movement with its complex use of off-stage bands. From both the recollections of Klemperer and the published score, it is clear that Mahler was concerned that the off-stage musicians should sound as distant as possible and should be arranged in a particular manner.[509] Barbirolli was conscious of this and it seems that he placed the off-stage band at Fig. 22 as far away as possible in Berlin. Aware that this passage can present particular spatial and dynamic difficulties in the concert hall, he noted clearly in his score that mutes should be used if necessary ('*sord.* [*sordini*] if necessary'). As Barbirolli was also keen to avoid a lack of communication between the on-stage podium and the off-stage bands, he always used a second conductor at these critical junctures, which can be confirmed from his annotation above Fig. 29, where he writes '2 conductors necessary' in big print.

TEMPO

Barbirolli's approach to tempo in the Second Symphony was highly organised and he regularly used speed as an architectonic indicator. Taking his lead from the composer's '*Anmerkung für den Dirigenten*' ('note for conductors') at the beginning of the first movement, Barbirolli constructs a detailed tempo plan for the work based on the two printed metronome marks found in that note: $\quarternote$ = 144 and $\quarternote$ = 84–92. Using $\quarternote$ = 144 as the first of two main tempo anchors, J.B. relates that speed directly to his intended tempi at bars 254 and 291 and to that of the fourth movement, where he inserts the metronome mark, '$\quarternote$ = 66–72'. His score also indicates that he wanted the tempo at the opening of the last movement, $\quarternote$ = 72, and the material heard from bars 48 ($\quarternote$ = 69–72), 62 ($\quarternote$ = 69–72) and 162 ($\quarternote$ = 72) to be related to $\quarternote$ = 144.

Barbirolli's second main tempo anchor, $\quarternote$ = 84–92, and its near neighbour, $\quarternote$ = 80–4, were also inserted at key points and were the bases for his speeds from bar 117 in the first movement, the central section of the fourth movement ($\quarternote$ = 84), and bar 618 in the last movement ($\quarternote$ = 88). While it is obvious from the tempo chart found in Appendix Two of this volume that he did not always follow his intentions strictly in the heat of performance, the general contour of his manipulations indicates clearly that he used speed as a means by which to define the architectonics of both individual movements and the work as a whole.

Where anomalies occur between the marked score and the recordings, they are often the result of Barbirolli reinterpreting a passage after the initial annotation was made. At the *coda* to the first movement, for example, he writes and underlines in his score 'No change of tempo to the end $\quarternote$ = 80–84'. He also writes above the stave '*Tempo sostenuto* (in the tempo of a Funeral March.)[510] he [Mahler] evidently discarded this in the revision'. When the annotated comments and metronome mark are compared with the recordings, it seems that Barbirolli agreed initially with Mahler's revised thoughts, but later reconsidered his position and conducted the opening of the section at a speed more traditionally associated with a funeral march. And while he does begin the passage in the recordings at $\quarternote$ = 66, a tempo that is related directly to the speed of other architectonically important passages, he considered that tempo inappropriate for the *coda* as a whole. In order to reach $\quarternote$ = 84, one of the work's core tempi, and the speed necessary to balance the opening and closing of the movement, Barbirolli again contradicts his annotations in bars 392 and 393 and conducts an *accelerando* from approximately bar 407. This directs the music to bar 418 and, later, to bar 441, the *Tempo I*, where his original goal of $\quarternote$ = 84 is finally achieved.

A fundamental element of Barbirolli's conducting style was the way in which he paced individual movements within the context of the whole. While the internal direction and shape of a movement was of considerable importance to him, J.B. also argued that symphonic works have only one true climax. And from his increased flurry of tempo and metronome marks from Fig. 39 in the last movement, it seems that he considered bar 712 (Fig. 48) to be the work's principal climatic point. As elsewhere in his marked scores when realising such passages, he turns to Italian, rather than German or English, to express his intentions. After beginning his journey to the climax from bar 560 (Fig. 39), where he inserts the metronome mark, '♩ = 92–96', Barbirolli then shadows Mahler's instructions at bar 576 by adding '*poco accel[erando]*' before inserting '*accel[erando] ed appass[ionato]*' in bars 588–91. He then continues to shadow Mahler's instructions with a '*sempre movendo*' ('always moving') at bars 603 and 604 and with 'again somewhat *ritenendo*' at bars 616 and 617. At bar 618 (Fig. 42), he reduces the tempo to ♩ = 88 before reducing the speed still further to ♩ = 60 at bar 629 (Fig. 43), a tempo that is linked directly to the brass chorale at bar 142. From bar 640 (Fig. 44), he indicates that the speed should rise to '♩ = 100' and should be played '*Con passione (ma senza corerre)*' ('with passion but without rushing ahead'). As if to reinforce that marking and to highlight the forward motion of the music, he writes '*avanti*' ('forward') at bars 645 and 660. He continues in Italian at bars 664 and 669, where he marks '*accel[erando]*' and '*senza slargare*' ('without broadening') respectively. At bar 684, he again underlines the music's sense of forward motion with another '*avanti*'. Having begun to beat in two from four bars after Fig. 46 (bar 676), he interrupts the direction of the music before Fig. 47 (bar 696) by observing the printed '*Rit[ardando]*' and '*luft[pause]*'. From Fig. 47 (bar 696), he continues to beat in two – '*Immer 2*' – but prepares the chorus for the work's climax by inserting large wedge-like marks in the voice parts at the bar directly preceding Fig. 48 (bar 711). He then signals the work's climax by writing boldly '4 (*Meno*) *Maestoso*' at Fig. 48 (bars 712–15).

Little more than three months after conducting that great climax for the final time at Stuttgart in April 1970, Barbirolli was dead. With bad health afflicting his later years, J.B. looked increasingly to the music of Mahler for solace and inspiration. Speaking directly to his artistic soul, the composer's inimitable sound-world touched Barbirolli in a way that he had hitherto never experienced. Increasingly evangelical in bringing Mahler's music before the public during the last decades of his career, J.B. believed passionately that his efforts on the composer's behalf were amongst his greatest, and most enduring, professional achievements. Taking time to reflect on what Mahler meant to him personally and artistically, Barbirolli explained to the German newspaper, *Die Welt*, shortly before his death:

So I began to study the Mahler symphonies – if you want to conduct Mahler well his music must be under your skin and in your bones. Because I subsequently spent two years studying one of these scores, I have, as it were, enriched myself in doing so, and it is a joy to me in my advancing years that I have found something which, apart from the connoisseurs, is new to people and is also of such mighty dimensions. Mahler's name is no longer a mystery – he has at long last become a monument.[511]

BARBIROLLI ON THE ART AND CRAFT
OF CONDUCTING

Conductors make no sound, they only change sound. A source of endless fascination for concert-goers and musicians alike, this phenomenon is a curiosity that has defied even the most searching of musicological and psychological investigations. The fact that two conductors conducting the same piece with the same orchestra on two consecutive days under similar conditions can produce very different sounds is no secret, but to define precisely how these differences come about has proven far from easy. Questions have been asked and theories have been investigated. But answers have been few and far between, with the mysterious art of conducting being unwilling to give up its secrets freely. Yet, as important as these differences undoubtedly are, conductors are not simply engaged in a kind of out-of-body experience that hovers somewhere between time and space; they are constantly involved in a series of very practical decision-making processes that often require both snap and long-term judgements. Questions of programming, choice of edition, score preparation, the engaging of players and the disposition of the orchestra are but a few of the issues that a conductor has to deal with on a day-to-day basis. And while these less-than-glamorous elements of the conducting profession might be of only passing interest to those intent on being mesmerised by the elegant gestures of an equally elegant *maestro*, they are the basis for the craft, if not the art, of conducting.

Perhaps one of the most important interpretative issues that a conductor has to grapple with is tempo. Clearly defined tempo plans are the skeletons upon which conductors' readings are based and directly affect artists' decisions about bowing, phrasing, articulation and architectonic management. A seminal guide to the treatment of tempo for artists trained in the late nineteenth and early twentieth centuries was Richard Wagner's 1869 article, *On Conducting*.[512] Read and digested by at least five generations of musicians, *On Conducting* is a treasure trove of ideas that addresses important aspects of performance practice and performance style. Central to Wagner's argument in the article is the relationship between tempo and *melos*.[513] Something of an amorphous term that loosely equates to what singers call 'line', *melos* was for Wagner the key to revealing the true meaning of a work based on a sympathetic understanding of vocal technique. A passionate advocate of the Master's theories, Barbirolli confirmed his affinity with them when he wrote:

Wagner laid it down that the two fundamental principles underlying the art [of conducting] were: (1) giving the true tempo to the orchestra; (2) finding the "melos," by which he means the unifying thread of line that gives a work its form and shape. Given these two qualities, of course, we have the conductor *in excelsis*, and most of our lives must be spent in trying to obtain these qualities, more especially the first. [514]

Another model for Barbirolli was Felix von Weingartner, who declared that 'no slow tempo must be so slow that the melody of the piece is *not yet* recognisable, and no fast tempo so fast that the melody is *no longer* recognisable'.[515] Although Barbirolli probably would have nodded in agreement after reading this astute piece of advice, he would have also been aware that the viability of any individual tempo depended on its place within a broader whole. Yet, like Wilhelm Furtwängler, a conductor with whom Barbirolli was later compared favourably, J.B. understood that *appearing* to be too rigid when it came to speed might not always be in the music's best interest. A master of *tempo rubato* within a fixed tempo plan, Furtwängler often created the false impression that his speeds were the result of an artistic free spirit. The violinist, Szymon Goldberg,[516] knew the truth about Furtwängler's musical confidence trick, however, and let the cat out of the bag when he let slip:

> Furtwängler knew exactly what he did. His way of music-making created the impression that he would permanently improvise, but it really was not so. He conducted according to a very definite plan, and what was generally supposed to be improvisation was just imaginative planning.[517]

Barbirolli was also a master of *tempo rubato* and his readings of works from the Austro-German cannon were the beneficiaries of a 'very definite plan'. In practice, this meant that J.B. regularly adopted a series of well-considered core tempi that not only acted as architectonic indicators, but also as interpretative hubs around which his equally well-considered *rubati* revolved. This approach was, in fact, a response to Wagner's plea for 'things which formerly existed in separate and opposite forms, each complete in itself, [to be] placed in juxtaposition, and further developed, one from the other, so as to form a whole'.[518] A simple, but good, example of this can be heard on Barbirolli's 1947 disc of Beethoven's Fifth Symphony with the Hallé Orchestra, where he adopts a single tempo area – ♩ = 82–4 – as the basis for a broader temporal plan. First heard at the beginning of the symphony, this tempo zone is then pressed in to service again at key structural moments later in the work. (see below)

MOVT.	SECTION/ SUBJECT	NIKISCH (Berlin Philharmonic 1913)	WEINGARTNER (Royal Philharmonic Orchestra, 1927 & London Philharmonic, 1933)	STRAUSS (Berlin Staatskapelle, 1928)	BARBIROLLI (Hallé Orchestra, 1947)
1	First subject	𝅗𝅥 = 84	𝅗𝅥 = 92 (1927) 𝅗𝅥 = 92 (1933)	𝅗𝅥 = 88	𝅗𝅥 = 84
1	Second subject	𝅗𝅥 = 84 (bridge 𝅗𝅥 = 88)	𝅗𝅥 = 84 (1927) 𝅗𝅥 = 84 (1933)	𝅗𝅥 = 92 (bridge 𝅗𝅥 = 100)	𝅗𝅥 = 84 (bridge 𝅗𝅥 = 89)
1	Development	𝅗𝅥 = 80	𝅗𝅥 = 92–96 (1927) 𝅗𝅥 = 92–96 (1933)	𝅗𝅥 = 88 rising to 𝅗𝅥 = 100	𝅗𝅥 = 84
2	Opening	♪ = 80	♪ = 92–96/100 (1927) ♪ = 80 (1933)	♪ = 84—8	♪ = 74 (From bar 124 ♪ = 83)
2	*Più mosso*	♪ = 84	♪ = 112 (1927) ♪ = 96 (1933)	♪ = 104 rising to ♪ = 108	♪ = 97
3	*Scherzo*	From bar 19: 𝅗𝅥. = 84	From bar 19: 𝅗𝅥.= 92 (1927) 𝅗𝅥.= 88 (1933)	𝅗𝅥. = 96	𝅗𝅥. = 82
3	*Trio*	𝅗𝅥. = 84	𝅗𝅥. = 92 (1927) 𝅗𝅥. = 88 (1933)	𝅗𝅥. = 92	𝅗𝅥. = 84
4	First & second subjects	𝅗𝅥 = 84	𝅗𝅥 = 84 (1927) 𝅗𝅥 = 80 (1933)	𝅗𝅥 = 88 (𝅗𝅥 = 84 second subject)	𝅗𝅥 = 84
4	*Tempo I*	𝅗𝅥.= 84	𝅗𝅥. = 92 (1927) 𝅗𝅥. = 84 (1933)	𝅗𝅥. = 96	𝅗𝅥. = 85
4	*Presto*	𝅝 = 92	𝅝 = 92–100 (1927) 𝅝 = 92–96 (1933)	𝅝 = 104 rising to 𝅝 = 108	𝅝 = 98 rising to 𝅝 = 101

By so doing, J.B., much like Nikisch, Weingartner and Strauss before him, was better able to define the architecture of the individual movements, to create unity within the work as a whole and to secure points of reference when organising his expressive use of *rubati*.

Instrumental retouching and the doubling of woodwind and brass instruments in loud passages were also issues that concerned Wagner.[519] In a world swamped by *Urtext* scores of all types, and at a time when professional musicians are increasingly interested in simply realising the printed page, absolute textual fidelity has become something of a *sine qua non*. Yet, that was not always so. For conductors born, raised and educated in central Europe during the late nineteenth and early twentieth centuries, the printed text was only the point of departure for a wider aesthetic discussion that benefitted from a less literal approach to the score. Take Bruno Walter, for example. He argued that 'whatever can be adduced against [altering a score] on the grounds of *literary fidelity*, I must declare myself against the radical rejection of retouching.'[520] Then there was Furtwängler. While he did not deny that 'literal rendering plays a major role in the practice and reception of music today… and [that] [p]lacing the creator above the private person is naturally quite self-evident', he also believed that to 'propagate [a] literal rendering … as an 'ideal[,]' [if] it is an ideal, … is at best a pedantic one.'[521] And what of Barbirolli? True, he was outraged when he heard Toscanini adjust the orchestration of a Brahms symphony in 1937,[522] but that did not prevent him from engaging in the occasional textual indiscretion himself in later years, as, for example, in Bruckner's Eighth and Mahler's Second Symphonies where he added an extra note or two.[523] But these minor transgressions did little to define J.B. either culturally or musically, and to do that it is necessary to turn once again to his 1947 reading of Beethoven's Fifth Symphony.

From that disc, it is not only immediately obvious that Barbirolli had much in common with the central European school of conducting when it came to tempo, but also in the ways in which he responded to the score's printed text. Listen, for example, to his treatment of bar 303 in the first movement. Here, he doubles the bassoon material with the horns, an emendation that was strongly recommended by Strauss and Weingartner and that was later adopted by Sir Henry Wood and Sir John Pritchard,[524] two other British conductors who also looked to central Europe for guidance. And then there was J.B.'s use of double woodwind and brass in loud passages. Again, he fell into line behind Wagner, and from the film of his 1959 performance of Brahms's Second Symphony with the Boston Symphony

Orchestra,[525] it is clear that double woodwind was his preference when realising late Classical and Romantic works from the Austro-German canon. It seems, then, that although J.B. was trained within the British music education system, he looked to central Europe for direction when it came to the works of its composers.

For many aspiring *maestri*, the physical gestures associated with conducting are all-consuming. Yet, the potential for disagreement over what actually constitutes conducting technique is huge. Were Fritz Reiner's minimal movements any less effective than those of his flamboyant pupil, Leonard Bernstein, for example? Absolutely not. Both were in complete command of their players and both produced readings of character and integrity. And for most orchestral musicians, it is of little consequence whether conductors stand on their heads and wiggle their toes or beat time like metronomes as long as their intentions are clear. As a former orchestral musician himself, Barbirolli probably would have agreed with this. But he also believed passionately that a conductor should have 'a natural gift of gesture which should be at once clear and eloquent'.[526] And as every '"gesture" is included [in the] beat', J.B. also argued that each movement 'should have a definite meaning, and only be inspired by the most complete sincerity towards the music, oneself, and the public'. In other words, the physical gestures used by conductors must always be a natural consequence of the music and should invariably act as a conduit between the composer, the players and the audience.

Avoiding excessive and extraneous movement was central to the Barbirolli approach as a whole and was the inevitable consequence of him being a jobbing conductor. With a schedule that regularly saw J.B. give in excess of two hundred concerts a year, it was necessary for him to channel his energies strategically and to pace himself physically. By so doing, he was able to focus his attention on the players and to deal with them in a sympathetic and sensitive manner. Particularly aware of the problems faced by musicians occupying principal chairs, Barbirolli was always alert to the fact that 'some players need more guidance than others'. And, from his own experiences as an orchestral cellist, he understood that it was 'dangerous to worry a very sensitive player too much'. Quite 'the contrary', he argued. Rather, it was incumbent on the conductor 'during an important and difficult solo … [to] provide him with a background of sympathy, trust, and help'.[527] But J.B. was also quick to point out that this 'freedom' was not a licence for 'anachronisms in phrasing' on the part of the musician and that 'no "selfish" player, however good, should ever be tolerated in any first-class orchestra'.[528] In a nutshell: Barbirolli had no truck with instrumental *prima donnas*.

One of the tools most associated with the conductor is the baton. Although they can vary significantly in length and weight, they are generally made of light wood, have a grip made of cork at one end and are often constructed according to a conductor's own detailed specifications. Sir Henry Wood, for example, had his batons made by Palmer's of Great Yarmouth, and in his book, *About Conducting*, he quotes a letter to the firm in which he set out his requirements precisely:

WEIGHT: Slightly under 1 ounce

LENGTH   of exposed Shaft   19 inches

             of Handle   5 [inches]

TOTAL LENGTH   24 [inches]

SHAFT made of seasoned straight-grain poplar wood, carefully rived by hand to ensure that the grain runs straight. Painted white with two coats of water paint. The shaft runs right through the handle.

HANDLE of cork 5 inches long, diameter at base 1¼ inches, diameter at shaft end 1⅛ inch.[529]

Sir Henry's love of long batons was not shared universally, however. Herbert von Karajan preferred a short baton, while Barbirolli opted for a stick of moderate length.[19] Unlike Bruno Walter, who argued vociferously that to conduct without the baton 'carries the seeds of decay',[530] Barbirolli was more sanguine when it came to the choice and use of a stick. For him, these matters were simply a question of 'good taste and good sense'.[531] But he was quick to warn that 'it is as absurd to use a baton which resembles a diminutive lead pencil as it is to wave a weapon of exceeding length and frailty'.[532]

Concerned that 'few people … realise that conducting at the performance is the least important part of the business of conducting', Barbirolli was always at pains to point out at the lectures that he gave on the subject, that much of what he did musically was the result of an arduous, and to a degree mundane, preparatory process.[534] Conscious of the fact that audiences were blissfully unaware of the importance of 'annotating parts, editing, [and of] the one hundred and one points of technical elucidation of scores which has to go on always',[535] J.B. felt duty bound to open their eyes to what the craft of conducting really involved. And for anyone familiar with Barbirolli's working practices, and the ways in which he prepared his scores and parts for performance, his remarks have a particular resonance.

154

With a calligraphic style that was as elegant as it was expressive, he annotated his performance material so that it acted not only as a detailed *aide-memoire*, but also as a powerful statement of interpretative intent. Even without the advantage of a matching recording, musicians can recreate a clear sound-image of a Barbirolli interpretation by closely examining these documents. Aware that these cartographic expressions of musical intent were only of limited value unless they were supported by a carefully-crafted programming policy, he also cast in stone a creed that was as simple as it was effective: 'programs [*sic*] … must have as a basis the great classical masterpieces[,] … a representative selection of modern classics, and such contemporary music as might interest the public to hear'.[536]

When it came to the seating arrangement of orchestras, Barbirolli's approach changed over time. Having been a cellist in a professional string quartet during the 1920s, he initially looked to his experiences as a chamber musician as a possible seating model. Writing in 1938 as Music Director of the New York Philharmonic-Symphony Orchestra, he explained that:

I personally seat the orchestra in the more conservative way of having the violins on either side which is much in the manner of the Joachim Quartet, because after all the string choir of an orchestra is but an enlarged quartet. I was very interested to find only a few nights ago when visiting some friends who have a collection of Wagneriana to find a sketch for the seating of an orchestra for a concert in Wagner's own handwriting, with the strings disposed of in very much the same manner as the strings in the Philharmonic-Symphony are today.[537]

But aware that changes were afoot, Barbirolli continued by observing that:

It has become usual of late years both here and abroad to mass the deeper-toned string families on the outside of the orchestra to the right of the conductor in the place for so long traditionally occupied by the second violins. Sometimes the violas are placed immediately on the right of the conductor or sometimes even the cellos, and the first and second violins are massed together on the conductor's left.[538]

While this seating arrangement did have the potential to create a more brilliant violin tone and 'a deep somber-hued [*sic*] sonority' in the lower strings, it had two drawbacks for Barbirolli. First, it tended to a preponderance of the bass parts and, second, when the violins were massed together, it became hard to distinguish between the first and second violins when they were playing antiphonally. Yet, after his return to Britain in 1943, he had a complete change of heart and adopted this seating plan. He continued with this new approach for the rest of his career and only reverted to his earlier disposition when working with orchestras from the German-speaking countries, such as the Berlin and Vienna Philharmonics.

When conducting piano concertos, Barbirolli placed the conductor's podium between the audience and the piano. The preferred choice of Sir Henry Wood, Basil Cameron, Constant Lambert and Richard Strauss when working in Britain, this disposition also had its detractors. Sir Adrian Boult was particularly vociferous in his disapproval of this arrangement and complained that:

> This [approach] has many drawbacks; the conductor will have to be mounted uncomfortably high, and … [this] can be [awkward] for the front desk of the strings, and even then he will find the piano lid in the way of his contact with the orchestra and in danger of its breaking his stick for him. Certain of my more unscrupulous colleagues arrange for the stick which supports the piano lid to be shortened somewhat. This upsets the angle chosen by the maker to reflect the sound straight into the hall; with a short stick the sound is thrown at the feet of the people in the front row of the stalls. No, a short stick is most unfair to soloists, whose tone will be misdirected and muffled. Moreover, the most serious objection to the conductor's being in that position is that he has the whole weight of the piano tone just under his nose and ears, and cannot possibly judge accurately whether the orchestra is drowning the soloist.[539]

As compelling as Boult's words might well have been when they first appeared in 1963, they made no impact on Barbirolli. Undaunted by conducting on a high podium, J.B. never lost faith in this arrangement, as he believed it to be an essential tool in realising his thesis that a 'concerto [was] not [just] a virtuosic display by one individual, but … [a] collective musical accomplishment … [that should] always [be] considered part of the orchestral repertoire.'[540]

A firm advocate of conducting from memory, Hans von Bülow famously made it clear to his young protégé, Richard Strauss, after a less-than-impressive performance of his tone poem, *Macbeth*, at Berlin in 1892 that 'the score should be in your head and not your head in the score'.[541] Sage advice, no doubt. But Strauss's great contemporary, Felix von Weingartner, was not convinced that the thorny issue of conducting from memory was as straightforward as Bülow seemed to suggest:

> If the conductor is so dependent on the score that he can never take his eyes from it to look at the players, he is of course a mere time-beater, a bungler, with no pretension to the title of artist. Conducting from memory, however, that makes a parade of virtuosity is also inartistic, since it diverts attention from the work to the conductor ... But I hold that it is entirely the conductor's own concern whether he will use the score or not. A good performance from the score has value; a bad one done from memory has none.[542]

Bruno Walter was also an advocate of conducting from memory, and having freed himself from the score, he felt that nothing stood between him, the music and his players. But he was also aware that for those with a poor memory, the score was indispensable and that a photographic recollection of it was not necessarily a sign of true musicianship.[543] Barbirolli agreed completely with Weingartner and Walter and was keen to point out that:

> It is foolish to imagine that a man knows less about a work because he uses [a score]. On the other hand, it is just as foolish to accuse all those who dispose of them of being bluffers and charlatans ... To some a score may be an impediment, to others, even though they refer to it very seldom, it is a release from any anxiety which enables them to give a much freer vent to their imagination ... [But] what I [conduct] from memory, I should also be able to write down from memory.[544]

A firm believer that 'a conductor is born and not made',[545] Barbirolli understood that conducting might not be for everyone and that the craft behind the art was not simply a series of mundane tasks to be endured and overcome. Aware that conducting carried with it a cultural and spiritual responsibility that only those who were prepared to commit themselves to years of hard work could fully realise, J.B. considered it a near-religious experience that had the potential to shape the human condition. That being so, perhaps the final word should go to the *Maestro Glorioso* himself:

> In conclusion I would like to say to any young musician who contemplates this most arduous and responsible of careers to make his watchwords[:][546] "Integrity and sincerity to yourself and loyalty to the man whose music you are seeking to interpret." Never think "What can I make of this piece?" but try to discover what the composer meant to say. We must bear in mind that the conductor has become one of the most important and responsible personalities in the musical world, and by fine <u>stylistic</u> performances can do much towards a purification of musical perception amongst the general public. On the other hand performances that are merely the vehicle to indulge the vanity of a personality, however talented, can only tend to lead us further from that which should be the goal of all true musicians: Service to that great art which it is our privilege to practise.[547]

APPENDIX ONE

BRUCKNER'S EIGHTH SYMPHONY

TEMPO CHART AND SCORE EXAMPLES

Tempo Table and Beating Instructions derived from Barbirolli's marked score and the BBC Legends recording of Bruckner's Eighth Symphony[548]

Movement	Bar number	Printed metronome marks, superscription and supplementary instructions	Barbirolli's tempo, beating and metronome marks	Recorded tempi
I (first theme)	1	Allegro moderato	♩ = 54 Circa; [beaten in] 2	♩ = 54
I (second theme)	51	breit und ausdrucksvoll		♩ = 56
I (third theme)	97			♩ = 58
I (development)	140	Ruhig		♩ = 54 (molto rubato)
I (first theme, recapitulation)	225	Feierlich breit	Grande	♩ = 58
I (second theme, recapitulation)	311	breit und ausdrucksvoll	Breit	♩ = 56
I (third theme, recapitulation)	341		Ein wenig fliessend	♩ = 58 (accelerando)
II (Scherzo)	1	Allegro moderato	♩ = 104 [crossed-out, top left-hand corner, p. 39]; Früh Takt [on bassoon staves]; ♩ = circa 120 [between the trumpet & trombone staves]; [beaten in] 3 [between the trombone & contra-bass tuba staves]	♩ = 120
II (Scherzo)	49			♩ = 138
II (Scherzo)	65			♩ = 132
II (Scherzo)	135			♩ = 126
II (Scherzo)	183			♩ = 138

II (Trio)	1	Langsam	♪ = ♪ of 3/4 [crossed-out between trumpet & contra-bass tuba staves]; [beaten in] 4 (♪ circa 104 [crossed-out and replaced with] 96✓) [above the harp stave]	♪ = 88–92
II (Trio)	37	sanft hervortretend	dolcemente fuori	♪ = 84
II (Trio)	45			♪ = 72
II (Trio)	61			♪ = 88
II (Trio)	85	sanft hervortretend	dolcemente fuori; sempre 4	♪ = 84
III (first theme)	1	Adagio: Feierlich langsam: doch nicht schleppend	overall circa ♪ = 100: In 4; *Solenne*	♩ = 46–48
III (second theme)	47			♩ = 50
III	129	poco a poco accel.	*sehr fliessend; poco a poco accel[errand]*	♩ = 66 (accelerando)
III	134			♩ = 76
III	185	a tempo (wie anfangs)	nicht schleppend [viola figure]	♩ = 46
III	197–198		*aber nicht schleppend; S.[lesso] T.[empo] (non troppo)*	accelerando
III	205			♩ = 66
III	211–226		*poco movendo (sempre)✓* [bars 211–212]; *muovere* [bar 215]; *S.[lesso] T.[empo]* [bar 218]; *poco a poco cresc[endo] al f [orte] e sempre movendo un poco cresc[endo] sempre* [above bars 220–226]	♩ = 66 [bar 211]; (accelerando); ♩ = 84 [bar 226]
III	227–236		12 bars to Höhepunkt. (F.[ar] too fast); Ruhig (aber nicht schleppend)	♩ = 66 [bar 227]; (accelerando); ♩ = 80 [bar 236]

III	237–238		sempre marc. [ato] [bar 237]	♩ = 76; (rallentando) [bar 238]
III	239–243	Etwas bewegter	Höhepunkt [bar 239]; S.[tesso] T.[empo] [bar 239]	♩ = 60 [bars 239–243]
IV (first theme)	1	♩ = 69; Feierlich, nicht schnell	♩ = 80 ♩ = 69 (too slow) [top left-hand corner of p. 105]; ♩ = 69 [inserted between the trumpet and trombone staves but, later, erased]; Solenne [inserted above the timpani stave]; Feierlich [superscription above the violins]	♩ = 84
IV (second theme)	69	♩ = 60; Langsamer	♩ = 66 circa; (aber nicht schleppend); Meno immer 2	♩ = 58
IV	89–95		breit [bar 93]	♩ = 58 [bar 89]; (accelerando); ♩ = 63 [bar 95]
IV	99	noch langsamer	[beaten in] 4; ♩ = 88	♩ = 88
IV	111	a tempo	Breit; ♩ = 60 [crossed-out]; too slow ♩ = 66 circa. (aber nicht schleppend)	♩ = 63
IV (third theme)	135		(S.[tesso] T.[empo]) [bar 136]	♩ = 60; (accelerando)
IV (first theme, recapitulation)	437	Erstes Zeitmass	sub. [ito] Tempo Primo	♩ = 84
IV (second theme, recapitulation)	547	♩ = 60; (Langsamer)	♩ = 66; Meno	♩ = 58
IV	567–73	noch langsamer	In 4; ♩ = 84-88 [with a vertical arrow joining 'this one' to ♩ = 84]; In 4 (aber nicht schleppend)	♩ = 72 [bar 567]; ♩ = 80 [bar 573]
IV (third theme, recapitulation)	583	viel langsamer	superscription (viel langsamer), above the top system, crossed-out; Not in Haas [above the crossed-out superscription]; Molto meno; still 4 (♩ = 112); S.[tesso] T.[empo]	♩ = 92

IV	647			♪ = 52; (accelerando)
IV	697			♪ = 66
IV	708	riten.	In 4	(rallentando)

SCORE EXAMPLES   (Barbirolli's annotations marked in red)

Example 1 (Movement 1, bars 1–9)

Example 2 (Movement 3, bars 1–4)

Example 3 (Movement 1, bars 51–4)

Example 4 (Movement 1, bars 403–17)

Example 5 (Movement 3, bars 129–35)

APPENDIX TWO

MAHLER'S SECOND SYMPHONY

TEMPO CHART AND SCORE EXAMPLES

Tempo Table derived from Barbirolli's marked score
and recordings (1965 and 1970) of Mahler's Second Symphony

Movement/ Bar Number	Marked Score (Inserted metronome mark)	Berlin Philharmonic (1965)	Radio-Symphonieorchester Stuttgart (1970)
1/1	♩ = 84–92	*Quasi fermata*	*Quasi fermata*
1/2	♩ = 144	♩ = 144	♩ = 144
1/3	♩ = 84	*Quasi fermata*	*Quasi fermata*
1/4	♩ = 144	♩ = 144	♩ = 144
1/5	♩ = 84–92	♩ = 80 (♩ = 84 from bar 17)	♩ = 72 (♩ = 84 from bar 31)
1/97	♩ = 92	♩ = 84	♩ = 80
1/117	*Circa* ♩ = 80	♩ = 69	♩ = 66
1/123	*Circa* ♩ = 88	♩ = 76	♩ = 76
1/147	♩ = 88	♩ = 88	♩ = 88
1/179	♩ = 108	♩ = 112	♩ = 104
1/230	♩ = 138	♩ = 144	♩ = 132
1/254	♩ = 72	♩ = 72	♩ = 92
1/291	♩ = 144	♩ = 144	♩ = 138
1/301	♩ = 108	♩ = 108	♩ = 120
1/329	♩ = 84–92	♩ = 84	♩ = 92
1/392	♩ = 80–84	♩ = 66 (♩ = 84 at bar 441 [*Tempo I*])	♩ = 66 (♩ = 84 at bar 441 [*Tempo I*])
2/1	♪ = 96	♪ = 76 (♪ = 88 at bar 64)	♪ = 88 (♪ = 92 at bar 64)

2/133	♪ = 108	♪ = 100	♪ = 100
3/1	♪ = 160	*Circa* ♪ = 174	*Circa* ♪ = 174
4/1	♩ = 66–72	♩ = 66 (from bar 15)	♩ = 66 (from bar 15)
4/36	♩ = 84	♩ = 80	♩ = 84
4/60	♩ = 66	♩ = 42	♩ = 48
5/26	♩ = 72	*Circa* ♩ = 56	*Circa* ♩ = 56
5/48	♩ = 69–72	♩ = 69–72	♩ = 72
5/62	♩ = 69–72	♩ = 72	♩ = 72–6
5/142	♩ = 60	♩ = 60	♩ = 60
5/162	♩ = 72	♩ = 63	♩ = 72
5/196	♩ = 132	♩ = 138	♩ = 126
5/203	♩ = 132	♩ = 132	♩ = 132
5/220	♩ = 126	♩ = 132–8	♩ = 126–132
5/242	♩ = 96	♩ = 144	♩ = 132
5/251	♩ = 126	♩ = 144	♩ = 132
5/289	♩ = 92–104	♩ = 126	♩ = 116
5/342	♩ = 138	♩ = 126	♩ = 120
5/380	𝅗𝅥 = 100	𝅗𝅥 = 84	𝅗𝅥 = 80
5/472	♩ = 63	♩ = 46	♩ = 46
5/493	♩ = 63	♩ = 56	♩ = 63
5/560	𝅗𝅥 = 92–96	𝅗𝅥 = 92	𝅗𝅥 = 92
5/618	♩ = 88	♩ = 88	♩ = 80
5/629	♩ = 60	♩ = 60 (bar 636)	♩ = 60
5/640	𝅗𝅥 = 100	𝅗𝅥 = 100	𝅗𝅥 = 100
5/712		[♩ = 66]	[♩ = 66]

APPENDIX TWO

SCORE EXAMPLES   (Barbirolli's annotations marked in red)

Example 1 (Movement 2, bars 1–4)

Example 2a (Movement 3, bars 190–3)

Example 2b (Movement 3, bars 209–10)

Example 3 (Movement 1, bar 282)

Example 4 (Movement 5, bars 433–46)

Example 5 (Movement 5, bars 194–9)

Example 6 (Movement 1, bars 48–50)

Example 7 (Movement 2, bars 22–4)

NOTES

ESSAY ONE

[1] O. A. H. Schmitz, *Das Land ohne Musik: englishe Gesellschaftsprobleme* (Munich, 1914). The book was first published in 1904, details unknown.

[2] After studies in Scotland and Germany, Mackenzie joined the Hofkapelle Sonderhausen in Thuringia. On his return to Britain, he studied at the Royal Academy of Music, after which he played under the Italian-born, British conductor, Sir Michael Costa. Mackenzie's compositions were performed by Hans von Bülow, Pablo Sarasate and August Manns and, as a conductor, Mackenzie took charge of the Philharmonic Society of London's prestigious subscription series between 1892 and 1899. Appointed Principal of the Royal Academy of Music in 1888, Mackenzie retired from that post in 1924.

[3] The performances of Rossini's opera under Barbirolli at Hammersmith ran from 25 to 30 July. Perhaps Mackenzie had been invited to a dress rehearsal on 24 July.

[4] Letter from Sir Alexander Mackenzie to John Barbirolli, dated 24 July 1927. Barbirolli Collection, Royal Academy of Music, London.

[5] With the Scottish Orchestra, Barbirolli conducted Mackenzie's Overture to *The Cricket on the Hearth* on 22 December 1933, *Benedictus* on 12, 13 and 14 November 1935 and the Funeral March from *Coriolanus* on 27 January 1936. Barbirolli also gave two complete performances of Mackenzie's opera, *The Cricket on the Hearth*, with students from the Royal Academy of Music at the New Scala Theatre, London, on 15 and 17 July 1936.

[6] The exact date and programme is unknown. The members of the Music Society String Quartet were André Mangeot (violin), Boris Pecker (violin), Henry J. Berly (viola) and John Barbirolli (cello). André Mangeot and John Barbirolli also played together in the Philharmonic String Quartet, while Henry J. Berly was also a member of the London Piano Quartet with Barbirolli.

[7] After joining Sir Henry Wood's Queen's Hall Orchestra in July 1912, Goossens became second violin of the Langley-Mukle Quartet. In 1923, he was appointed the first Music Director of the Rochester Philharmonic Orchestra and, in 1931, Music Director of the Cincinnati Symphony Orchestra. From 1947 to 1956, he took charge simultaneously of the Sydney Symphony Orchestra and the New South Wales State Conservatorium of Music (now Sydney Conservatorium of Music).

[8] 20 March 1925.

[9] The Kutcher Quartet's members for that recording were Samuel Kutcher (violin), Max Salpeter (violin), Raymond Jeremy (viola) and John Barbirolli (cello).

[10] Barbirolli joined the 1st Reserve Garrison Battalion, Suffolk Regiment, on 2 February 1918. The Isle of Grain is in Kent at the mouths of the Medway and Thames Rivers.

[11] 'JB: a Portrait of Sir John Barbirolli', *Monitor*, BBC, 1965.

[12] Uncatalogued programme. Barbirolli Collection, Royal Academy of Music, London.

[13] A traditional route for an aspiring conductor to take after joining an opera company is to start as a répétiteur before becoming a chorus master and, finally, a conductor. As Barbirolli was not a proficient pianist, this avenue was closed to him.

[14] *The Times*, 5 May 1921.

[15] The Guild performed at the Steinway Hall, the People's Palace, 93 Harley Street, the Marylebone Court House and the Crowndale Road Working Men's College.

[16] *The Times*, 20 July 1926.

[17] Ibid, 26 January 1925.

[18] The Chenil Gallery was opened in 1906 by the art dealer, Jack Knewstub, on a site next to the Chelsea Town Hall in the King's Road. The premises were extended in 1925 to include live

performance spaces and were renamed the New Chenil Galleries. The new premises were officially opened on 5 June 1925 by Sir Augustine Birrell 'with an important Exhibition of Paintings, Drawings, Etchings, and Sculpture organized by the Chelsea Arts Club' (*The Times*, 11 May 1925) and closed in 1927 after Knewstub was made bankrupt.

[19] 'Peter Warlock' was the pseudonym of the composer Philip Heseltine.

[20] M. Kennedy, *Barbirolli: Conductor Laureate* (Uttoxeter, 2003), p. 50.

[21] The Queen's Hall was situated at Portland Place and the Royal Albert Hall at Kensington Gore.

[22] 'Chenil Gallery Music', *The Musical Times*, 1 March 1927, pp. 261–2.

[23] *The Tailor* was composed by van Dieren between 1917 and 1930.

[24] Barbirolli must have felt some connection with van Dieren's music, as he went on to give the composer's *Serenata* (Serenade) with the John Barbirolli Chamber Orchestra at the Wigmore Hall on 10 November 1928.

[25] Cf. R. Holden, 'Austin, Frederick William (Frederic) (1872–1952), singer, composer, and impresario', *Oxford Dictionary of National Biography* (Oxford, 2019).

[26] *The Musical Times*, 1 January 1926, p. 45.

[27] The Kutcher String Quartet recorded Gibbon's Fantasias Nos. 3, 6, 8 and 9 for Vocalion in June 1925 (exact day unknown) and Purcell's (eds. Mangeot and Warlock) Fantasia in Five Parts, Fantasia No. 3 in G minor and Fantasia No. 4 in C minor for the National Gramophonic Society in February 1926 (exact day unknown).

[28] *The Musical Times*, 1 October 1926, p. 919.

[29] *The Times*, 26 January 1925.

[30] Barbirolli performed Warlock's *Serenade* for the final time on 13 March 1928 at the Aeolian Hall with the Chenil Chamber Orchestra.

[31] Barbirolli conducted 'The Walk to the Paradise Garden' from *A Village Romeo and Juliet* with the Vienna Philharmonic at the Salzburg Festival on 20 August 1947.

[32] This figure only includes concerts by the Boston Symphony Orchestra and not its engagements as the Boston Pops Orchestra. The British conductors that performed Delius's music with the orchestra were Sir Eugene Goossens (3), Sir Thomas Beecham (7), Stanley Chapple (2), Guy Fraser Hamilton (2), Sir John Barbirolli (9), Sir Andrew Davis (4), Grant Llewellyn (8) and Sir Mark Elder (5).

[33] While Sir Mark Elder is a distinguished and committed interpreter of *Sea Drift*, Barbirolli never performed it.

[34] R. Holden, *Elder on Music: Sir Mark Elder in Conversation with Raymond Holden* (London, 2019), p. 144.

[35] Barbirolli recorded Delius's *Summer Night on the River* with the National Gramophonic Society Chamber Orchestra on 3 January 1927 and the composer's *Appalachia* and *Brigg Fair* with Alun Jenkins (baritone), the Ambrosian Singers and the Hallé Orchestra between 15 and 17 July 1970.

[36] A detailed study of Barbirolli's activities as an Elgarian can be found in Essay Six: 'From the Cradle to the Grave: Barbirolli, Elgar and *In the South (Alassio)*'.

[37] Although considered to be the first complete recording of a Mozart opera, Busch's discs of *Le nozze di Figaro* largely excluded the work's *secco recitatives*.

[38] The majority of Barbirolli's recordings of British music during his first HMV period were of short works or extracts. Along with Elgar's *Introduction and Allegro for Strings*, he documented the composer's 'Leap, leap to light' and 'O my warriors' from *Caractacus* (Peter Dawson, bass-baritone) and 'Where corals lie' from *Sea Pictures* (Maartje Offers, contralto), Purcell's Hornpipe from *The Married Beau*, Sullivan's 'The Night is Calm' from *The Golden Legend* (Florence Austral, soprano) and *The Lost Chord* (Beniamino Gigli, tenor), Adam's *The Holy City* and *The Star of Bethlehem*, Quilter's *A Children's Overture*, Delius's *A Song Before Sunrise*, Balfe's Overture to *The Bohemian Girl* and Bishop's 'Lo! Here the gentle lark' from *Clari* (Lily Pons, soprano).

[39] At Barbirolli's concert with the Orchestra of the Royal Philharmonic Society at the Queen's Hall

on 17 January 1929, he conducted Delius's Cello Concerto with Alexandre Barjansky as soloist. At his concert for the society at the Queen's Hall on 5 November 1931, he performed Bax's Second Symphony.

[40] Carlo Maria Giulini was Music Director of the Los Angeles Philharmonic between 1978 and 1984.

[41] Amongst the soloists who appeared with the Scottish Orchestra during Barbirolli's tenure were Arthur Rubinstein, Vladimir Horowitz, Benno Moiseiwitsch, Solomon, Adolf Busch, Jacques Thibaud, Jascha Heifetz, Bronislaw Hubermann, Carl Flesch, Leopold Godowsky, Isobel Baillie and Alexander Kipnis.

[42] J. Barbirolli, 'Fourth speech given before the Lord Provost of Glasgow', as found in R. Holden, *Glorious John: a Collection of Sir John Barbirolli's Lectures, Articles, Speeches and Interviews* (Uttoxeter, 2007), p. 167.

[43] Ibid.

[44] Barbirolli conducted music by 112 composers with the Scottish Orchestra.

[45] With the Scottish Orchestra, Barbirolli performed Bax's Third and Fourth Symphonies, *The Garden of Fand* and *The Tale the Pine Trees Knew*, Vaughan Williams's *Job*, *Fantasia on a Theme by Thomas Tallis* and *Toward the Unknown Region* and Walton's Viola Concerto (Eileen Grainger, viola).

[46] Gibilaro arrived in London in 1891 and married Barbirolli's sister, Rosa, in 1916. Barbirolli also conducted the *Scottish Fantasia* at one of the New York Philharmonic-Symphony Orchestra's children's concerts at Carnegie Hall on 18 December 1938.

[47] A good example of this type of mixed programme was Barbirolli's concert on 1 January 1935 at St. Andrew's Hall, Glasgow. Works performed that night were Sullivan's Overture to *The Yeoman of the Guard*, Wagner's 'Gerechter Gott' from *Rienzi*, Tchaikovsky's Sixth Symphony ('*Pathétique*'), Mozart's Serenade No. 13 ('*Eine kleine Nachtmusik*'), Elgar's 'In Haven' and 'Where Corals Lie' from *Sea Pictures* (Mary Jarred, contralto), Delius's *On Hearing the First Cuckoo in Spring*, Boccherini's (arr. Barbirolli) *Minuet*, Grainger's *Shepherd's Hey* and Gibilaro's *Scottish Fantasia*.

[48] On 19 and 20 November 1934, Barbirolli performed Elgar's 'Funeral March' from *Grania and Diarmid* and his Violin Concerto (David McCallum, violin), Delius's *Eventyr* and Holst's *The Planets* ('Mars', 'Venus' and 'Jupiter' only). The first concert was held at the Usher Hall, Edinburgh, and, the second, at St. Andrew's Hall, Glasgow.

ESSAY TWO

[49] Lorenzo Barbirolli's *I Trojani in Laurento* was performed at Ferrara's Teatro Apollo in 1837. Library of Congress: https://www.loc.gov/resource/musschatz.12696.0?st=gallery.

[50] Verdi supervised the rehearsals for the premiere of *Otello* and his thoughts and comments were passed on to Barbirolli by his father and grandfather.

[51] After the Royal Opera House, Covent Garden, was used solely for opera from 1847 until the establishment of the Covent Garden Opera Company in 1947, some of the troupes that played in the theatre included the Royal Italian Opera (1847–91), the Royal English Opera Season (1858–66), the Autumn Opera and Royal Opera Season (1891–1914), the Grand Opera Season and the Beecham Opera Company (1919–20), the Carl Rosa Company (1920–2), the British National Opera Company (1922–4) and the Grand Opera Season (1924–40).

[52] The pianist for that Edison Bell recording was Barbirolli's sister, Rosa. Along with 'O Star of Eve', Barbirolli recorded van Biene's *Broken Melody*, Thomé's *Simple aveu* and Pergolesi's (attributed) *Tre giorni son che Nina* with his sister in October 1911.

[53] Barbirolli, 'The Noblest Traditions of Italian Art', as found in Holden, *Glorious John*, pp. 104–7. (*I Zingari* was an amateur cricket club that was formed by former Harrovians on 4 July 1845).

[54] Ibid. (Here, Barbirolli is referring to the trombones' three-bar theme at Fig. 54 in Ricordi's full score of the opera)

[55] Ibid. (Here, Barbirolli is referring to the bassoon material at Fig. 1 in the Ricordi's full score of the opera).

[56] Ibid.

[57] Ibid.

[58] Ibid.

[59] Ibid.

[60] J. Kerman, *Opera as Drama* (Berkley and Los Angeles, 2005), p. 205.

[61] Barbirolli, 'The Noblest Traditions of Italian Art', as found in Holden, *Glorious John*, pp. 104–7.

[62] Ibid.

[63] Barbirolli, 'Speech to the New York Philharmonic-Symphony League on 1 November 1938', as found in Holden, *Glorious John*, pp. 133–42.

[64] *Newcastle Chronicle*, 27 September 1926.

[65] Barbirolli conducted *Madama Butterfly* (afternoon) and *Aïda* (evening) on 25 September 1926 at Newcastle-upon-Tyne's Hippodrome Theatre.

[66] Barbirolli did not conduct at Covent Garden until 30 June 1928.

[67] Barbirolli, 'Becoming a Conductor: a Conference with John Barbirolli', as found in Holden, *Glorious John*, pp. 131–2.

[68] *The Manchester Guardian*, 18 November 1926.

[69] Barbirolli also conducted Puccini's *Tosca* and *La bohème* for the first time on this tour.

[70] Barbirolli also conducted Puccini's *Madama Butterfly* at the Golders Green Hippodrome in January 1927.

[71] *The Daily Mail*, 13 January 1927.

[72] *The Morning Post*, 14 January 1927.

[73] Ibid.

[74] Ibid.

[75] *The Daily Telegraph*, 14 January 1927.

[76] Barbirolli repeated the opera at Birmingham and Golders Green the following month.

[77] *The Yorkshire Post*, 3 February 1927.

[78] *Yorkshire Observer*, 11 February 1927.

[79] Barbirolli and Bartlett played sonatas for cello and piano by Delius, Beethoven and Brahms.

[80] Mrs Mulholland was the mother of Joan Mulholland, who had attended the London Violoncello School with Barbirolli.

[81] *Daily Express*, 1 August 1927.

[82] The Wimbledon performances began on 1 August 1927.

[83] *Daily Express*, 1 August 1927.

[84] *The Times*, 26 July 1927.

[85] Barbirolli conducted *Il barbiere di Siviglia* at Newcastle-upon-Tyne's Hippodrome on 19 September 1927.

[86] Barbirolli conducted *Il barbiere di Siviglia* on 23 October 1927 and *Die Meistersinger von Nürnberg* on 27 October 1927. Both were given at His Majesty's Theatre, Aberdeen.

[87] Unidentified review held in the Barbirolli Collection, Royal Academy of Music, London.

[88] *Aberdeen Journal*, 28 October 1927.

[89] *Die Meistersinger von Nürnberg* was given at the Lewisham Hippodrome.

[90] In addition to the venues that Barbirolli had already visited with the BNOC, he performed at Cardiff's Empire Theatre. There, he conducted *Il barbiere di Siviglia* on 13 February 1928, *La bohème* on 19 February 1928, *Madama Butterfly* on 25 February 1928 and *Die Meistersinger von Nürnberg* on 27 February 1928.

[91] Barbirolli conducted *Falstaff* for the first time on 19 October 1928 at His Majesty's Theatre, Aberdeen.

[92] Barbirolli's last performance for the BNOC was with *Falstaff* at the Golders Green Hippodrome on 3 April 1929.

[93] The Covent Garden Opera Syndicate's first season ran from 30 April to 14 July 1928.

[94] *The Times*, 2 July 1928.

[95] Miriam Licette sang the title role and Hans Clemens sang Pinkerton under Barbirolli. Rosetta Pampanini sang Butterfly and Dino Borgioli sang Pinkerton under Bellezza on 31 May.

[96] *The Times*, 2 July 1928.

[97] Ibid.

[98] Walter conducted three performances of *Don Giovanni* at Covent Garden in 1926.

[99] Barbirolli conducted *Don Giovanni* on 27 and 30 May and 4 June 1929.

[100] *Daily Express*, 27 May 1929.

[101] *The Times*, 28 May 1929.

[102] *The Gramophone*, June 1929.

[103] *The Times*, 24 September 1929.

[104] Ibid, 30 September 1929.

[105] 'Bleeding chunks' was a term first found in Donald Tovey's *Essays in Musical Analysis, Vol.II.* (Oxford, 1935), p. 71.

[106] With the Scottish Orchestra, Barbirolli gave all-Wagner programmes on 26 December 1933 and 3 December 1934. With the New York Philharmonic-Symphony Orchestra, he gave all-Wagner programmes on 11 December 1937; 1 May, 19 November and 20 November 1938; 29 April, 27 October, 14 December and 15 December 1939; 13 April 1941, and 5 April 1942.

[107] *The New York Times*, 6 April 1942.

[108] With the Houston Symphony Orchestra, Barbirolli gave all-Wagner concerts on 18 and 19 November 1963 and on 22 and 23 November 1965.

[109] Barbirolli conducted Act 2 from *Tristan und Isolde* at the Royal Albert Hall (Proms) on 26 August 1954. He conducted *Madama Butterfly* on 11 and 12 May 1966 and *Otello* on 14 and 16 May 1968 at the Free Trade Hall, Manchester.

[110] Bülow conducted the premiere of *Tristan und Isolde* at the Munich Hofoper on 10 June 1865.

[111] Letter from Hans von Bülow to Eduard Lassen, dated 31 July 1865. As found in K. Birkin, 'Une organisation musicale de plus rares', *Richard Strauss-Blätter* (Vienna, June 2002), Heft 47, p. 17.

[112] *The Times*, 27 August 1954.

[113] Ibid.

[114] The cast included Elizabeth Vaughan (Cio-Cio San), David Hughes (Pinkerton), Monica Sinclair (Suzuki) and John Shaw (Pinkerton).

[115] *The Guardian*, 12 May 1966. (*The Manchester Guardian* changed its name to *The Guardian* on 24 August 1959).

[116] Ibid.

[117] The cast for *Otello* included Pier Miranda Ferraro (Otello), Elizabeth Vaughan (Desdemona), John Shaw (Iago), David Hughes (Cassio), Neil McKinnon (Roderigo) and Gwynne Howell (Lodovico).

[118] *The Guardian*, 15 May 1968.

[119] 14 May 1968. As found in Barbirolli's engagement book 1967–8. Author's private collection.

[120] Between 5 September and 19 October and between 4 and 10 November 1946, the San Carlo company performed Rossini's *Il barbiere di Siviglia*, Puccini's *La bohème*, *Tosca* and *Madama Butterfly*, Verdi's *Rigoletto* and *La traviata*, Mascagni's *Cavalleria rusticana* and Leoncavallo's *I Pagliacci*. The theatre had official reopened in February 1946 with a season of ballet.

[121] Rankl had sought refuge from Nazi oppression in London in 1939 and was clearly an anti-fascist. Yet, that mattered little to some commentators in the years directly following the Second World War.

[122] H. Rosenthal, *Two Centuries of Opera at Covent Garden* (London, 1958), p. 614.

[123] Barbirolli's Rome sessions were also recorded in city's Teatro dell'Opera.

[124] Barbirolli conducted *Aïda* in Rome on 14, 16, 20, 23, 26 and 29 April 1969.

[125] G. Jones, 'A Reminiscence', as found in R. Holden, *Barbirolli: a Chronicle of a Career* (Uttoxeter, 2016), p. xi.

ESSAY THREE

[126] Hans Richter's comment to the London Symphony Orchestra at the start of the first rehearsal for the London premiere of Elgar's First Symphony at the Queen's Hall on 7 December 1908. W. H. Reed, *Elgar* (New York, 1949), p. 97.

[127] M. Pearton, *The LSO at 70: a History of the Orchestra* (London, 1974), p. 37.

[128] Benjamin Britten and Evelyn Barbirolli (née Rothwell) both attended the Royal College of Music, London.

[129] Britten's Violin Concerto was given on 28 and 29 March 1940.

[130] *New York World-Telegram*, 29 March 1940.

[131] Britten's *Sinfonia da Requiem* was given on 29 and 30 March 1941.

[132] *The New York Times*, 30 March 1941.

[133] *The Sun*, 31 March 1941.

[134] *The New York Times*, 31 March 1941.

[135] *New York Herald Tribune*, 31 March 1941.

[136] Barbirolli's performance of the *Sinfonia da Requiem* from 30 March 1941 has since been released on NMC Recordings.

[137] E. Barbirolli, *Life with Glorious John* (London, 2002), p. 66.

[138] Barbirolli performed the *Concerto Accademico* with the violinist, Sybil Eaton, and the Chenil Chamber Orchestra at the Aeolian Hall, London, on 13 March 1928.

[139] *Toward the Unknown Region* appeared as *Towards the Unspecified Region* in the promotional material of the Scottish Orchestra for Barbirolli's performance of the work at the Usher Hall, Edinburgh, on 3 February 1936.

[140] Barbirolli gave a second performance of the symphony with the New York Philharmonic-Symphony Orchestra at Carnegie Hall on 17 February 1939. He performed the symphony again with the orchestra at Carnegie Hall on 25 and 26 February 1943.

[141] *The New York Times*, 18 February 1938.

[142] *The Sun*, 17 February 1938.

[143] Barbirolli gave a second performance of the symphony on 9 February 1940.

[144] *The Sun*, 9 February 1940.

[145] Vaughan Williams was unhappy that the symphony was viewed in this way and argued that it had no underlying extra-musical thesis.

[146] With the Houston Symphony Orchestra, Barbirolli toured with Vaughan Williams's Sixth Symphony to St. Petersburg (FL), Jacksonville (FL), University Park (PA), Brunswick (GA), Columbia (SC), Albany (NY), Staten Island (NY). With the Boston Symphony Orchestra, he also performed it in New London (CT).

[147] Letter (date unspecified) from Adeline Vaughan Williams to Ursula Wood (later Ursula Vaughan Williams). As found in U. Vaughan Williams, *R.V.W.: a Biography of Ralph Vaughan Williams* (London, New York and Toronto, 1964), p. 291.

[148] While all six symphonies were given during the first season (1951–2), they were not heard in chronological order. Included in the programme for the first concert at the hall on 16 November 1951 was Vaughan Williams's *Serenade to Music* in the version for orchestra alone.

[149] Barbirolli conducted the premiere of the *Sinfonia antartica* with the Hallé Orchestra at the Free Trade Hall, Manchester, on 14 January 1953.

[150] Barbirolli conducted Vaughan Williams's Tuba Concerto with the London Symphony Orchestra

at the Royal Festival Hall, London, on 13 June 1954. The soloist was the orchestra's principal tuba, Philip Catelinet. The conductor recorded the concerto with the same forces on 14 June 1954. On 4 and 5 July 1955, Barbirolli also recorded the composer's Oboe Concerto with same orchestra; his wife, Evelyn Rothwell, was the soloist. Barbirolli conducted the premiere of the Eighth Symphony with the Hallé Orchestra at the Free Trade Hall, Manchester, on 2 May 1956.

[151] The *Sinfonia antartica* used music from Vaughan Williams's score for Ealing Studio's 1947 film, *Scott of the Antarctic*.

[152] *The Times*, 14 June 1954.

[153] Barbirolli, 'A Tribute to Vaughan Williams', as found in Holden, *Glorious John*, pp. 101–2.

[154] Barbirolli recorded the Second Symphony ('A London Symphony') (1957 and 1967), the Fifth Symphony (1944 and 1962), the *Sinfonia antartica* (1953) and the Eighth Symphony (1956). With the exception of his 1962 recording of the Fifth Symphony with the Philharmonia Orchestra, Barbirolli's discs of Vaughan Williams's symphonies were all made with the Hallé Orchestra.

[155] EMI and Pye were Barbirolli's principal recording companies during his Manchester period.

[156] While Vaughan Williams gave the premiere of *A Sea Symphony* in 1910, Sir Adrian Boult conducted the first performances of the Third ('A Pastoral Symphony'), Fourth and Sixth Symphonies in 1922, 1935 and 1948 respectively. Sir Malcolm Sargent gave the premiere of the Ninth in 1958.

[157] Kennedy, *Barbirolli: Conductor Laureate*, p. 264.

[158] This total excludes the works of Arnold van Wyk, John Joubert, Arthur Benjamin, Percy Grainger, Malcolm Williamson and Mátyás Seiber which were also given by Barbirolli at Cheltenham.

[159] On 4 July 1966, Barbirolli performed McCabe's First Symphony ('Elegy'), Janáček's *Taras Bulba*, Martinů's Concerto for Oboe and Small Orchestra (Evelyn Rothwell, oboe) and Vaughan Williams's Eighth Symphony.

[160] *The Times*, 5 July 1966.

[161] Each of Barbirolli's touring concerts including at least one work by either Delius, Elgar, Walton, Holst, Arnold, Vaughan Williams or himself.

[162] During his 1958–9 North American tour, Barbirolli performed Delius's 'The Walk to the Paradise Garden' from *A Village Romeo and Juliet*, Elgar's 'Enigma' Variations, *Introduction and Allegro for Strings* and *The Dream of Gerontius*, Arnold's 'Tam O'Shanter' Overture, Vaughan Williams's Eighth Symphony, Walton's Violin Concerto (John Corigliano, violin) and his own *An Elizabethan Suite*.

[163] *New York Journal-American*, 2 January 1959.

[164] Between 1 and 25 January 1959, Barbirolli gave three performances of Elgar's *Introduction and Allegro for Strings* and four of *The Dream of Gerontius*, three performances of Vaughan Williams's Eighth Symphony, one performance of Arnold's 'Tam O'Shanter' Overture, one performance of Walton's Violin Concerto (John Corigliano, violin), four performances of Holst's *The Planets* and four performances of his own *An Elizabethan Suite*.

[165] Given between 22 and 25 January 1959, Barbirolli's soloists for *The Dream of Gerontius* were Maureen Forrester (contralto), Richard Lewis (tenor) and Morley Meredith (bass). The chorus was the Westminster Choir.

[166] *The New York Times*, 24 January 1959.

[167] *Musical America*, February 1959.

[168] The composers arranged by Barbirolli are William Byrd ('The Earl of Salisbury's Pavane'), Anon ('The Irish Ho Hoane'), Giles Farnaby ('A Toye' and 'Giles Farnaby's Dreame') and John Bull ('The King's Hunt').

[169] Barbirolli either performed or recorded *An Elizabethan Suite* on no fewer than 147 occasions during the last twenty-nine years of his career.

[170] *The New York Times*, 10 January 1959.

[171] *New York Herald Tribune*, 10 January 1959.

[172] During Barbirolli's 1960 tour of North America, he performed Vaughan Williams's Eighth Symphony, Elgar's 'Enigma' Variations, Arnold's 'Tam O'Shanter' Overture, Delius's Intermezzo from *Fennimore and Gerda*, Purcell's Suite for Strings, Four Horns and Cor Anglais (arr. Barbirolli) and his own *An Elizabethan Suite*.

[173] During Barbirolli's 1968 tour of Central America, South America and the Caribbean, he conducted Britten's *Sinfonia da Requiem*, Walton's Violin Concerto (Martin Milner, violin), Elgar's Second Symphony, Rawsthorne's 'Street Corner' Overture and Piano Concerto No. 2 (Denis Matthews, piano) and Vaughan Williams's *The Lark Ascending*. During the tour, eighteen of the concerts contained a work by a living British composer.

[174] Conversation between the author and Sir John Pritchard, London, 1989.

[175] Karajan recorded Vaughan Williams's *Fantasia on a Theme by Thomas Tallis* and Britten's *Variations on Theme of Frank Bridge* with the Philharmonia Orchestra in the 1950s. He also conducted Britten's *War Requiem* with the Berlin Philharmonic in 1963.

[176] Barbirolli conducted seventy-four public concerts with the Berlin Philharmonic of which twenty-two contained British works. All the British works performed were composed between 1899 and 1943. The composers heard were Elgar (*Introduction and Allegro for Strings*, 'Enigma' Variations and Cello Concerto), Delius (*A Song of Summer*), Vaughan Williams (*Fantasia on a Theme by Thomas Tallis* and Fifth Symphony), Barbirolli (*An Elizabethan Suite*), Britten (*Sinfonia da Requiem*) and Walton (Viola Concerto).

[177] During the 1961–2 season, Barbirolli conducted Delius's Intermezzo from *Fennimore and Gerda* and *A Song of Summer*, Arnold's 'Tam O'Shanter' Overture and Walton's Violin Concerto (Berl Sanofsky, violin).

[178] Living American composers who Barbirolli performed with the Houston Symphony Orchestra included Piston, Floyd, Hovhaness, Copland, Creston, Trubitt, Nelson and Kirk.

[179] A detailed study of Barbirolli's approach to Elgar's music can be found in Essay Six: 'From the Cradle to the Grave: Barbirolli, Elgar and *In the South (Alassio)*'.

ESSAY FOUR

[180] Barbirolli was little more than five feet tall.

[181] Edison's early sound experiments took place in 1877.

[182] Barbirolli's first recording session with his sister was in October 1911 at the Edison Bell Studios at the Elephant and Castle, London.

[183] Barbirolli recorded Casals's *Sardana* with the London Violoncello School for HMV in 1927.

[184] Barbirolli performed Elgar's Cello Concerto at the Winter Gardens, Bournemouth, on 27 January 1921.

[185] For these recordings, Barbirolli worked with leading ensembles, such as the London Symphony Orchestra, the London Philharmonic Orchestra and the New Symphony Orchestra of London.

[186] Rubinstein and Barbirolli recorded Chopin's Second Piano Concerto in 1931, Tchaikovsky's First Concerto in 1932 and Chopin's First Concerto in 1937. All the discs were made with the London Symphony Orchestra.

[187] *The Times*, 23 December 1931.

[188] *The Manchester Guardian*, 16 December 1931.

[189] Ibid.

[190] Purcell's suite was recorded at Carnegie Hall, New York, on 7 February 1938.

[191] *New York World-Telegram*, 7 September 1940.

[192] *The New York Times*, 8 September 1940.

[193] *PM's Weekly*, 2 September 1940.

[194] Over the next twenty-seven years, Barbirolli and the Hallé went on to perform and to record

together on a staggering 3,168 occasions.

[195] *The Gramophone*, February 1944, p. 134.

[196] Barbirolli recorded Mozart's 25th Symphony with the New York Philharmonic-Symphony Orchestra on 3 November 1941 for Columbia.

[197] *The Gramophone*, June 1958, p. 12.

[198] Sir Thomas Beecham and the Royal Philharmonic Orchestra, 1957, Columbia (ML4313). Bruno Walter and the Columbia Symphony Orchestra, 1960, Columbia (ML 5655).

[199] Deutsche Grammophon (Matrix 180bm-186bm; Polydor 6984569848; US Brunswick 25017-25020; Koch CD re-issue 3-7076-2H1; Deutsche Grammophon CD re-issue DG 431874-2).

[200] *The Gramophone*, June 1958, p. 12.

[201] Concert Hall Records (UK) documented Mendelssohn's Fourth Symphony ('Italian') and Rimsky-Korsakov's *Capriccio espagnol* with Barbirolli and the Hallé Orchestra at the Kultur-Casino, Bern, on 13 April 1961; Electrecord set down Schubert's Fifth Symphony with Barbirolli and the Orchestra Filarmonicii 'George Enescu' at the Filarmonica George Enescu, Bucharest, on 16 and 17 September 1961; and Supraphon recorded Franck's Symphony in D minor with Barbirolli and the Czech Philharmonic at the Rudolfinum, Prague, between 23 and 25 March 1962.

[202] A detailed study of Barbirolli's approach to Mahler's music can be found in Essay Nine: 'From Mystery to Monument: Barbirolli, Mahler and the Second Symphony'.

[203] Barbirolli recorded the *Lieder eines fahrenden Gesellen*, the *Rückert-Lieder* and the *Kindertotenlieder* with Janet Baker.

[204] *The Gramophone*, September 1964, p. 133.

[205] Barbirolli recorded Brahms's four symphonies, the 'Academic Festival' and 'Tragic' Overtures and the 'Haydn' Variations with the Vienna Philharmonic for EMI between in 1966 and 1967 at the Grosser Musikvereinssaal, Vienna.

[206] Conversation between the author and Evelyn Barbirolli, London, 19 September 2005.

[207] With the exception of his 1962 recording of the Second Symphony with the Royal Philharmonic Orchestra for *Reader's Digest*, the other discs were all made with the Hallé Orchestra.

[208] Along with the seven symphonies, Barbirolli also recorded *Pohjola's Daughter*, the 'Karelia' Suite, *Valse Triste*, *Pelléas et Mélisande*, *The Swan of Tuonela*, *Lemminkäinen's Return*, *Finlandia*, *Scènes historiques*, *Rakastava* and the Romance in C major.

[209] The recordings were made between 23 January 1966 and 22 May 1970.

[210] Of the recording taken from the performances on 5 and 10 May with Turner, *The Gramophone* reported that she 'completely vanquished the London Philharmonic Orchestra and Puccini's scoring'. *The Gramophone*, August 1937, p. 100.

[211] Barbirolli conducted *Madama Butterfly* on 11 and 12 May 1966 at the Free Trade Hall, Manchester.

[212] *The Gramophone*, September 1967, p. 170.

[213] Ibid.

[214] Ibid.

[215] The cast included James McCracken, Dietrich Fischer-Dieskau and Gwyneth Jones. The orchestra was the New Philharmonia. The recording was made between August and October 1968.

[216] Barbirolli conducted *Otello* on 14 and 16 May 1968 at the Free Trade Hall, Manchester.

ESSAY FIVE

[217] Typed transcript of a 1964 BBC television documentary held at the Royal Academy of Music, London.

[218] Originally called the Australian Broadcasting Company in 1929, the organisation changed its name to the Australian Broadcasting Commission in 1931 before becoming the Australian

Broadcasting Corporation in 1983.

[219] Charles Moses's letter to W. G. James, dated 15 January 1947. National Archive of Australia (NAA), Villawood, New South Wales.

[220] The concerts would consist of '11 original programmes and 14 repeats'. Ibid.

[221] King George VI, Queen Elizabeth and Princess Margaret were scheduled to visit Australia in 1949 but cancelled the tour because of the King's ill health.

[222] ABC internal memo, dated 10 April 1948. NAA.

[223] 'Extract from a report from Dr. [Keith] Barry in London', dated 24 November 1948. NAA.

[224] Ibid.

[225] 'Extract from letter from G[eneral]. M[anager] to Dr. [Keith] Barry, London', dated 10 December 1948. NAA.

[226] Ibid.

[227] Keith Barry's response to a letter from T. W. Bearup. Response dated 7 February [1949]. NAA.

[228] Ibid.

[229] Ibid.

[230] ABC internal memo, recorded 8 March 1949. NAA.

[231] 'Extract from Mr Bearup's letter dated 5th August, 1949'. ABC internal memo, recorded 15 August 1949. NAA.

[232] Telegram from the ABC's London office, dated 9 December 1949. NAA.

[233] [Paul] Klecki was a misspelling of Paul Kletzki.

[234] ABC internal memo by W. G. James for the attention of Sir John Barbirolli, dated 19 July 1950. NAA.

[235] Charles Moses's letter to Sir John Barbirolli, dated 1 August 1950. NAA.

[236] Sir John Barbirolli's letter to Charles Moses, dated 24 August 1950. NAA.

[237] Kenneth Crickmore's undated letter to T. W. Bearup. NAA.

[238] For both the 1950–1 and 1955 tours of Australia, the ABC paid for two return, first-class airfares to Australia and all ABC-related travel within the country for Barbirolli and his wife, Evelyn.

[239] Barbirolli's grandfather, Antonio, was born in Rovigo in 1838; his father, Lorenzo, was born in Padua in 1864, and, his mother Louise, was born in Arcachon, France, in 1870.

[240] Concerning an exchange of orchestras between Sydney and Manchester, Barbirolli said 'it would be a fine thing for the Commonwealth – I mean the British Commonwealth. I think both Governments should realise how very well worthwhile it might be; a project that should surely not frighten us by its boldness; in fact, I think the sum involved would prove negligible compared with the great good it could do … You see, we are really most interested in the suggestion that the Sydney Symphony Orchestra would like to tour Britain. The way I would like to solve the problem is by an exchange with the Halle [sic] Orchestra on the lines that each should take the other's revenue. Besides that, all we would really need would be a grant sufficient to cover the flying part of the trip. We would find ready-made audiences in both countries, there would be no advertising to do, and we would simply take over each other's job. I know the idea has been turned down for the moment, but we have every intention of persevering with it. Yes, I would willingly see anybody in Australia who could help further such a proposition, and you certainly have my permission to say so'. *The ABC Weekly*, 13 January 1951, p. 4.

[241] *Daily Telegraph*, 4 January 1951.

[242] The Brahms symphony was part of the original programme but the other planned works – Rossini's Overture to *La gazza ladra*, Sibelius's *The Swan of Tuonela* and Vaughan Williams's Sixth Symphony – were not in the Conservatorium's library.

[243] *Daily Telegraph*, 29 December 1950.

[244] As found in 'Experts Review Main Events in Past Year', Ibid, 3 January 1951.

[245] *Daily Telegraph*, 30 December 1950.

[246] *Sydney Morning Herald*, 30 December 1950.

[247] *Daily Telegraph*, 6 January 1951.

[248] *Sydney Morning Herald*, 6 January 1951.

[249] Lindsay Hassett (1913–93) and Ken Archer (b. 1928) were both Australian cricketers.

[250] *Daily Mirror*, 8 January 1951.

[251] *Sydney Morning Herald*, 6 January 1951.

[252] *Truth*, 7 January 1951.

[253] *Daily Telegraph*, 11 January 1951.

[254] Ibid.

[255] On 15 January 1951, Barbirolli performed Wagner's Prelude to *Die Meistersinger von Nürnberg*, Mendelssohn's Fourth Symphony ('Italian'), Mozart's 'Batti, batti' from *Don Giovanni* and 'Non so più' from *Le nozze di Figaro* (Lorna McKean, soprano) and Sibelius's Second Symphony.

[256] On 20 February 1951, Barbirolli performed Rossini's Overture to *Semiramide*, Delius's 'The Walk to the Paradise Garden' from *A Village Romeo and Juliet*, Tchaikovsky's *Romeo and Juliet*, Mozart's 29th Symphony and Elgar's 'Enigma' Variations.

[257] *The Courier-Mail*, 16 January 1951.

[258] *The Telegraph*, 22 January 1951.

[259] *The Courier-Mail*, 22 January 1951.

[260] On 26 January 1951, Barbirolli performed his own *An Elizabethan Suite*, Vaughan Williams's Sixth Symphony and Sibelius's Second Symphony.

[261] On 27 January 1951, Barbirolli performed Wagner's Prelude to *Die Meistersinger von Nürnberg*, his own *An Elizabethan Suite*, Johann Strauss II's *Kaiser-Walzer*, Rimsky-Korsakov's *Capriccio espagnol* and Tchaikovsky's Fourth Symphony.

[262] On 28 January 1951, Barbirolli performed Wagner's Prelude to *Die Meistersinger von Nürnberg*, Bizet's Suite from *L'Arlésienne* (number unspecified), Johann Strauss II's *Kaiser-Walzer* and Tchaikovsky's Fourth Symphony.

[263] *Argus*, 27 January 1951.

[264] *Listener In*, 20 January 1951.

[265] The programme also contained Rossini's Overture to *Semiramide*, Mozart's 29th Symphony and Elgar's 'Enigma' Variations.

[266] *The Age*, 12 February 1951.

[267] ABC's financial report, 30 June 1951. NAA.

[268] ABC's telegram to its London office, dated 12 September 1951. NAA.

[269] ABC internal memo, dated 12 December 1951. NAA.

[270] Charles Moses's letter to Sir John Barbirolli, dated 14 May 1952. NAA.

[271] As found in 'Extract from Mr Bearup's Letter Dated 13th June, 1952. Sir John Barbirolli', ABC internal memo, received 19 June 1952. NAA.

[272] The German bass-baritone, Hans Hotter, who also toured Australia in 1955, was particularly appalled by the standard of Australian hotels. Conversation between the author and Hans Hotter's daughter, Gabriele Strauss-Hotter, Garmisch-Partenkirchen, August 1993.

[273] The rental of 'Cherwood' was for two weeks and three days. The cost for the extra three days was £3/3/- per day. Charles Moses's undated draft letter to Evelyn Barbirolli. NAA.

[274] The heating cost was estimated at £2 per week. The rental was for three weeks and the maisonette was retained by the Barbirolli's during their five-day visit to Brisbane. Ibid.

[275] Ibid.

[276] Evelyn Barbirolli's letter to Charles Moses, dated 3 March 1955. NAA.

[277] The Australian first performances given by Barbirolli during the tour were of works by Bates, Geoffrey Bush, Moeran, Finzi, Rubbra, Ibert and Castelnuovo-Tedesco.

[278] The eight works repeated by Barbirolli were Brahms's First Symphony (Adelaide, 1951; Sydney, 1955), Delius's 'The Walk to the Paradise Garden' from *A Village Romeo and Juliet* (Brisbane,

1951; Sydney, 1955), Sibelius's Second Symphony (Brisbane and Melbourne, 1951; Sydney, 1955), Beethoven's Overture to *Egmont* (Adelaide, 1951; Sydney, 1955), Wagner's Prelude to *Die Meistersinger von Nürnberg* (Sydney, 1950, Brisbane and Melbourne, 1951; Adelaide, 1955), Barbirolli's *An Elizabethan Suite* (Melbourne, 1951; Adelaide, 1955), Elgar's 'Enigma' Variations (Brisbane and Melbourne, 1951; Adelaide, 1955) and Tchaikovsky's Fourth Symphony (Sydney and Melbourne, 1951; Brisbane, 1955).

[279] Barbirolli's wife, Evelyn, was his soloist at four concerts in 1955 and also recorded four oboe recitals for broadcast in Melbourne in June that year.

[280] On 11 and 12 May 1955, Barbirolli performed Kabalevsky's Overture to *Colas Breugnon*, Wagner's *Wesendonck Lieder* (Sylvia Fisher, soprano), Bate's Third Symphony and Brahms's First Symphony.

[281] *Sydney Morning Herald*, 12 May 1955.

[282] On 14, 16 and 17 May 1955, Barbirolli performed Geoffrey Bush's 'Yorick' Overture, Delius's 'The Walk to the Paradise Garden' from *A Village Romeo and Juliet*, Strauss's *Tod und Verklärung*, 'Von einem Kahn' from Wagner's *Tristan und Isolde* (Sylvia Fisher, soprano) and Sibelius's Second Symphony.

[283] On 19 May 1955, Barbirolli performed Elgar's *Introduction and Allegro for Strings*, Haydn's 104th Symphony ('London'), Stravinsky's Suite from *L'oiseau de feu* (1919) and Rubbra's Sixth Symphony.

[284] On 21 May 1955, Barbirolli performed Beethoven's Overture to *Egmont*, Moeran's *Serenade*, Castelnuovo-Tedesco's *Concerto da Camera for Oboe and Strings* (Evelyn Rothwell, oboe) and Beethoven's Third Symphony ('Eroica')

[285] *The Bulletin*, 25 May 1955.

[286] *Sydney Morning Herald*, 23 May 1955.

[287] On 26, 27 and 28 May 1955, Barbirolli performed Wagner's Prelude to *Die Meistersinger von Nürnberg*, Mozart's Concerto for Oboe and Orchestra (Evelyn Rothwell, oboe), Moeran's *Serenade*, his own *An Elizabethan Suite* and Elgar's 'Enigma' Variations.

[288] On 4 and 6 June 1955, Barbirolli performed Purcell's (arr. Barbirolli) Suite for Strings, Four Horns, Flute and Cor Anglais, Finzi's *Romance*, Ibert's Suite from *Le chevalier errant* and Dvořák's Seventh Symphony.

[289] On 10 and 11 June 1955, Barbirolli performed Geoffrey Bush's 'Yorick' Overture, Finzi's *Romance*, Mozart's Concerto for Piano and Orchestra No. 20 (Monique Haas, piano) and Tchaikovsky's Fourth Symphony.

[290] On 14 June 1955, Barbirolli performed Rossini's Overture to *La gazza ladra*, Butterworth's *A Shropshire Lad*, Haydn's (arr. Barbirolli) Concerto for Oboe and Orchestra (Jiří Tancibudek, oboe), the 'Liebestod' from Wagner's *Tristan und Isolde* (Sylvia Fisher, soprano) and Stravinsky's Suite from *L'oiseau de feu* (1919).

[291] Ronald Dowd sang the tenor part at Barbirolli's last major choral concert on 16 May 1970. Again, the work was Elgar's *The Dream of Gerontius*.

[292] On 24 and 25 June 1955, Barbirolli performed Geoffrey Bush's 'Yorick' Overture, Finzi's *Romance*, Rachmaninoff's Concerto for Piano and Orchestra No. 2 (Colin Horsley, piano) and Brahms's First Symphony.

[293] 'Copy of Confidential Letter to General Manager from London Representative, Dated 29th May, 1959'. ABC internal memo. NAA.

ESSAY SIX

[294] Barbirolli, 'Forty Years with Elgar's Music', as found in Holden, *Glorious John*, p. 96.

[295] See Essay One: 'In Defence of the Realm: Barbirolli and British Music (Part One)'.

[296] It was not until 7 May 1957 at the Lesser Free Trade Hall, Manchester, that Barbirolli played Elgar's String Quartet (Laurance Turner, violin, Sydney Partington, violin, and Rachel Goodlee, viola) and Quintet for Piano and Strings (Wilfred Parry, piano, Laurance Turner, violin, Sydney Partington, violin, and Rachel Goodlee, viola). That concert was the first of four all-Elgar concerts

that Barbirolli gave that month. On 9 May, he conducted *The Dream of Gerontius* with Norma Procter, Ronald Dowd, Marian Nowakowski, the Montgomery County Music Festival Chorus and the Hallé Orchestra at the County Pavilion, Newtown. And, on 11 and 12 May, he conducted the *Introduction and Allegro for Strings*, the Cello Concerto (Derek Simpson, cello) and the Second Symphony with the Hallé Orchestra at the Town Hall, Middlesbrough, and the City Hall, Newcastle-upon-Tyne, respectively. All of the above performances were given during the centenary of the composer's birth: 1857.

[297] Barbirolli played the second movement of Goltermann's Cello Concerto No. 1 and Saint-Saëns's Cello Concerto (number unknown) with the Trinity College of Music Orchestra at the Queen's Hall on 16 December 1911 and 11 July 1912 respectively. On 14 July 1914, he played Bruch's *Kol Nidrei* with the Royal Academy of Music Orchestra at the same venue.

[298] 27 January 1921.

[299] Richard Strauss, for example, gave the first performance of his Violin Concerto with Benno Walter at the Bösendorfersaal in Vienna on 5 December 1882 and the premiere of his First Horn Concerto with Bruno Hoyer at Munich in March 1883 (exact date and venue unknown) with piano.

[300] At the Aeolian Hall on 12 June 1923, Barbirolli and Craxton played Sammartini's (arr. Salmon) Sonata in G major, Elgar's Cello Concerto, Delius's Sonata for Cello and Piano, Cui's *Cantabile*, Bartlett's *An Ancient Lullaby*, Fauré's (trans. Casals) *Après un rêve* and Popper's *Sérénade espagnole*.

[301] Barbirolli's programme at the New Chenil Galleries on 16 October 1925 consisted of Vivaldi's *Concerto grosso*, Op. 3 No. 4 ('L'estro armonico'), Mozart's *Andante* from *Cassation* No. 2, two unidentified minuets by Rameau, Debussy's *Danse sacrée et danse profane* (Ethel Bartlett, piano) and Elgar's *Elegy for Strings*.

[302] *The Times* critic also reported that the string strength of the orchestra was '4, 3, 2, 2, 1'. In other words, four first violins, three second violins, two violas, two celli and one double-bass. *The Times*, 19 October 1925.

[303] Ibid.

[304] Compton Mackenzie founded *Gramophone* with his brother-in-law, the broadcaster Christopher Stone, in 1923.

[305] *The Gramophone*, April 1928, p. 450.

[306] An undated copy of the composer's note to Compton Mackenzie was made available to the present author by Lady Barbirolli in 2006.

[307] Conversation between the author and Lady Barbirolli, London, 2006.

[308] Barbirolli recorded 'Oh! My Warriors' and 'Leap, Leap to Light' from *Caractacus* on 24 September 1928 and 'Sabbath Morn at Sea' and 'Where Corals Lie' from *Sea Pictures* on 15 April 1929. Barbirolli made his second recording of the *Introduction and Allegro for Strings* with the John Barbirolli Chamber Orchestra on 28 January 1929.

[309] Barbirolli's 1947, 1953 and 1955 recordings of the *Introduction and Allegro for Strings* were all made with the Hallé Orchestra. His 1962 recording was made with the Sinfonia of London.

[310] The programme was comprised of Haydn's 104th Symphony ('London') and Cello Concerto in D major (Pablo Casals, cello) and Elgar's Second Symphony.

[311] Barbirolli and R. Kinloch Anderson, 'Barbirolli talks about the Elgar Second', as found in Holden, *Glorious John*, pp. 108–10.

[312] Ibid.

[313] *The Manchester Guardian*, 13 December 1927.

[314] Kennedy, *Barbirolli: Conductor Laureate*, p. 61.

[315] Barbirolli performed the *Introduction and Allegro for Strings* and the 'Enigma' Variations' at the Usher Hall, Edinburgh, on 16 January and 20 November 1933 respectively.

[316] Barbirolli conducted the Violin Concerto with Adolf Busch at the Usher Hall, Edinburgh, and St. Andrew's Hall, Glasgow, on 27 and 28 November 1933 respectively.

[317] Barbirolli's performances of the Violin Concerto with David McCallum were given at the Usher Hall, Edinburgh, and St. Andrew's Hall, Glasgow, on 19 and 20 November 1934 respectively.

[318] During his career, Barbirolli either performed or recorded Elgar's Second Symphony on 103 occasions, while he either recorded or performed the First on thirty-eight occasions.

[319] Barbirolli performed the *Introduction and Allegro for Strings* twice, the 'Enigma' Variations eleven times, the Violin Concerto four times, 'Pomp and Circumstance' March No. 1 nine times, *Cockaigne (In London Town)* three times, Handel's Overture in D minor (arr. Elgar) three times, the *Elegy for Strings* once, the 'Funeral March' from *Grania and Diarmid* twice, 'In Haven' and 'Where Corals Lie' from the *Sea Pictures* (Mary Jarred, contralto) once each, the Second Symphony three times, the First Symphony once, the *Romance* for Bassoon (A. T. Wood, bassoon) once and the Prelude to *The Light of Life* once. Barbirolli also gave a performance of the First Symphony's Third Movement but that has not been included in the overall statistics for complete performances. 'In Haven' and 'Where Corals Lie' from the *Sea Pictures* have been counted separately.

[320] Barbirolli conducted Elgar's Second Symphony with the London Philharmonic Orchestra at the Colston Hall, Bristol, on 19 March 1937.

[321] The soloist for the Violin Concerto was Albert Sammons.

[322] *The Manchester Guardian*, 16 February 1934.

[323] Ibid.

[324] Ibid.

[325] Ibid.

[326] Elgar died at Worcester on 23 February 1934.

[327] Barbirolli, 'Elgar the Man', as found in Holden, *Glorious John*, pp. 97–9.

[328] 7 and 8 November 1936.

[329] The work was repeated on 5 November 1937.

[330] *The New York Times*, 5 November 1937.

[331] *The Sun*, 5 November 1937.

[332] *New York Post*, 5 November 1937.

[333] Barbirolli gave at least 266 performances of the 'Enigma' Variations during his career.

[334] With the New York Philharmonic-Symphony Orchestra as Music Director, Barbirolli performed the *Introduction and Allegro for Strings* eleven times, the 'Enigma' Variations twenty-one times, the Violin Concerto twice with Jascha Heifetz and once with John Corigliano, Handel's Overture in D minor (arr. Elgar) twice, the Second Symphony twice, *Cockaigne (In London Town)* four times, the Cello Concerto with Gregor Piatigorsky once and the Cello Concerto (arr. Tertis for viola) with Zoltan Kurthy once. These figures include concerts in New York and on tour but do not include Barbirolli's engagements as a guest conductor with other North American orchestras. While the total number of performances of Elgar's works that J.B. gave with the orchestra is not dissimilar to that which he gave with the Scottish Orchestra, it was given over a greater number of concerts and is, therefore, proportionally much less.

[335] *New York Herald Tribune*, 10 November 1940.

[336] Barbirolli conducted the Hallé Orchestra for the first time as a guest conductor on 12 January 1933. The programme included Purcell's (arr. Barbirolli) Suite for Strings, Delius's *In a Summer Garden*, Mozart's 40th Symphony and Franck's Symphony in D minor.

[337] At the King's Hall, Belle Vue, Manchester, on 15 August 1943, Barbirolli conducted Wagner's Prelude to *Lohengrin*, Debussy's *Prélude à l'après-midi d'un faune*, Elgar's 'Enigma' Variations and Tchaikovsky's Fifth Symphony.

[338] Barbirolli conducted Elgar's *Falstaff* for the first time on 28 January 1944 at the City Hall, Sheffield.

[339] For Associated-Rediffusion, Barbirolli performed Elgar's *Nursery Suite* on 23 April 1956, *Cockaigne* on 11 November 1958 and 'Pomp and Circumstance' March No. 4 on 9 June 1959.

[340] Barbirolli also conducted excerpts from the work on seven occasions. The tally of forty-nine

complete performances includes his recording of the work for EMI in 1964.

[341] Barbirolli conducted *The Dream of Gerontius* with the Orchestra Sinfonica Roma at the Auditorium RAI, Rome, on 20 November 1957.

[342] Barbirolli, 'The Dream of Gerontius: a Personal Note', as found in Holden, *Glorious John*, pp. 110–2.

[343] 29 September 1958.

[344] Barbirolli, 'The Dream of Gerontius: a Personal Note', as found in Holden, *Glorious John*, pp. 110–2.

[345] *The Guardian*, 1 May 1970.

[346] As at the concerts at the Free Trade Hall, Manchester, on 30 April and at the City Hall, Sheffield, on 1 May, the concert at the Royal Festival Hall, London, included Bruckner's Eighth Symphony as the companion work to *In the South (Alassio)*.

[347] Barbirolli had conducted the Städtischer Opernhaus- und Museums-Orchester at the Schauspielhaus, Frankfurt am Main, on 22 and 23 March 1970, the Radio-Sinfonieorchester Stuttgart des SWR at the Konzerthaus-Liederhalle, Stuttgart, on 5 April 1970 and the Symphonieorchester des bayerischen Rundfunks at the Herkulessaal, Munich, on 9 and 10 April 1970.

[348] *The Guardian*, 21 May 1970.

[349] Elgar's *In the South* can be heard on BBC Legends 4013. Bruckner's Eighth Symphony, the other work on the programme, can be heard on the same label (4067–2).

[350] On the first page of Walter's annotated score of Mozart's 40th Symphony, for example, he wrote, '*Mein Gott, warum hast Du mich verlassen?*' ('My God, why hast Thou forsaken me?'). Universitätsbibliothek der Universität für Musik und darstellende Kunst, Wien, BW II-38.566.

[351] The British Library holds marked scores of *Falstaff* (Music Collections E.1307.n.), 'Pomp and Circumstance' Marches Nos. 3 and 5 (Music Collections I.348.b. & Music Collections I.348.c.) and *The Dream of Gerontius* (Music Collections E.1307.m. & Music Collections I.348.o.). The score of *In the South (Alassio)* discussed in this essay is part of the author's private collection. The present author was also shown a partially marked score of Elgar's Second Symphony held at the Hallé Orchestra's library. But the minimal number of annotations in that artefact make it highly unlikely that Barbirolli conducted from it. A more detailed description of The British Library's collection of the conductor's marked materials is included in Essay Seven: 'Bruckner 8: Sir John Barbirolli's London Swansong'.

[352] Although Barbirolli had visited German-speaking countries from near the beginning of his career, the 1960s saw him work increasingly closely with many German orchestras, and it was during that decade that he became a regular guest conductor with the Berlin Philharmonic.

[353] Barbirolli conducted from Novello and Company's 1904 full conducting score of *In the South*. All references to figure numbers and page numbers in this essay pertain to that score. A copy of the Novello score can be found online at the IMSLP Petrucci Music Library: https://ks.imslp.net/files/imglnks/usimg/1/1d/IMSLP112638-SIBLEY1802.15836.6252-39087009279466score.pdf.

[354] Conversation between the author and Lady Barbirolli, London, 2006.

[355] Elgar conducted *In the South* with the London Symphony Orchestra on 8 March 1905, 25 November 1912 and 26 April 1926. While it is highly unlikely that the annotation in Barbirolli's marked score refers to the first two performances, it could relate to the third. Barbirolli could well have noted the timing at that concert had he attended. Sir Henry Wood also made similar annotations in his marked scores when observing composers conducting their own works.

[356] The dot after the minim is missing from Barbirolli's inserted metronome mark.

[357] Barbirolli adds hairpin accents (>) above the first violins on the fourth quaver in the fourth bar before Fig. 6, the first and fourth quavers of the third and second bars before Fig. 6 and the first quaver of the first bar before Fig. 6.

[358] Barbirolli also indicates that he beats in three at Fig. 9 (noting '(*immer* 3)' at bars 7 and 8 after

Fig. 9), Fig. 17 (noting '*tranquillo Stesso*'), Fig. 25 (noting '*Quasi 3*'), Fig. 33 (noting 'very gradual'), Fig. 34, Fig. 43 (noting '(small 3 here)'), Fig. 53 (returning to one in a bar at Fig. 54). At Figs. 13 and 46, he reinforces the meter change by inserting the numeral '2' at the beginning of both passages and, at Fig. 20, he writes '*immer Ein*' ('always in one').

[359] By adding a *crescendo-diminuendo* to the second violins in those bars, Barbirolli also rationalises their dynamic with that of the woodwind and celli.

[360] On the tour, Barbirolli conducted Elgar's Second Symphony in Mexico City, Kingston (Jamaica) and Santiago.

[361] Barbirolli and Kennedy, 'Interview with Michael Kennedy', as found in Holden, *Glorious John*, pp. 216–7.

ESSAY SEVEN

[362] Barbirolli, 'Elgar the Man', as found in Holden, *Glorious John*, p. 98.

[363] The programme also included Weber's Overture to *Oberon* and Beethoven's First Piano Concerto (Serge Rachmaninoff, piano). The concert was repeated the following evening.

[364] *New York Mirror*, 11 January 1940.

[365] *New York Herald Tribune*, 11 January 1940.

[366] *The New York Times*, 11 January 1940.

[367] H. J. Wood, *My Life of Music* (London, 1938), p. 174.

[368] Ibid.

[369] Barbirolli conducted Bruckner's Seventh Symphony with the Hallé Orchestra at the Albert Hall, Manchester, on 26 and 27 March 1947. The other works in the programme were Weber's Overture to *Der Freischütz*, Bach's 'Liebster Jesu, mein Verlangen' from Cantata No. 32 and Mozart's Bassoon Concerto (Archie Camden, bassoon).

[370] *The Manchester Guardian*, 27 March 1947.

[371] Ibid.

[372] Ibid.

[373] Barbirolli conducted the Seventh Symphony with the Israel Philharmonic Orchestra on 26, 27, 28, 29 June and 1 and 2 July 1961, the Houston Symphony Orchestra on 20 and 21 November 1961 and the Berlin Philharmonic on 9 and 10 June 1965.

[374] *The Guardian*, 1 May 1970.

[375] Ibid, 21 May 1970.

[376] Ibid.

[377] BBC Legends, 4067–2.

[378] Shelf-marks (Music Catalogue): First to Seventh Symphonies, I.348.f.-l. respectively; Eighth Symphony (pianoforte arrangement), G.1503.bb.; Ninth Symphony, I.348.m.; Tenth Symphony (*Andante*) G.1503.cc..

[379] These include Beethoven's First and Eighth Symphonies, Dvořák's Eighth and Ninth Symphonies, Elgar's First and Second Symphonies, Nielsen's Fourth Symphony, Mozart's 29th and 41st Symphonies, Schubert's Fifth and Ninth Symphonies and Sibelius's First, Second, Third and Seventh Symphonies.

[380] Shelf-mark (Music Catalogue): E.1307.t..

[381] Shelf-mark (Music Catalogue): E.1307.b.. There is also a marked C. F. Peters Edition (Leipzig) conducting score of Beethoven's Ninth Symphony (Shelf-mark (Music Catalogue): G.1503.i.).

[382] Stokowski's recording was made in 1934 and has since been re-released on Music & Arts CD 846.

[383] i. Haas (Fourth Symphony): *Anton Bruckner Sämtliche Werke, 4. Band*, VEB Breitkopf & Härtel Musikverlag, Leipzig (Nr. 3618). Shelf-mark (Music Catalogue): E.1307.g..

ii. Gutmann (Seventh Symphony): *Eulenburg's kleine Orchester-Partitur-Ausgabe Symphonien No. 65*, Ernst Eulenburg, Leipzig. Shelf-mark (Music Catalogue): E.1307.h..

iii. Nowak (Ninth Symphony): *Anton Bruckner Sämtliche Werke, Musikwissenshaftlicher Verlag der Internationalen Bruckner-Gesellschaft, Wein 1951* (copyright 1959). Shelf-mark (Music Catalogue): E.1307.i..

[384] Shelf-mark (Music Catalogue): G.1503.s.. The score measures 24.4 cm. x 33 cm..

[385] Those that were inserted before the score was enlarged.

[386] *Anton Bruckner Sämtliche Werke, 8. Band, Brucknerverlag Wiesbaden G.M.B.H.*, 1949.

[387] From some of the annotations, it is unclear whether Barbirolli considered conducting a performance of the Nowak edition. In the first movement, above the first violins' material (bars 169 with the anacrustic semiquaver to 171), for example, he writes before enlargement: '*Trem[olo]* cont.[inued] [underline inserted after enlargement] in Haas wind only'. This passage was bracketed before enlargement but, later, bowed in pencil; the material is then crossed-through in pencil.

[388] In the *Adagio*, Barbirolli pencils in the first clarinet's B in bar 66 (last quaver) — the bar numbers in this essay match those found in the Nowak edition — and the first violins' material in bar 160. Curiously, in the first movement, he does not correct the horn passage in bars 101 and 102, or its derivative in bars 345 and 346; these corrections are, however, in the orchestral parts and can be heard in the recording.

[389] These were inserted in short score and correspond to the following in the Haas edition:

i. *Adagio* bars 209 to 218 inclusive. This insertion is sellotaped between pp. 92 and 93 and measures 24.3 cm. x 23.1 cm.. It is written in black ink with the annotations marked in pencil. There are two systems of four staves each (one stave empty).

ii. Finale bars 211 to 231 inclusive. Barbirolli draws a vertical line in pencil between bars 210 and 211 (Nowak); he crosses through bars 211 to 214 (Nowak) and inserts an arrow above them in pencil. He writes, on the bar line that divides bars 211 and 212 (Nowak), 'Haas 15 [*sic*] longer here'. This manuscript insertion is sellotaped between pp. 122 and 123 and measures 24.8 cm. x 31.4 cm.. It is written in black ink with the annotations marked in pencil. There are four systems of three staves each.

iii. Finale bars 253 to 258 inclusive. This insertion is glued to the top left-hand corner of p. 123 and measures 19.7 cm x 12.7 cm.. It is written in black ink with the annotations inserted in pencil and blue ink. There is one system of three staves (one stave blank). At the bottom right-hand corner of p.123, Barbirolli brackets bars 237 and 238 (Nowak) and writes: 'Haas 4 bars longer here'.

iv. Finale bars 583 to 598 inclusive. This insertion is sellotaped between bars 562 and 563 (Nowak) and measures 24.5 cm. x 26.3 cm.. It is written in black ink with the annotations inserted in pencil, blue pencil and blue ink. There are three systems of three staves each (one stave blank). Barbirolli draws a bracket in pencil beside bar 567 (left-hand side, Nowak) and writes: 'Haas edition [illegible] more bars here.'

v. Finale bars 609 to 616 inclusive. This insertion is sellotaped and glued over the top system of p. 156 (oboes exposed) and measures 14.2 cm. x 10.9 cm.. It is written in black ink and pencil with the annotations inserted in pencil and blue ink. There is one system of three staves. Barbirolli crosses out the superscription, *viel langsamer*, in bar 583 (Nowak) and writes: 'Not in Haas..'.

vi. Finale bars 671 to 675 inclusive. This insertion is sellotaped to the bottom right-hand corner of p. 161 and measures 24.5 cm. x 15.6 cm.. It is written in black ink with the annotations inserted in pencil. There is one system of four staves (one stave blank).

[390] In the Finale, Barbirolli annotates the following doublings: the second bass tuba with the double-basses (bars 557 to 560 beat 1 first half), and the second tenor tuba with the second bass tuba (bars 652 to 656 inclusive). The first was inserted before enlargement, while the second was inserted before enlargement and, later, confirmed in pencil. Of these, only the latter can be verified from the recording. But Bruckner was strongly against such modifications and implored Weingartner 'not to alter the score and it is one of my most burning wishes to have the orchestral parts printed without alterations.' As found in E. Doernberg, *The Life and Symphonies of Anton Bruckner* (London, 1960), p. 118.

[391] *a2* meaning two instruments to a part and *a4* meaning four instruments to a part.

[392] Strauss, in his 1926 recording of Mozart's 39th Symphony with the Berlin Staatskapelle, for example, differentiates between the first movement's first and second subjects by applying a *meno mosso* at the arrival of the latter: ♩. = 52 (bars 26–53) to ♩. = 48 (bar 98). Further, the speed at the opening of the Introduction (♪ = 96 [♩ = 48]) is related to both the first movement's second subject (♩. = 48) and the overall pulse of the Finale (♩ = 144). Moreover, his tempo at bar 25 (second half) of the Introduction (♪ = 92) is the speed of the second movement's first subject; while his pulse at the first movement's first subject (♩. = 52) is related to the speed of the bridge passage in the *Andante* (♪ = 104). Deutsche Grammophon Matrix 347bg-352bg; single side nos. B20640-1-2-3-4-5; Polydor 69833-69835; Heliodor LP re-issue 88022; Koch CD re-issue 3-7076-2H1.

[393] It could be argued, however, that the speed at bar 67 (♩ = 63) undermines this tempo scheme. As this speed is transitory rather than architectonic, this thesis cannot be sustained. That said, the pulse at this bar is significant for two reasons: first, the *accelerando* between bars 59 and 67, followed by the *rallentando* from bar 69, emphasises the contour of the arched dynamic within the second theme area; and, second, the tempo at bar 67 acts as a kind of fulcrum, balancing the tempo of the second theme's statement in bar 51 with its restatement in bar 74.

[394] As the first theme group is modified significantly in the recapitulation (bar 225), Barbirolli directs it at ♩ = 58, the tempo of the third theme group.

[395] This impression is strengthened from bar 107, where Barbirolli consciously sets out to confuse the ear by taking a marginally broader tempo.

[396] At the reprise of the *Trio*'s opening material, Barbirolli returns to ♪ = 88–92.

[397] Beside ♩ = 69, Barbirolli writes in pencil after enlargement: '(too slow)'.

[398] At the second theme group, Barbirolli sets up a complex series of tempo relationships that have wider implications. This theme group can be divided into three sub-sections: bars 69 to 98; bars 99 to 110, and bars 111 to 122. These sub-sections are linked melodically and, from the printed tempo instructions, must be realised symmetrically. But as these speeds were only part of Barbirolli's overall scheme, it was necessary to adjust his tempi in the following manner. First, to achieve greater structural definition between bar 69 and bar 99, the rise from ♩ = 58 at bar 69 to ♩ = 63 at bar 95 was imperative. Second, the new speed at bar 99 (♩ = 88) acts as a foil to the tempo that immediately precedes and succeeds this sub-section (♩ = 63). Third, the speed at bar 99 is directly related to that heard at bar 183 (♩ = 84–8) and closely linked to that of the first theme (♩ = 84).

[399] For Barbirolli's thoughts and definition of *melos*, see Essay Ten: 'Barbirolli on the Art and Craft of Conducting'.

[400] Above the trombone staves.

[401] On the tuba staves.

[402] These accents are inserted above the horn, tuba and trumpet staves (beat 3 second quaver & beat 4 first and second quavers).

[403] This annotation was inserted before enlargement and is faint. In a similar passage, from bar 129 (with the anacrustic semiquaver), '*Punta*', also inserted before enlargement, is reinforced in pencil.

[404] Barbirolli maintains the last printed up-bow in bar 1 (beat 4 second half).

[405] In bar 2, Barbirolli inserts '*sim.[ile]*', indicating that these instruments should continue bar 1's bowing pattern.

[406] Barbirolli shapes the first violins' *crescendo-diminuendo* in bars 3 and 4 asymmetrically. The *decrescendo*'s decay is brief, highlighting the semitone's melodic rise and fall at the end of the phrase.

[407] Between bars 130 and 133. In bar 129 (first half), Barbirolli marks two up-bows.

[408] When beaten in four.

[409] *The Guardian*, 21 May 1970.

ESSAY EIGHT

[410] As found in Holden, *Elder on Music*, p. 128.

[411] Anthony Collins's complete set of Sibelius's symphonies with the London Symphony Orchestra from 1952 to 1955 was the second on record. The first set was with Sixten Ehrling and the Stockholm Philharmonic from 1952 and 1953.

[412] Wood, *My Life of Music*, p. 206.

[413] 1937.

[414] Wood, *My Life of Music*, p. 206.

[415] *The Scotsman*, 3 January 1933.

[416] Barbirolli conducted Sibelius's *Finlandia* on 9 January 1933 (Usher Hall, Edinburgh), 22 November 1933 (St. Andrew's Hall, Glasgow), 10 January 1934 (St. Andrew's Hall, Glasgow), 27 January 1934 (St. Andrew's Hall, Glasgow) and 26 December 1934 (Usher Hall, Edinburgh).

[417] *The Scotsman*, 10 January 1933.

[418] 26 December 1934 at the Usher Hall, Edinburgh.

[419] *The Scotsman*, 27 December 1934.

[420] Barbirolli then performed Sibelius's Second Symphony at the Usher Hall, Edinburgh, on 16 January 1933.

[421] *The Scotsman*, 4 January 1933.

[422] Barbirolli conducted the Fifth Symphony at the Usher Hall, Edinburgh, and St. Andrew's Hall, Glasgow, on 11 and 12 December 1933 respectively.

[423] *The Scotsman*, 12 December 1933.

[424] Ibid, 13 December 1933.

[425] Ibid, 4 October 1934.

[426] Barbirolli had already conducted Sibelius's First Symphony with the Leeds Symphony Orchestra at Leeds Town Hall on 21 October 1933 and with the Eastbourne Municipal Orchestra at the Devonshire Park Theatre, Eastbourne, on 23 November 1933. He then went on to give it twice with the Resident Orchestra of The Hague on 18 and 19 March 1936.

[427] *The Scotsman*, 12 November 1934.

[428] Ibid.

[429] Ibid.

[430] Ibid, 8 January 1935.

[431] Ibid, 2 February 1937.

[432] Given at the Usher Hall, Edinburgh, on 8 February 1937, the concert also contained Mendelssohn's 'Hebrides' Overture, Mozart's 34th Symphony and Brahms's Fourth Symphony.

[433] Barbirolli had performed *The Swan of Tuonela* with the Scottish Orchestra at St. Andrew's Hall, Glasgow, on 16 January 1934. He then gave the work in the same hall on 16 February 1937 (along with *Lemminkäinen's Return*). Between these performances he conducted *Pohjola's Daughter* for the first time with the Scottish Orchestra at St. Andrew's Hall, Glasgow, on 18 December 1934.

[434] *The Scotsman*, 9 February 1937.

[435] At St. Andrew's Hall on 16 February 1937, the programme included Mozart's Overture to *Die Zauberflöte* Brahms's Concerto for Piano and Orchestra No. 2 (Arthur Rubinstein, piano), Delius's *In a Summer Garden* Chopin's *Scherzo* in C sharp minor and *Études* Op. 25 No. 1 and Op. 10 No. 4 (Arthur Rubinstein, piano), Ravel's *Alborada del gracioso* and Sibelius's *The Swan of Tuonela* and *Lemminkäinen's Return*.

[436] *The Scotsman*, 17 February 1937.

[437] This figure does not included the New York Symphony Orchestra's performances of Sibelius's works but does include performances given at Lewisohn Stadium by the Philharmonic.

[438] The Seventh Symphony was given by Otto Klemperer with the Stadium Symphony Orchestra on

13 and 16 January 1927.

[439] Barbirolli's first concerts as a guest conductor with the New York Philharmonic-Symphony-Orchestra were given at Carnegie Hall on 5 and 6 November 1936.

[440] *Mid-Week Pictorial* reported: 'By the time of their first rehearsal together, members of the orchestra had grown to revere and love Barbirolli. Today he is reported to be one of the most popular conductors they have had. Within a few weeks he won their respect and affection, as he has won the acclaim of critics and of his national radio audience'. *Mid-Week Pictorial*, 9 December 1936, p. 37.

[441] Barbirolli conducted the Violin Concerto (Jascha Heifetz, violin) on 3 and 4 December 1936 and the First Symphony on 17, 18 and 27 December 1936. All five performances were given at Carnegie Hall.

[442] Barbirolli gave ten performances of the First Symphony and three of the Third Symphony in North America between 1937 and 1943.

[443] *Valse triste* was given by Barbirolli with the Philharmonic Orchestra of Los Angeles on 29 November 1942.

[444] *The New York Times*, 20 December 1937.

[445] *New York World-Telegram*, 20 December 1937.

[446] Barbirolli conducted the Violin Concerto with Efrem Zimbalist as soloist on 3, 4 and 6 March 1938 and the Third Symphony on 30 March and 1 April 1938.

[447] *The New York Times*, 31 March 1938.

[448] Rodzinski conducted the Second Symphony on 25, 26, 27 and 28 February 1937 with the New York Philharmonic-Symphony Orchestra at Carnegie Hall.

[449] Barbirolli's appointment as Music Director of the New York Philharmonic-Symphony Orchestra was announced in the American press at the end of 1936, but he did not actually take up the position until the November of the following year.

[450] *The New York Times*, 4 November 1938.

[451] Arturo Toscanini conducted Sibelius's Fourth Symphony on 19, 20, 21 and 22 March 1931 and on 22 and 23 February 1934 with the New York Philharmonic-Symphony Orchestra.

[452] Barbirolli conducted the First Symphony on 4 October 1944, the Second Symphony on 1 November 1944, the Third Symphony on 29 November 1944, the Fourth Symphony on 14 February 1945, the Fifth Symphony on 14 March 1945, the Sixth Symphony on 11 April 1945 and the Seventh Symphony on 25 April 1945. All performances were given at the Albert Hall, Manchester. Barbirolli conducted all seven symphonies again in the 1949–50 season at the same venue.

[453] *The Manchester Guardian*, 15 February 1945.

[454] Conversation between the author and Herbert von Karajan, Salzburg, July 1989.

[455] Barbirolli conducted Sibelius's Sixth Symphony at the Albert Hall, Manchester, on 11 April 1945 and on 22 and 23 March 1950, and at the Free Trade Hall, Manchester, on 3 May 1970.

[456] *The Manchester Guardian*, 12 April 1945.

[457] *The Sun*, 7 December 1940.

[458] *The New York Times*, 4 February 1943.

[459] *New York World-Telegram*, 6 February 1943.

[460] Barbirolli recorded the Second Symphony (1949), the Fifth Symphony (1952) and *The Swan of Tuonela* (1955) for HMV and the Fifth Symphony (1957), *Valse triste* (1957), the First Symphony (1957) and *Pohjola's Daughter* (1958) for Pye.

[461] *Gramophone*, October 1976. (*The Gramophone* became *Gramophone* from the June 1969 issue.)

[462] Ibid, June 1991.

[463] *Hi-Fi News*, February 1967.

[464] *Records and Recordings*, April 1967.

[465] Ibid, September 1970.

ESSAY NINE

[466] The rehearsal to which Barbirolli was referring preceded a performance of Mahler's Fourth Symphony conducted by Oskar Fried at a 'B.B.C. concert' at the Queen's Hall, London, on 4 April 1930. *The Times*, 5 April 1930.

[467] Barbirolli to D. C. Parker, as found in Kennedy, *Barbirolli Conductor Laureate*, p. 76.

[468] Sir Henry Wood conducted the First Symphony, the Fourth Symphony and the *Adagietto* from the Fifth Symphony at the Proms between 1903 and 1934. Sir Hamilton Harty conducted Mahler's Ninth Symphony with the Hallé Orchestra on 27 February 1930 followed by *Das Lied von der Erde* on 11 December 1930. He had previously given the Fourth Symphony with the orchestra on 24 November 1927.

[469] After a performance of Mahler's Sixth Symphony on 26 July 1965 at the Royal Albert Hall, London, Barbirolli was presented with the Gustav Mahler Medal of Honor [*sic*] at the request of the Bruckner Society of America. The concert was part of the 1965 Proms and the orchestra was the Hallé. https://www.bbc.co.uk/events/ev58gw.

[470] Barbirolli performed the *Kindertotenlieder* with the Orchestra of the Royal Philharmonic Society on 29 January 1931.

[471] *The Times*, 30 January 1931.

[472] Barbirolli gave the local premiere of the *Adagietto* from the Fifth Symphony at Glasgow's St. Andrew's Hall on 21 November 1933.

[473] *The Scotsman*, 22 November 1933.

[474] Barbirolli conducted the *Adagietto* from the Fifth Symphony with the New York Philharmonic-Symphony Orchestra at Carnegie Hall on 26 and 27 October and on 16 and 17 December 1939. He also conducted it with the Cincinnati Symphony Orchestra on 13 February 1942 and the Chicago Symphony Orchestra on 4 and 5 February 1943.

[475] *The New York Times*, 27 October 1939.

[476] Barbirolli conducted *Das Lied von der Erde* at Sheffield, Bradford, Manchester (twice), Huddersfield and Birmingham between 9 and 30 April 1946. He then gave a further ten performances of the work with the Hallé Orchestra between 1952 and 1968 with Kathleen Ferrier (1952), Kerstin Meyer (1957), Janet Baker (1968), Richard Lewis (1952 and 1957) and Ronald Dowd (1968) as soloists. Barbirolli conducted the *Adagietto* at Manchester (twice), Bradford, Wolverhampton, Leicester and Hanley between 2 and 24 October 1946.

[477] This tally includes *Das Lied von der Erde* but not the other song cycles or individual songs with orchestra.

[478] *Houston Post*, 20 March 1962.

[479] Mahler's works were heard at 6.2% of Barbirolli's concerts with the Houston Symphony Orchestra and at only 2.6% of his concerts with the Hallé Orchestra.

[480] Barbirolli made his debut with the Berlin Philharmonic at the Edinburgh Festival on 22 August 1949 and conducted it on a further seventy-seven occasions either at Berlin, on tour or in the recording studio.

[481] Barbirolli conducted the Second Symphony with the Radio-Sinfonieorchester Stuttgart des SWR at the Konzerthaus-Liederhalle, Stuttgart.

[482] W. Stresemann, … *und abends in die Philharmonie: Erinnerungen an grosse Dirigenten* (Munich, 1981), p. 237.

[483] Barbirolli recorded Mahler's First Symphony for Pye on 11 and 12 June 1957 at the Free Trade Hall, Manchester.

[484] *The Gramophone*, September 1957, pp. 137–8.

[485] Ibid.

[486] Ibid.

[487] Barbirolli recorded Mahler's Ninth Symphony with the Berlin Philharmonic on 10, 11, 14 and 16 January 1964 at Jesus-Christuskirche, Berlin, for HMV.

[488] *The Gramophone*, September 1964, p. 133.

[489] Ibid.

[490] Ibid.

[491] Ibid.

[492] *Gramophone*, December 2002, p. 59.

[493] Ibid.

[494] Barbirolli conducted Mahler's Ninth Symphony with the Berlin Philharmonic at the Konzertsaal der Hochschule für Musik, Berlin, 4 and 5 January 1963.

[495] Barbirolli recorded Mahler's Sixth Symphony with the New Philharmonia Orchestra at the Kingsway Hall, London, between 17 and 19 August 1967.

[496] *The Gramophone*, July 1968, pp. 153–4.

[497] *Gramophone*, October 1996, p. 56.

[498] Barbirolli recorded *Lieder eines fahrenden Gesellen* and the *Kindertotenlieder* with Janet Baker and the Hallé Orchestra at Studio One, Abbey Road, London, between 4 May and 13 July 1967. At those sessions they also recorded 'Ich bin der Welt abhanden gekommen' from the *Rückert-Leider*. Then, between 16 and 18 July 1968, Barbirolli recorded the complete *Rückert-Lieder* and the Fifth Symphony with Janet Baker and the New Philharmonia Orchestra for the same company at the Town Hall, Watford.

[499] 15 July 1969. The programme also included Haydn's 83rd Symphony ('*La poule*').

[500] *The Gramophone*, December 1969, pp. 967–8.

[501] In the German-speaking countries, Mahler's music was heard regularly after his death. Modern commentators frequently stress the notion that these works were often neglected before the 1960s. But their inclusion at 8% of the Berlin Philharmonic's concerts during the 1920–1 season suggests that further research is needed before any conclusions can be drawn. That said, Mahler's music was heard less frequently in Britain during the first half of the twentieth century, and when Wilhelm Furtwängler asked to perform a Mahler symphony at his debut with the Royal Philharmonic Society in 1924, his request was denied because it was felt that the work would attract a small audience. For performance data concerning Mahler's music during the nineteenth and early twentieth centuries, cf. R. Holden, *The Virtuoso Conductors* (London and New Haven, 2005).

[502] Barbirolli conducted 266 performances of the 'Enigma' Variations and 228 performances of Brahms's Second Symphony.

[503] Barbirolli conducted Mahler's Second Symphony on 14 and 15 May 1958. For both performances at the Free Trade Hall, Manchester, with the Hallé Orchestra and Choir, the soloists were Joan Sutherland (soprano) and Eugenia Zareska (mezzo-soprano). The first of these performances was also Barbirolli's first of the symphony.

[504] *The Manchester Guardian*, 15 May 1958.

[505] Barbirolli's 1970 performance with the Radio-Symphonieorchester Stuttgart is available on EMI Classics (72435751002) and his 1965 performance with the Berlin Philharmonic is available on Testament (SBT2 1320).

[506] Barbirolli adds some additional breath-marks to the vocal parts in the bars after Fig. 31 in the last movement.

[507] O. Klemperer, ed. P. Heyworth, *Conversations with Klemperer* (London, 1985), p. 34.

[508] As found in Kennedy, *Barbirolli Conductor Laureate*, p. 147.

[509] Klemperer recalled 'I met him [Mahler] twice in Berlin. The first time was in 1905 when [Oscar] Fried was conducting his Second Symphony and asked me to conduct the off-stage orchestra. Mahler came to the last rehearsal, and afterwards I went to him and asked. "Excuse me, but was it all right?" He said, "No, it was terrible. It was too loud. It should sound very quietly from behind."

I said, "But it says *sehr schmetternd* [very blaring] in the score." He replied, "But from a long way away; it was much too close." It wasn't possible to get that far away, so I said to the musicians. "Play it *piano*: the whole thing." They did so and the performance was an enormous success. Mahler embraced Fried on the stage and when he came into the artists' room he shook my hand and said, "Very good." I was proud'. Klemperer, *Conversations*, pp. 29–30.

[510] The words in brackets were crossed out by Barbirolli.

[511] Taken from an unidentified extract of an interview given by Barbirolli to *Die Welt* held at the Royal Academy of Music, London.

ESSAY TEN

[512] *Über das Dirigieren* (*On Conducting*) was first published in the *Neue Zeitschrift für Musik* and the *New Yorker Musik-Zeitung* in 1869. It was later incorporated into the *Gesammelte Schriften und Dichtungen von Richard Wagner* (Leipzig, 1871–83). http://www.gutenberg.org/cache/epub/4523/pg4523.txt.

[513] In *On Conducting*, Wagner wrote that 'whole duty of a conductor is comprised in his ability always to indicate the right *tempo*' and that 'the right comprehension of the melos is the sole guide to the right tempo'. Ibid.

[514] Barbirolli, 'Speech to the New York Philharmonic-Symphony League on 1 November 1938', as found in Holden, *Glorious John*, p. 136.

[515] F. Weingartner, *On Conducting*, trans. E. Newman (London, 1906), p. 5.

[516] Szymon Goldberg was the leader of the Berlin Philharmonic between 1929 and 1934.

[517] As found in H-H. Schönzeler, *Furtwängler* (London, 1990), p. 155.

[518] Wagner, *On Conducting*. http://www.gutenberg.org/cache/epub/4523/pg4523.txt.

[519] Wagner explored these issues in his 1873 article, *Zum Vortrage der neunten Symphonie Beethoven's* (*Performing Beethoven's Ninth Symphony*).

[520] B. Walter, trans. P. Hamburger, *Of Music and Music-making* (London, 1961), pp. 136–40.

[521] W. Furtwängler, *Notebooks 1924–1954*, trans. S. Whiteside, ed. M. Tanner (London 1995), pp. 46–7.

[522] For a more detailed description of Barbirolli's thoughts on Toscanini and Brahms, please refer to Essay Nine: 'From Mystery to Monument: Barbirolli, Mahler and the Second Symphony'.

[523] For a more detailed description of Barbirolli's approach to Bruckner and Mahler, please refer to Essays Seven and Nine, 'Bruckner 8: Sir John Barbirolli's London Swansong' and 'From Mystery to Monument: Barbirolli, Mahler and the Second Symphony'.

[524] In Wood's marked score, held at the Royal Academy of Music, the bassoon's material is replicated in the horns in black ink with the word, 'Nobly', written and circled above the stave. In Pritchard's score, part of the author's private collection, the emendation is indicated by '+ Hn' being added in blue pencil on the horns' stave.

[525] The film of Barbirolli conducting Brahms's Second Symphony with the Boston Symphony Orchestra is available on a commercial DVD published by VAI Music.

[526] Barbirolli, 'Speech to the New York Philharmonic-Symphony League on 1 November 1938', as found in Holden, *Glorious John*, p. 136.

[527] Ibid, p. 137.

[528] Ibid.

[529] H. J. Wood, *About Conducting* (London, 1945), p. 70.

[530] Two of Barbirolli's batons are held at the Royal Academy of Music, London; they measure 449 and 450 millimetres respectively.

[531] Walter, *Of Music and Music-making*, pp. 136–40.

[532] Barbirolli, 'Speech to the New York Philharmonic-Symphony League on 1 November 1938', as found in Holden, *Glorious John*, p. 139.

[533] Ibid.

NOTES

[534] Barbirolli regularly lectured on various aspects of conducting on both sides of the Atlantic, including speeches to the New York Philharmonic-Symphony League in 1938 and 1939.

[535] Barbirolli, 'Speech to the New York Philharmonic-Symphony League on 1 November 1938', as found in Holden, *Glorious John*, p. 137.

[536] Ibid.

[537] Ibid, p. 139.

[538] Ibid, p. 138.

[539] A. Boult, *Thoughts on Conducting* (London, 1963), p. 36.

[540] Barbirolli, 'Speech to the New York Philharmonic-Symphony League on 1 November 1938', as found in Holden, *Glorious John*, p. 139.

[541] R. Strauss, ed. W. Schuh and trans. L. J. Lawrence, *Recollections and Reflections* (London, 1953), p. 121.

[542] Weingartner, *On Conducting*, p. 43.

[543] Walter, *Of Music and Music-making*, pp. 131–2.

[544] Barbirolli, 'Speech to the New York Philharmonic-Symphony League on 1 November 1938', as found in Holden, *Glorious John*, p. 139.

[545] Ibid, p. 141.

[546] Barbirolli's original typed text read 'make his watchwords' but he later crossed this out and added in pencil 'realise the mental & physical discipline & strength required & to make his watchwords'. Ibid, p. 142.

[547] Ibid.

APPENDIX ONE

[548] The information in this table has been restricted to passages of structural and interpretative importance.

INDEX

Aberdeen, 29, 35, 36

Aberdeen Journal, 35

Adelaide, 71, 72, 77–8, 80, 81

Adorno, Theodor, 117

Aeolian Hall, 19, 84

Age, The, 78

Ahne Carse, Adam von, 53

Albert Hall (Manchester), 124

Alhambra Theatre (Bradford), 34

Alwyn, William, 50

America, United States of, 24, 26, 40, 45–8,
    49, 51–3, 54–5, 57, 59, 60–1, 69, 83,
    90–1, 93, 102, 103, 121–4, 126, 133

Angeles, Victoria de los, 66

Anson, Hugo, 19

Arcadia, 138

Archer, Ken, 75

Aristotle, 101

Arnaud, Yvonne, 59

Arnold, Malcolm, 50, 52, 54;
    'Tam O'Shanter' Overture, 52

Arts Council of Great Britain, 29, 43

Associated-Rediffusion, 92–3

Atlanta, 52

Austin, Frederic, 22–3, 34; Sonata for Cello,
    23; *Paalsgard*, 23; *Spring*, 23

Austral, Florence, 64

Australia, 49, 69–82, 93, 141

Australian Broadcasting Commission (ABC),
    69–82

Austria, 24, 43, 69, 103, 106, 139

Bach, Johann Sebastian, 25; *Ouvertüren*, 25;
    'Brandenburg' Concertos, 25; Cello
    Suites, 25; *Das wohltemperierte Klavier*,
    25

Backhaus, Wilhelm, 59

Bad Homburg, 19

Baker, Janet, 58, 93, 137

Barbirolli, Evelyn, 44, 45, 46, 73, 77, 80, 96,
    144

Barbirolli, John, as a cellist, 17, 19, 23, 29,
    34, 57, 67, 72, 83–4, 87, 90, 111,
    130, 155; as a champion of British
music, 17–27, 45–55, 57, 61–2, 74–6,
78, 80–1, 83–100; early professional
and conducting experiences, 18–9,
20–3; as an opera conductor, 18, 22–3,
25, 29–44, 57, 65–7, 84, 87, 118; as an
orchestral cellist, 18, 25, 29, 30, 65,
90, 153; as a chamber musician, 17–9,
23, 47, 57–8, 59, 155; as a champion
of new music, 17–27, 45–55, 61–2, 75,
76, 78, 80–1; as a recording artist, 19,
20, 23, 25, 29, 41, 46, 47, 48, 50, 57–67,
83–6, 126–8, 133–8, 150–1, 152; as a
soldier in the British army, 19–20, 29,
84; adaptability and quickness to learn,
20; lack of keyboard skills, 20; as a
conductor of chamber orchestras, 20–5,
47, 58, 84–86, 118; orchestral sound,
21; programming, 21, 26–7, 31, 39–40,
45–55, 75, 76, 77–8, 79, 80, 88, 91, 103,
118–25, 131, 132, 155; as conductor of
the Scottish Orchestra, 23, 25–7, 39–40,
47, 88–9, 118–21, 130; as conductor of
the Hallé Orchestra, 23, 24, 25, 40–1,
42, 43, 47–51, 53, 57, 58, 61–2, 63, 64,
65, 66, 67, 69, 70, 71, 72, 73, 75, 76, 78,
80, 82, 86, 89, 91–2, 94–6, 100, 103–5,
115, 124–5, 127–8, 131, 132, 133, 134,
135, 137, 139, 142, 150, 151; conducting
technique, 26, 32, 35, 36, 37, 38, 39, 46,
59, 91, 134–5, 149–58; responsibilities
as a music director, 26; educational
responsibilities of conductors, 26, 34,
39, 62, 67, 92, 93, 157; spiritual content
of music, 26; family members and
antecedents, 27, 29, 33, 42, 66, 67, 73,
87, 89, 94; impact of Puccini, 29–31, 66;
as a trainer of orchestras, 38, 48, 59–60,
61, 73, 76, 84, 86, 91–2, 125, 133, 135–6,
139; as conductor of the New York
Philharmonic-Symphony Orchestra,
38, 40, 45–8, 51–3, 60–1, 64, 90–1, 102,
121–4, 126, 130, 138, 155; as conductor
of the Houston Symphony Orchestra,
40, 54–5, 57, 82, 103, 131–2; as one

of Benjamin Britten's 'corpses', 46–7;
wartime concerts in Britain and Europe,
47, 49, 57, 61, 91–2; as an arranger, 23,
52, 77, 81; *An Elizabethan Suite*, 52, 77,
81; string sound, 52, 58, 64, 65, 67, 77,
84, 86, 91, 111–4, 140–3; as a performer
of American music, 54; as a violinist,
57; religious and spiritual beliefs, 58,
93–4, 138, 157; personal, eating and
musical idiosyncrasies, 72–3, 79–80;
score preparation and the marking and
annotating of performance materials,
95–100, 105–15, 139–47, 149, 154–5;
seating arrangements of orchestras, 155–
6; on conducting from memory, 156–7
Barbirolli, Rosa, 57, 58
Barbirolli Society, The, 138
Barenboim, Daniel, 64
Bartlett, Ethel, 19, 34
Basel, 105
Bate, Stanley, 50, 80–1; Third Symphony,
80–1
Bavagnoli, Gaetano, 30
Bax, Arnold, 21, 22, 27, 45, 50, 52, 61, 62;
Romantic Overture, 22; Third Symphony,
61
BBC Classics, 138
BBC Legends, 86, 95, 104
BBC Symphony Orchestra, 25, 74, 78
BBC Television Service, 92
Beecham, Thomas, 22, 24, 25, 29, 57, 59, 62,
65, 69, 70, 86, 87, 90, 117, 134, 140, 143
Beethoven, Ludwig van, 25, 45, 71, 78, 81,
89, 92, 101, 102, 105, 117, 124, 150–1,
152; complete piano sonatas, 25;
Overture to *Fidelio*, 71; First Symphony,
71; Overture to *Egmont*, 78; Third
Symphony ('Eroica'), 81; Overture
to *Coriolan*, 81; Ninth Symphony
('Choral'), 105; last quartets, 124; Fifth
Symphony, 150–1, 152
Belgium, 19
Bell, Donald, 93
Bellezza, Vincenzo, 36
Bergonzi, Carlo, 66
Berkeley, Lennox, 50
Berlin, 17, 53–4, 69, 82, 134, 137, 144, 157
Berlin Philharmonic, 53–4, 82, 103, 133,
134–6, 139, 141, 142, 151, 156
Berlin Staatskapelle, 62, 151
Berlioz, Hector, 62, 75, 77, 129; '*Le carnaval
romain*' Overture, 75, 77
Bernstein, Leonard, 57, 136, 153
Biancolli, Louis, 46
Biene, Auguste van, 57
Bingley, 34
Birmingham, 33, 34, 36
Bishop, Christopher, 65
Bizet, Georges, 77; Suite from *L'Arlésienne*,
77
Bliss, Arthur, 45
Blois, Eustace, 36, 37
Blom, Eric, 88
B.O.A.C., 73
Böhm, Karl, 106
Borg, Kim, 58, 93
Boston, 24, 49, 51
Boston Symphony Orchestra, 24, 51, 152
Boult, Adrian, 50, 74, 78, 83, 90, 156
Bournemouth, 57, 84
Bournemouth Municipal Orchestra, 57, 84
Bow Street, London, 29, 36, 38
Bradford, 33, 34, 61, 128, 131, 133
Bradford Education Committee, 34
Brahms, Johannes, 19, 50, 60–1, 63, 64–5,
74, 78, 80, 81, 92, 98, 101, 121, 138, 144,
152; Second Symphony, 60–1, 64, 74,
78, 138, 152; Fourth Symphony, 63, 64;
'Ye that now are sorrowful' from *Ein
deutsches Requiem*, 64; Third Symphony,
64, 65; 'Academic Festival' Overture, 64;
First Symphony, 78, 81, 144
Bridge, Frank, 19
Brisbane, 71, 72, 76–7, 80, 81, 83
British Broadcasting Corporation (BBC), 19,
70, 92, 95
British Library, The, 105–6, 139, 140
British National Opera Company (BNOC),
22–3, 25, 31–6, 38, 42, 84, 87
Britten, Benjamin, 45–7, 50, 51, 53, 54,
55; Violin Concerto, 45–6, 47;
Sinfonia da Requiem, 45–7, 51, 55;
*The Young Person's Guide to the
Orchestra*, 54
Brosa, Antonio, 45
Bruch, Max, 84
Bruckner, Anton, 50, 57, 94, 97, 101–15,
144, 152; Eighth Symphony, 94, 103,

104–15, 144, 152; Seventh Symphony, 102, 103, 105; First Symphony, 103; Second Symphony, 103; Fifth Symphony, 103; Sixth Symphony, 103; Third Symphony, 103; Fourth Symphony, 103, 105; Ninth Symphony, 103, 106
Bruckner Society of America, 101, 129
Brussels, 19
Bulawayo, 83
Bull, John, 52, 77; 'The King's Hunt', 77
Bulletin, The, 81
Bülow, Hans von, 40, 156, 157
Busch, Adolf, 20, 25, 26, 88
Busch, Fritz, 25
Bush, Geoffrey, 81
Butterworth, George, 54, 62, 81
Byrd, William, 77

Cameron, Basil, 156
Campoli, Alfredo, 64
Canada, 47, 51, 52, 93
Capitol Theatre (Perth), 81
Cardiff, 29
Cardus, Neville, 63, 95, 104–5, 115, 131
Caribbean, 53
Carnegie Hall (New York), 40, 52, 91, 102, 122, 124, 126, 130
Casals, Pablo, 25, 88
Castel Gandolfo, 94
Castelnuovo-Tedesco, Mario, 81
Cecchele, Gianfranco, 43
Central America, 53, 100
Chapman, Henry G., 105
Charthouse School (Carthusian), 30
Chausson, Ernest, 24; *Poème*, 24
Chelsea, 21–2, 34, 84
Cheltenham, 49, 50, 51
Cheltenham Music Festival, 49, 50, 51
Chenil Chamber Orchestra, 21–2, 23, 47, 58, 84
'Cherwood' (King's Cross, Sydney), 80
Chicago, 47, 52, 122
Chicago Symphony Orchestra, 122
Chopin, Frédéric, 59, 121
Chotzinoff, Samuel, 91
City Hall (Brisbane), 76–7, 81
Clark, Petula, 62
Clarke, Ashley, 93
Coates, Albert, 38, 83, 90

Coleridge-Taylor, Samuel, 20; *Petite Suite de Concert*, 20
Collins, Anthony, 45, 117
Colonial Mutual Life Insurance, 80
Columbia Records, 60, 126, 134
Columbia Symphony Orchestra, 62, 133
Concert Hall (UK), 63
Cooper, John, 21, 23
Corelli, Arcangelo, 58, 77; Oboe Concerto (arr. Barbirolli), 77
Cortot, Alfred, 59
Cossotto, Fiorenza, 43
Courier-Mail, The, 76–7
Covent Garden Opera Company, 25, 39
Covent Garden Opera Syndicate, 36–8, 39, 42
Craxton, Harold, 19, 84
Crozier, Eric, 47
Czech Philharmonic, 53
Czech Republic, 37, 133

Daily Express, 37
Daily Mail, The, 33
Daily Mirror (Sydney), 75
Daily Telegraph (Sydney), 73, 74, 75
Daily Telegraph, The, 33
Damrosch, Walter, 45
Dawson, Peter, 86
Debussy, Claude, 19, 20, 58, 84, 91
Delius, Frederick, 19, 20, 21, 23, 24–5, 27, 45, 50, 53, 54, 55, 58, 62, 81, 83, 121; *Summer Night on the River*, 23; *Sea Drift*, 24; *A Song Before Sunrise*, 25; *In a Summer Garden*, 121
Detroit, 51
Detroit Symphony Orchestra, 51
Dewsbury, 34
Dieren, Bernard van, 22–3, 25; Third String Quartet, 22, *The Tailor*, 22–3
Donegan, Lonnie, 62
Dowd, Ronald, 81, 93
Downes, Olin, 90, 123–4, 130
Duke's Hall (Royal Academy of Music), 17
Dundee, 18, 36
Dvořák, Antonín, 62, 71, 81; Fourth Symphony, 71; Slavonic Dances, 71
Dyson, George, 53

East 58th Street (New York), 126
Eastern Europe, 53

Edinburgh, 18, 33, 35, 59, 88, 118, 119, 120, 121

Edison, Thomas, 57

Edison Bell, 58

Elder, Mark, 24, 25, 117

Electrecord (Romania), 63

Elgar, Edward, 21, 22, 23, 24, 25, 27, 45, 50, 52, 53, 54, 55, 57, 58, 62, 63, 72, 76, 78, 79, 81, 83–100, 104, 136, 137, 138; *Introduction and Allegro for Strings*, 23, 25, 58, 84–5, 86, 88, 90–1, 92; Second Symphony, 25, 76, 86–88; 'Enigma' Variations, 45, 77, 88, 89, 90, 91–2, 138; First Symphony, 45, 86, 88; *The Dream of Gerontius*, 52, 58, 79, 81, 91, 92, 93–4, 138; Cello Concerto, 53, 57, 72, 83, 84, 88–9, 91; *Serenade for Strings*, 78; String Quartet, 83; Piano Quintet, 83; *Elegy for Strings*, 84; *Caractacus*, 86; *Sea Pictures*, 86; Violin Concerto, 88, 89, 92; Funeral March from *Grania and Diarmid*, 88; *Romance* for Bassoon and Orchestra, 89; Prelude to *The Light of Life*, 89; 'Pomp and Circumstance' March No. 1, 89, 100; *Froissart*, 89; *Cockaigne (In London Town)*, 89, 92; Cello Concerto (arr. Tertis), 91; *Falstaff*, 92; *In the South (Alassio)*, 92, 94–100, 104

Elman, Mischa, 59

Elsenheimer, Nicholas, 52

EMI, see His Master's Voice (HMV)

English Chamber Orchestra, 66

Epstein, Jacob, 22

Esplanade, The (Perth), 80

Eton, 30

Farnaby, Giles, 77

Ferrara, 29

Ferrier, Kathleen, 78, 93

Figueras, 23

Finland, 117

Finzi, Gerald, 54, 81

First World War, 19

Fischer, Edwin, 20, 25, 59

Fisher, Sylvia, 78

Foreign Office, 100

Franck, César, 63; Symphony in D minor, 63

Fraser-Simson, Harold, 20; Suite from *The Maid of the Mountains*, 20

Free Trade Hall (Manchester), 40, 41, 49, 89

Furtwängler, Wilhelm, 53–4, 57, 60, 105, 134, 150, 152

Gaisberg, Fred, 25, 59

Galliera, Alceo, 71

Galliver, David, 94

Gardiner, John Eliot, 20

Gerhardt, Elena, 130

Germany, 17, 19, 32, 39, 49, 53–4, 65, 95, 117, 133, 139, 146; cultural imperialism, 17; cultural chauvinism, 19, 53–4, 117

Gibbons, Orlando, 19, 21, 23, 58

Gibilaro, Alfonso, 27; *Scottish Fantasia*, 27

Girona, 23

Giulini, Carlo Maria, 26, 57

Glasgow, 33, 35, 59, 88, 118, 119, 120, 121

Glenelg (Adelaide), 80

Glossop, Peter, 66

Gluck, Christoph Willibald, 43; *Orfeo ed Euridice*, 43

Godfrey, Dan, 57, 84

Godowsky, Leopold, 26

Goldberg, Szymon, 150

Golders Green, 33, 36

Gold Seal (RCA), 127

Golschmann, Vladimir, 126

Goltermann, Georg, 83

Goossens, Eugene, 19, 21, 23, 25, 45, 58, 74; 'Phantasy' Sextet, 19; *By the Tarn*, 19, 23; *Jack O'Lantern*, 19, 23

Goss, John, 20, 21, 22

Gounod, Charles, 23, 32, 33; *Roméo et Juliette*, 32, 33

Gramophone, (*The*), 38, 62, 66, 85, 127, 133–4, 134–5, 137

Greevy, Bernadette, 93

Guardian, The, 42, 60, 88, 89, 94, 95, 104–5, 125, 138

Guild of Singers and Players, 20–1

Guild of Singers and Players Chamber Orchestra, The, 58

Guildhall (London), 92

Gustav Mahler Medal of Honor, 129

Gutmann, Albert, 106

Haas, Elsa, 81

Haas, Robert, 104, 105, 106

Halifax, 34, 38–9

Hallé Choir, 139
Hallé Orchestra, 23, 24, 25, 40–1, 42, 43, 47–51, 53, 57, 58, 61–2, 63, 64, 65, 66, 67, 69, 70, 71, 72, 73, 75, 76, 78, 80, 82, 86, 89, 91–2, 94–6, 100, 103–5, 115, 124–5, 127–8, 131, 132, 133, 134, 135, 137, 139, 142, 150, 151
Hamilton, Iain, 50
Hammersmith, 18, 34, 35
Handel, George Frideric, 79; *Messiah*, 79
Harnoncourt, Nikolaus, 20
Harty, Hamilton, 22, 117, 129, 131
Harewood, Lord, 47
Hassett, Lindsay, 75
Haydn, Joseph, 59, 63, 76, 81, 87; 104th Symphony ('London'), 59, 63; 83rd Symphony ('*La poule*'), 63, 76; 88th Symphony, 63; 96th Symphony, 63; Cello Concerto in D major, 87
Heifetz, Jascha, 59
Heming, Percy, 18
Hi-Fi News, 127
Hippodrome Theatre (Golders Green), 33, 36
Hippodrome Theatre (Newcastle-upon-Tyne), 32
His Master's Voice (HMV), 25, 41, 43, 50, 58, 59–60, 61–2, 63–7, 86, 127–8, 134–8
Hoddinott, Alun, 50
Holbrooke, Joseph, 53
Holst, Gustav, 21, 27
Horenstein, Jascha, 133, 135
Horowitz, Vladimir, 26
Houston, 40, 49, 52, 54–5, 57, 59, 67, 82, 131-2
Houston Symphony Orchestra, 40, 54–5, 57, 82, 103, 131-2
Howells, Herbert, 23
Hubermann, Bronislaw, 26
Hughes, Herbert, 19, 20
Humperdinck, Engelbert, 23, 34; *Hänsel und Gretel*, 34
Hungarian State Symphony Orchestra, 53

Iberia, 53
Ibert, Jacques, 81
Independent Television (ITV), 92–3
Internationalen Gustav Mahler Gesellschaft, Wien, 139

Ireland, 49, 81
Ireland, John, 19, 21, 45
Isle of Grain, 19
Israel, 133
Israel Philharmonic, 53, 103, 133, 134
Italy, 29, 41, 43–4, 53, 66, 93–4

Joachim Quartet, 155
John, Augustus, 22
John Barbirolli Chamber Orchestra, 22–3, 25, 58, 59
Jones, Gwyneth, 43, 44
Jones, Joan, 81
Jones, Parry, 34, 93
Joseph Eberle & Co (Wien), 139

Kabalevsky, Dmitry, 80
Kajanus, Robert, 126
Karajan, Herbert von, 53–4, 57, 125, 154
Kennedy, Michael, 94
Kensington Gore, 22
Kerman, Joseph, 31
Kilenyi Medal of Honor, 101
King's Cross (Sydney), 80
King's Lynn Festival, 86
King's Road (Chelsea), 21, 22
King's Theatre (Hammersmith), 18, 34–5
Kinloch Anderson, Ronald, 65
Kleiber, Carlos, 26
Klemperer, Otto, 60, 64, 69, 144
Kletzki, Paul, 71, 133, 134
Kolodin, Irving, 48
Koussevitzky, Serge, 126
Krauss, Clemens, 143
Kreisler, Fritz, 59, 64
Kubelik, Rafael, 69, 71, 133
Kurthy, Zoltan, 91
Kutcher String Quartet, 19, 22, 58

Lambert, Constant, 22, 156
Larner, Gerald, 94
'Lawson' (The Esplanade, Perth), 80
Leeds, 33, 36, 133
Lehmann, Lotte, 37
Leider, Frida, 37
Leinsdorf, Erich, 136
Leningrad, 83
Lennon's Hotel (Brisbane), 80
Levins, Leo, 17

INDEX

Lewis, Richard, 58, 93

Lewisham, 29, 36

Licette, Miriam, 34

Liederkranz Hall (New York), 126

Lisbon, 49

Liszt, Franz, 45

Liverpool, 33, 34, 36

Llewellyn, Ernest, 75

Locke, Matthew, 54

London, 17, 18, 19, 20–3, 27, 29–30, 33, 34,
35, 36–8, 39, 40, 42–3, 53, 57, 58, 59, 65,
67, 69, 71, 73, 76, 78, 79, 84, 86, 88, 89,
90, 92, 95, 97, 101, 103, 104, 105, 130,
133, 137

London Philharmonic Orchestra, 25, 89, 151

London Symphony Orchestra, 25, 45, 53,
86–8, 97

London Violoncello School, 57

Los Angeles, 26, 47, 51, 52, 59, 83, 122, 133

Los Angeles Philharmonic Orchestra, 26, 51,
122

Ludwig, Leopold, 135

MacCunn, Hamish, 27; 'The Land of the
Mountain and the Flood' Overture, 27

Mackenzie, Alexander, 17–8, 19, 27; Piano
Quartet, Op. 11, 17; Overture to *The
Cricket on the Hearth*, 27; *Benedictus*, 27;
Funeral March from *Coriolanus*, 27

Mackenzie, Compton, 84–5

Mackerras, Charles, 47

Mahler, Gustav, 45, 50, 57, 63–4, 79, 97,
98, 101, 104, 105, 129–47, 152; Fourth
Symphony, 63, 129, 131, 132; Ninth
Symphony, 63, 64, 131, 132, 134–6,
137; First Symphony ('Titan'), 63–4,
132, 133–4, 136; Fifth Symphony, 64,
131, 132, 137; Sixth Symphony, 64, 131,
132, 133, 136–7; *Leider eines fahrenden
Gesellen*, 64, 137; *Rückert-Leider*, 64,
137; *Kindertotenlieder*, 64, 130, 137;
Das Lied von der Erde, 79, 131, 132,
133; Second Symphony ('Resurrection'),
130, 132, 138–47, 152; *Adagietto* from
the Fifth Symphony, 130, 131; Seventh
Symphony, 131, 132, 133; *Adagio* from
the Tenth Symphony, 131, 132, 133;
Third Symphony, 132; Eighth Symphony
('Symphony of a Thousand'),138

Malipiero, Gian Francesco, 105; Third
Symphony, 105

Manchester, 24, 33, 36, 40, 47, 48, 49, 50,
57, 59, 61, 67, 69, 72, 79, 82, 83, 89,
91–2, 94, 101, 103, 104, 124–5, 133

Manchester Guardian, The, see *Guardian, The*,

Marriner, Neville, 20

Marylebone, 20, 21, 23

Marylebone Court House, 21, 23

McCabe, John 50, 51, 128; First Symphony
('Elegy'), 51, 128

McCallum, David, 88

McEwen, J. B., 19, 58; *Peat Reek*, 19

Melbourne, 49, 71, 72, 74, 77, 78, 80, 81

Mendelssohn, Felix, 19, 63, 71, 75; Fourth
Symphony ('Italian'), 63; 'Hebrides'
Overture, 71; Violin Concerto, 75

Mengelberg, Willem, 57, 60, 129

Mexico, 83

Mexico City, 83

Meyer, Kerstin, 86

Milan, 29, 66

Milner, Martin, 142

Mödl, Martha, 40

Moeran, E. J., 21, 50, 81

Moore, George, 91

Morning Post, The, 33

Moses, Charles, 70, 72, 80

Mottl, Felix, 105

Mozart, Wolfgang Amadeus, 20, 25, 37, 58,
59–60, 62–3, 71, 77, 81, 84, 121, 134;
Le nozze di Figaro, 25; *Don Giovanni*,
37; 23rd Piano Concerto, 59–60; 29th
Symphony, 62; 41st Symphony ('Jupiter'),
62–3, 77; 38th Symphony ('Prague'), 71;
Die Zauberflöte, 134

Mulholland, Mrs, 34

Münchinger, Karl, 20

Munich, 40, 49

Musical America, 52

Musical Times, The, 22, 23

Music Society String Quartet, 19, 23, 58

Musikwissenshaftlicher Verlag der
Internationalen Bruckner-Gesellschaft
Wien, 106

Nash, Heddle, 34

National Gramophonic Society, 19, 58, 84

National Gramophonic Society Chamber

Orchestra, 23–4, 58, 84

Navarra, André, 64

NBC Symphony Orchestra, 123

Newcastle Chronicle, 32

Newcastle-upon-Tyne, 32, 33, 34, 35, 36

New Chenil Galleries, 21–2, 34, 84

Newman, John Henry, 94

New Philharmonia Orchestra, 53, 136–7

New South Wales, 73, 74

New South Wales State Conservatorium of
    Music, 74

New Symphony Orchestra, 25

New York, 26, 40, 45–8, 49, 51–3, 57, 59,
    60–1, 69, 90–1, 102, 103, 121–4, 126,
    130, 155

New York Herald Tribune, 91, 102

New York Journal-American, 51

New York Mirror, 102

New York Philharmonic, see New York
    Philharmonic-Symphony Orchestra

New York Philharmonic-Symphony
    Orchestra, 38, 40, 45–8, 51–3, 60–1, 64,
    90–1, 102, 121–4, 126, 130, 138, 155

New York Post, 91

New York Times, The, 40, 46, 48, 52, 60,
    90–1, 102, 122, 123, 126, 130

New York World-Telegram, 45–6, 60, 122,
    126

Nicols, Robert, 23

Nikisch, Arthur, 45, 53, 130, 151, 152

Norwich, 19

Nowak, Leopold, 106

Nowakowski, Marian, 93, 94

O'Connell, Raymond, 78

Offers, Maartje, 86

Oklahoma, 52

Olof, Victor, 65

Oriana Madrigal Choir, 81

Ormandy, Eugene, 60, 69

Our Lady of Dublin, Choir of, 94

Oxford, 49

Palafrugell, 23

Pall Mall, 30

Palmers of Great Yarmouth, 154

Pan American Airways, 73

Pergolesi, Giovanni Battista, 57

Perth (Western Australia), 80, 81

Philadelphia Orchestra, 60, 105

Philharmonia Orchestra, 53

Philharmonic Orchestra of Los Angeles, see
    Los Angeles Philharmonic Orchestra

Philharmonic String Quartet, 19

Phillis Tate String Quartet, 19

Piatigorsky, Gregor, 59, 91

PM's Weekly, 60

Pope Pius XII, 73, 92, 93–4

Portland Place, 22

Portugal, 49, 53

Prague, 37, 133

Prince's Theatre (Bradford), 61

Pritchard, John, 24, 47, 53, 143, 152

Procter, Norma, 93

Promenade Concerts (Queen's Hall), 83, 92,
    103, 117

Puccini, Giacomo, 23, 29–31, 32, 34, 35, 36,
    37, 39, 40, 41–2, 43, 65–6; *Il Trittico*,
    29–31, 65; *Il Tabarro*, 30; *Suor Angelica*,
    30; *Gianni Schicchi*, 30, 31, 39; *La
    bohème*, 31, 34, 35, 36, 37, 43; *Madama
    Butterfly*, 31, 32, 34, 35, 36, 37, 40, 41–2,
    43, 66; *Turandot*, 31, 39, 43, 65–6; *Tosca*;
    31; *Manon Lescaut*, 31

Puerto Rico, 133

Purcell, Henry, 19, 20, 21, 23, 26, 52, 58, 60,
    62, 66, 81; Suite for Strings (arr.
    Barbirolli), 23; Suite for Strings, Four
    Horns, Flute and Cor Anglais (arr.
    Barbirolli), 60; *Dido and Aeneas*, 66

Pye, 50, 58, 62–3, 65, 86, 127, 133–4

Qantas, 80

Queen's Hall (London), 59, 84, 86, 88, 90,
    97, 103, 130

Queen's Hall Orchestra, 29

Queensland Symphony Orchestra, 76–7, 81

Quilter, Roger, 25; *A Children's Overture*, 25

Racine Fricker, Peter, 50, 51; First Symphony,
    51

Radford, Robert, 18, 34

Radio City (New York), 123

Radio-Symphonieorchester Stuttgart, 141

R.A.I. (Rome), Chorus and Orchestra of, 93

Rameau, Jean-Phillipe, 84

Rankl, Karl, 43

Ravel, Maurice, 19, 121

INDEX

Rawsthorne, Alan, 50, 51, 53; 'Street Corner' Overture, 51
RCA, 127
Reader's Digest, 65, 127
Reckless, Arthur, 93
Records and Recordings, 127, 128
Reed, W. H., 87
Reiner, Fritz, 153
Reynolds, Anna, 93
Richter, Hans, 105
Richter, Karl, 20
Rimsky-Korsakov, Nikolai, 36, 63, 77; *The Golden Cockerel*, 36; *Capriccio espagnol*, 63, 77
Robinson, Rae, 23
Rodzinski, Artur, 123
Rome, 41, 43–4, 66, 93
Ronald, Landon, 83
Rosa, Carl, 29
Rosenthal, Harold, 43
Rossini, Gioachino, 18, 23, 34, 35, 36, 74, 81; *Il barbiere di Siviglia*, 18, 34, 35, 36; Overture to *La gazza ladra*, 74
Rothwell, Evelyn, see Barbirolli, Evelyn
Roussel, Albert, 76; Second Suite from *Bacchus et Ariane*, 76
Royal Academy of Music (London), 17, 18, 47, 57
Royal Albert Hall (London), 22, 40–1
Royal Albert Hall Orchestra, 96
Royal Botanic Gardens (Melbourne), 77
Royal Family, 70
Royal Festival Hall (London), 95, 101, 103, 105, 137
Royal Melbourne Philharmonic Society, Choir of the, 81
Royal Opera House, Covent Garden, 29–30, 33, 36–8, 39, 42–3, 65
Royal Opera House, Covent Garden, Orchestra of the, 29–30, 59, 65
Royal Philharmonic Orchestra, 62, 127
Royal Philharmonic Society of London, 25, 47, 95, 103, 130
Royal Philharmonic Society of London, Orchestra of the, 25, 47, 151
Rubbra, Edmund, 50, 78, 81; Fifth Symphony, 78
Rubinstein, Arthur, 26, 59–60
Russia, 38

St. Andrew's Hall (Glasgow), 118, 119, 121
St. Andrew's Hall (Norwich), 19
St. Louis, 52
St. Louis Symphony Orchestra, 126
Saint-Saëns, Camille, 83
Salzburg, 24
Salzburg Festival, 24
Sammons, Albert, 92
San Antonio, 52
San Francisco, 47, 51
San Francisco Symphony Orchestra, 51
Sargent, Malcolm, 24, 35, 50, 69, 83, 92, 117
Scandinavia, 53, 120
Schiller, Friedrich, 105
Schmitz, Oscar Adolf Herman, 17; *Das Land ohne Musik*, 17
Schnabel, Artur, 25, 26
Schubert, Franz, 60, 63, 78; Fifth Symphony, 63; Ninth Symphony ('Great'), 78
Schumann, Elisabeth, 37
Schumann, Robert, 78; Piano Concerto, 78
Schuster, Frank, 88
Scotland, 25–7, 33, 35, 36, 39–40, 47, 59, 88–9, 91, 118–21, 130
Scotsman, The, 118–9, 120–1, 130
Scottish Orchestra, 23, 25–7, 39–40, 47, 88–9, 118–21, 130
Scotto, Renata, 66
Seattle, 47
Second World War, 42, 43, 48, 57, 129, 132
Seidl, Anton, 60
Serafin, Tullio, 66
Shacklock, Constance, 40, 93
Shadwick, Josef, 17
Sheffield, 93, 95, 104
Sheldonian Theatre (Oxford), 49
Shipley, 34
Shostakovich, Dmitri, 81
Sibelius, Jean, 60, 63, 65, 74, 81, 117–28; 'Karelia' Suite, 65, 118; complete symphonic cycle, 65, 117, 124, 125, 127; First Symphony, 65, 118, 119, 122, 126; Second Symphony, 65, 118, 122, 123–4, 126, 127–8; Fifth Symphony, 65, 118–9, 122, 126; Seventh Symphony, 65, 120, 122, 126, 128; *Pohjola's Daughter*, 65, 127; *The Swan of Tuonela*, 65, 74, 120–1, 122, 126; *Valse Triste*, 65, 122, 127; *Finlandia*, 118, 122; *Lemminkäinen's*

Return, 120–1, 122; Fourth Symphony, 122, 124–5; Third Symphony, 122, 123; Sixth Symphony, 122, 124, 125; Violin Concerto, 122, 123; *Pelléas et Mélisande*, 122

Simon, Henry W., 60

Simpson, Robert, 50

Small Queen's Hall (London), 59

Smetana, Bedřich, 39; *The Bartered Bride*, 39

Smyth, Ethel, 39, 53; *The Wreckers*, 39

Solti, Georg, 57

Somervell, Arthur, 53

South America, 53, 100

South Australia, 78

South Australian Symphony Orchestra, 77–8, 81

South Yarra (Melbourne), 80

Spain, 23, 53

Spen Valley, 34

Stabile, Marianno, 37

Steinbach, Fritz, 45, 60

Steinway Hall (London), 19

Stokowski, Leopold, 54, 105, 131

Straus, Noel, 46, 48

Strauss family, 19

Strauss I, Johann, 62

Strauss II, Johann, 39, 62, 77; *Die Fledermaus*, 39, 62; *Kaiser-Walzer*, 77

Strauss, Richard, 39, 45, 62, 63, 81, 98, 106, 129, 147, 151, 152, 156, 157; *Der Rosenkavalier*, 39; *Macbeth*, 147

Stravinsky, Igor, 26, 81

Stuttgart, 133, 139, 146

Suggia, Guilhermina, 59, 88

Suk, Josef, 71; 'Fairy-tale' Suite, 71

Sun, The (New York), 48, 91, 126

Sunday Concerts (Queen's Hall), 83

Suppé, Franz von, 20; Overture to *Dichter und Bauer*, 20

Supraphon, 63

Swift, Basil, 105

Switzerland, 53, 105

Sydney, 49, 71, 72, 73–6, 77, 79, 80–1

Sydney Conservatorium of Music, see New South Wales State Conservatorium of Music

Sydney Morning Herald, 75, 80–1

Sydney Symphony Orchestra, 73–6, 80–1

Szarvasy, Frederick, 36

Szell, George, 69

Tartini, Giuseppe, 20

Taubman, Howard, 52, 60, 122, 126

Taunus Mountains, 19

Tchaikovsky, Pyotr, 45, 59, 62, 75, 84, 91, 126; Fourth Symphony, 75; *Variations on a Rococo Theme*, 84; 'Theme and Variations' from Suite No. 3, 126

Teatro alla Scala (Milan), 29

Teatro Apollo (Ferrara), 29

Teatro dell'Opera (Rome), 43, 66

Teatro di San Carlo (Naples), 43

Tel Aviv, 133

Television Act (1954), 92

Tertis, Lionel, 91

Testament, 138

Theater an der Wien (Vienna), 43

Theatre Royal (Halifax), 38–9

Thomé, Francis, 57

Thompson, Oscar, 91

Times, The, 21, 36, 38–9, 41, 51, 59–60, 84, 130

Tippett, Michael, 50–51; Second Symphony, 51

Toronto, 52

Toscanini, Arturo, 44, 60, 111, 123, 124, 144, 152

Town Hall (Adelaide), 77–8, 81

Town Hall (Melbourne), 77, 81

Town Hall (Sydney), 73–4, 75, 76, 80–1

Trans Australia Airlines, 76, 77

Trevelyan, Marjorie, 121

Trinity College of Music (London), 57

Truth, 76

Turner, Eva, 66

Universal Edition, 139

Usher Hall (Edinburgh), 118, 120

Vancouver, 47, 51

Vancouver Symphony Orchestra, 51

Vaughan, Elizabeth, 42

Vaughan Williams, Ralph, 19, 21, 25, 27, 45, 47–50, 52, 53, 54, 55, 58, 61, 62, 63, 74, 75, 81; 'Phantasy' Quintet, 19; *Concerto Accademico*, 47; *Fantasia on Sussex Folk-Songs*, 47; Suite from

Job, 47; *Fantasia on a Theme by Thomas Tallis*, 47, 48, 50, 54; *Toward the Unknown Region*, 47; *Fantasia on Christmas Carols*, 47; Third Symphony ('A Pastoral Symphony'), 47–48, 50; Second Symphony ('A London Symphony'), 48; Sixth Symphony, 48–49, 50, 74, 75; Eighth Symphony, 48, 49, 52, 62; *Sinfonia antartica*, 49, 81; Tuba Concerto, 49; *Linden Lea*, 50; Fourth Symphony, 50; *Fantasia on 'Greensleeves'*, 50; Overture to *The Wasps*, 50; *Five Variants of Dives and Lazarus*, 50; *A Sea Symphony*, 50; Ninth Symphony, 50; Fifth Symphony, 61; *Serenade to Music* (orchestral version), 75

Veale, John, 50

Verdi, Giuseppe, 23, 29, 32, 34–6, 39, 40, 42, 43–4, 66–7, 79, 83; *Otello*, 29, 40, 42, 66–7; *Aïda*, 32, 34, 35, 36, 43–4; *Il trovatore*, 34; *Falstaff*, 36; *Rigoletto*, 39; Requiem, 79

Vich, 23

Vickers, Jon, 93

Victor Records, 60–1, 126

Victorian Symphony Orchestra, 70, 77, 78, 81, 82

Vienna, 43, 69, 106, 139

Vienna Philharmonic, 24, 64–5, 133, 156

Vienna Staatsoper, 43

Vienna Symphony Orchestra, 133

Vivaldi, Antonio, 20, 84

Vocalion, 19, 58

Voluntary Orchestra of the 1st Reserve Garrison Battalion, Suffolk Regiment, 20

Wagner, Richard, 23, 29, 35, 36, 38, 39–40, 41, 43, 45, 57, 74, 76, 80, 81, 83, 89, 91, 92, 129, 130, 149–50, 152, 155; 'O Star of Eve' from *Tannhäuser*, 29; *Die Meistersinger von Nürnberg*, 35, 36, 38, 40; *Der Ring des Nibelungen*, 36; *Tristan und Isolde*, 39, 40, 43, 130; *Parsifal*, 40; Act Two from *Tristan und Isolde*, 40–1; Prelude to *Die Meistersinger von Nürnberg*, 74, 76; *On Conducting*, 149

Walenn, Herbert, 57

Wall Street Crash, 26

Walter, Bruno, 36, 37, 60, 62, 95, 106, 129, 133, 135, 152, 154, 157

Walton, William, 27, 45, 50, 52, 53, 54, 55; Violin Concerto, 52; *Partita*, 55

Ward, David, 93

Warlock, Peter, 20, 21, 22, 23, 24, 25, 58; *Serenade*, 23–24

Weber, Carl Maria von, 45, 76, 121; Overture to *Der Freischütz*, 76

Weingartner, Felix von, 105, 150, 151, 152, 157

Welt, Die, 146

West Australian Symphony Orchestra, 81

Western Front, 19

Who's Who, 59

Wigglesworth, Mark, 20

Wigmore Hall (London), 19, 22–3

Williams, Morris, 81

Wimbledon, 34

Wimbledon Theatre, 34

Windgassen, Wolfgang, 40–1

Winnipeg Symphony Orchestra, 51

Wolfinsohn, Wolfe, 17

Wood, Henry, 22, 24, 29, 65, 75, 83, 95, 103, 117, 129, 152, 154, 156; *About Conducting*, 154

Wright, Adam, 23

Yorkshire Observer, 34

Yorkshire Post, The, 34

Zingari, I, 30

Photographs

All photographs are from Lady Barbirolli's Collection.

ALSO PUBLISHED BY THE BARBIROLLI SOCIETY

BARBIROLLI – Conductor Laureate
The authorised biography
by Michael Kennedy
ISBN: 1-85580-029-2

GLORIOUS JOHN
A Collection of Sir John Barbirolli's
Lectures, Articles, Speeches and Interviews
compiled and edited by Raymond Holden
ISBN: 978-0-9556710-0-5

BARBIROLLI: A CHRONICLE OF A CAREER
by Raymond Holden
Hardback, pp. 640 (and CDR) – ISBN: 978-09556710-2-9
Paperback, pp. 86 (and CDR) – ISBN: 978-09556710-3-6

*The CDR included provides a chronological listing
of the concerts and recordings as a pdf file*

SIR JOHN BARBIROLLI
A CAREER OF RECORD
includes Discography on CDR (updated 2020)
by David Ll. Jones
ISBN: 978-0-9556710-1-2